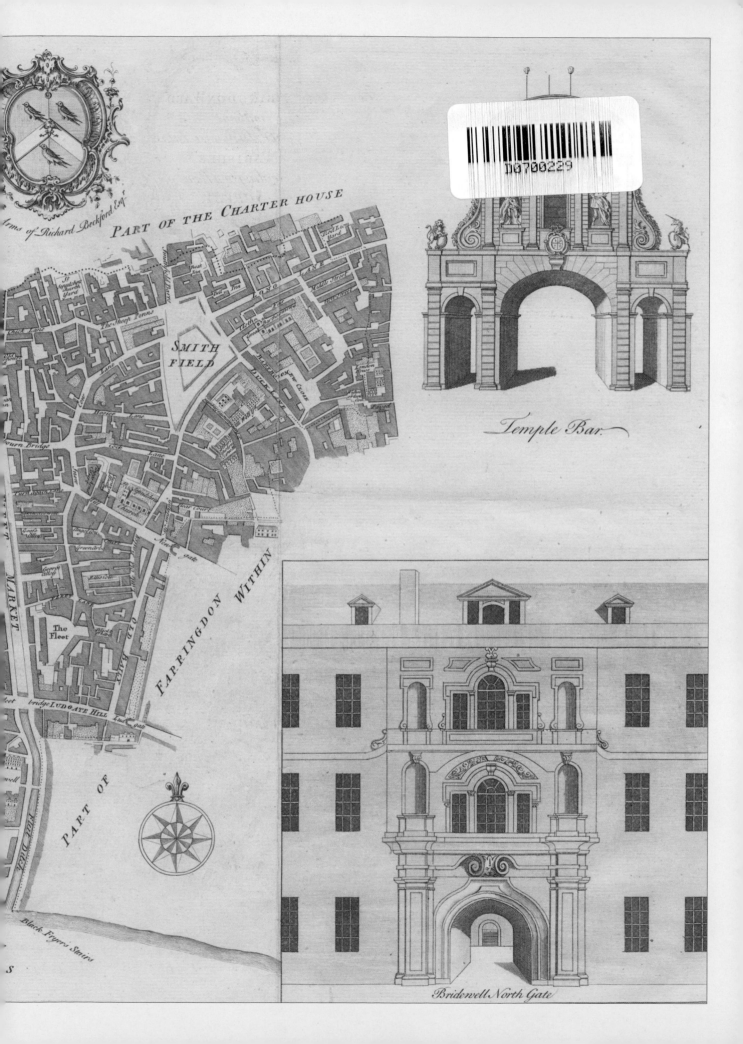

Arms of Richard Beckford Esq.

PART OF THE CHARTER HOUSE

SMITH
FIELD

FARRINGDON WITHIN

OLD BAILY

MARKET

The
Fleet

LUDGATE HILL

PART OF

FLEET DITCH

Black Fryers Stairs

Temple Bar.

Bridewell North Gate

CRIMINAL LONDON

Jack Sheppard: chained in Newgate Gaol
Sheppard was one of the most famous of London criminals in the 18th century. In this engraving, he is incarcerated in Newgate Gaol, weighed down with irons to prevent his escape. His story is told in this book.

CRIMINAL LONDON

A Pictorial History
from Medieval Times to 1939

MARK HERBER

PHILLIMORE

2002

Published by
PHILLIMORE & CO. LTD.
Shopwyke Manor Barn, Chichester, West Sussex

ISBN 1 86077 199 8

Printed and bound in Great Britain by
BUTLER & TANNER LTD
London and Frome

Contents

chapter 1

The Criminal in Action
Riots, Plots, Murders and Mayhem   1

chapter 2

Law and Order
Thieftakers and the Police   24

chapter 6

Some Political Trials and Executions   96

chapter 7

Victims of Crime   101

chapter 8

Executions   107

Foreword

WHEN I became Commissioner two years ago, I was excited yet humbled by the enormity of the job.

The Metropolitan Police Service and Scotland Yard are famed around the world and have a unique place in the history of policing. London is a vibrant and cosmopolitan city that offers a multitude of challenges to the blue light services. It is one of the biggest cities in the world and I'm determined to do all I can to make it the safest.

This is a considerable task and we are making real progress, but there is still work to be done. As this book demonstrates, part of the challenge is to keep up with the ever-changing nature of crime and the methods employed by criminals.

Neither policing nor crime stands still and the challenges of the 21st century are more than equal to any the Met has faced throughout our history. The first Met Bobbies who stepped out onto the streets of London in 1829 could not have imagined a world with multi-million pound fraud, computer hacking or human drug mules smuggling cocaine inside their bodies.

Whilst advances in technology such as fingerprinting and DNA testing have brought enormous benefits in catching criminals, so the methods employed by offenders to commit crime and evade capture have become more devious. To keep up, policing methods must continually become more sophisticated. It is vitally important that the police stay one step ahead and ensure we use technology to our advantage and focus on preventing crime, not just catching criminals after the act.

That said, and as this book shows, some things change very little. There is still the threat of terrorism; rioting, though far less common than in the past, has not disappeared from our streets. Youth crime is prevalent – although some of the 'artful dodgers' of yesteryear have become hard-core groups on the fringes of society, unafraid of the law, dismissive of the social order and responsible for more than 70 per cent of the capital's robberies.

So as well as moving forward we must learn the lessons of history. Britain, and London in particular, has given a tradition of firm and fair policing to the world and that is something of which we in the Met are fiercely proud and that we strive every day to uphold. It is something that too many of our colleagues have paid the ultimate price for. Some, such as the first Met officer to be killed on duty, PC Joseph Grantham, are mentioned in these pages. The rest are remembered in our hearts and the hearts of their loved ones.

We should be thankful that there are people of such courage, the bravest of the brave, willing to risk their lives as part of their everyday duties, in order to continue the battle against the perpetrators of crime and disorder. As long as these people continue to give their all, we can still hope that one day the worst crimes will exist only in the pages of history books.

I hope you enjoy reading this book.

SIR JOHN STEVENS QPM
Commissioner of the Metropolitan Police

Acknowledgements

IN RESEARCHING and preparing the material for this book, I have had the benefit of being able to consult many other works on London, the police and crime. Special mention must be made of *The London Encyclopaedia*, by Ben Weinreb and Christopher Hibbert and *The Official Encyclopedia of Scotland Yard* by Martin Fido and Keith Skinner. These books are indispensable to anyone interested in the history of London and the Metropolitan Police. Other works worthy of special mention are *The criminal prisons of London and scenes of prison life* by Henry Mayhew and John Binney, *Prisons and Punishments of London* by Richard Byrne and the series *Notable British Trials*, for example that on the poisoner Thomas Neill Cream by W. Teignmouth Shore.

I would like to express my gratitude to Sir John Stevens Q.P.M., Commissioner of Police of the Metropolis, for kindly agreeing to write the Foreword to this book and to John Ross, the Curator of the Metropolitan Police Crime Museum, for his fascinating talk about the exhibits there.

I would also like to thank Joslyn McDiarmid of Grosvenor Prints, in Shelton Street in London, Jeremy Smith of Guildhall Library, Roy Heywood of Wildy & Sons and Mel Menelaou for their assistance to me in locating so many of the prints and drawings for my collection and reproduction in this volume. Thanks are also due to Andy and Sue Parlour for their assistance with some of the illustrations and for their splendid research on the Whitechapel murders, which has added important information to our knowledge of this enduring mystery.

I must also thank my friends Michael Walsh, Managing Director of Decisions Strategies in London, and Detective Sergeant Colin Holder of the Metropolitan Police for their encouragement and example during our work against international fraudsters over the last few years.

I am grateful to the following for their kind permission to reproduce illustrations in this book: Guildhall Library, Corporation of London, extracts from Rocque's map (pages 119 and 158) and Whitecross Street Prison (page 141); Andy and Sue Parlour, Whitechapel horrors (page 22), Ten Pounds Reward (page 44) and the execution of Catherine Webster (page 126); The Directors of the Bank of England and the Curator of the Bank of England Museum & Archive, Cruickshank's Bank Restriction note (page 123); Museum of London, the central tower of Millbank Penitentiary (page 171). I am also grateful to the Clink Prison Museum for permission to reproduce my photographs of the museum and one of its exhibits (page 135).

Finally, but most importantly, I must thank Colleen Keck for her support of my work over the last few years, and in particular of her acceptance without complaint of my repeated absences abroad and the unsociable hours that I keep when writing. It is to her that I therefore dedicate this book.

MARK HERBER
April 2002

Introduction

WE SEEM to have an enduring fascination with crime and criminals, for reasons that have never been satisfactorily explained to me. We may recoil in horror at the atrocious crimes reported almost every day in newspapers and on the television, but we avidly read books about the crimes of years gone by and read or watch 'who-dunnits' in which crimes are expertly solved by the detectives of fiction.

Perhaps it is the cushion of history that turns a horrid murder into a fascinating story or even a compelling mystery. Perhaps the expertise of fictional detectives such as Sherlock Holmes and Inspector Morse gives us some form of subconscious comfort when we next see or read about some terrible crime on the streets around us. Whatever the reason, there is no denying the level of interest in historical crime, particularly those crimes that involve some mystery. Most of us would love to be the person who finally solves the riddles of who murdered the Princes in the Tower and the identity of Jack the Ripper. We all love to play detective.

London has always had its fair share of crimes (many of them still unsolved) and criminals, and of courts and prisons to deal with them. This book is a pictorial history of crime in the period up to 1939 in London; that is, in the City of London, the City of Westminster and those areas now within Greater London, such as Southwark (originally in Surrey) and Clerkenwell (originally in Middlesex).

Crime has always been a part of London life. The sparse records of medieval times contain many references to crimes such as murder, assault, treason, robbery, heresy and arson. London has always had its thieves, robbers and gangs of criminals. The wealth of London and its inhabitants attracted criminals, from throughout the country, who were looking for easy pickings. Certain parts of London, such as Southwark (infamous for its brothels, theatres and bear-baiting pits), were notorious for their crime and lawlessness. Alcohol and poverty fuelled the spiralling level of crime. In the 18th century, there were up to 6,000 shops selling cheap gin. Thousands of neglected children turned to crime to survive. Drunkenness, gambling and prostitution were rife. In the 19th century, it was estimated that London had about 6,000 brothels and 80,000 prostitutes. A newspaper of 1750 reported that there were three or more 'hold-up' street robberies each day in London. It also complained that, at least once a fortnight, a stage coach or gentleman's carriage was robbed by highwaymen or footpads on the outskirts of London, for example at Putney, Islington or on Hounslow Heath. As the financial centre of the country, London was the place in which forgery was most commonly committed. London was also the obvious centre for riots, revolts and conspiracies against the monarch or government.

The theme of this book could be that nothing really changes; riots, murders, fraud, burglary, robbery, bombings and forgery are still a part of London life. There is little from the history of crime that will surprise the reader of today. For example, the story of the career of Horatio Bottomley (see page 59), a Liberal MP for South Hackney, who was made bankrupt twice, acquitted of fraud twice but finally convicted and imprisoned in 1922, would not appear out of place in a modern newspaper. Poll tax riots are also not new; the imposition of a poll tax was a major cause of the Peasants' Revolt of 1381 that resulted in rioting in London and the burning of many prisons and other public buildings. Bombings by Irish terrorists, such as that in Ealing, appear regularly in the news today despite the advances made in the Irish peace process. However, in the 19th century the Fenian bombing campaigns in London were also a major problem for the police. The Fenians even managed to blow up part of the Metropolitan Police headquarters in Scotland Yard. Racism is also not new. Hundreds of Jews were falsely accused of coining, and then were killed, on the orders of Edward I and the whole Jewish population of England was expelled in 1290.

The criminal justice system has changed. It was plagued by corruption in previous centuries. The rich or well connected might escape prosecution or punishment for even the most serious of crimes, whilst a poor man might be hanged or transported for a petty theft. The forces of law and order were also inadequate to deal with day-to-day crime. A criminal might commit many crimes with little fear of detection. It was only if he were unlucky enough to be caught that he faced the prospect of a swift trial and violent punishment.

The most important courts in the land, the Royal Courts, were located in London, originally at Westminster. Many important criminal cases were heard there, especially in the Court of King's Bench. Show trials, for example that of Guy Fawkes, were held in Westminster Hall. The Royal Courts have now moved to the Strand but remain of importance to the criminal justice system. The Court of Appeal (Criminal Division) is located there and many High Court Judges hear urgent or important applications in criminal cases.

The charter of Henry I to the City of London granted its citizens the right to elect their own justices. This is the foundation of the City's privilege of holding trials of Crown pleas in the chief court of criminal justice in England; first at the Sessions House in Old Bailey and now at the Central Criminal Court in the same street. In addition, there were courts that were specifically for London and Londoners. Magistrates' Courts sat in the City at Guildhall and Mansion House. The Sessions Houses for Middlesex were located in Clerkenwell and at the Guildhall in Westminster and there were many Police Courts (later called Magistrates Courts) such as those at Bow Street and Marlborough Street.

The trials of criminals have been transformed over the centuries. One big change has been the speed with which the criminal justice system has operated. A murder trial or a complex fraud may now start a few months, or even years, after the commission of the crime. This was not the case in earlier days. Speed was the key, usually with a total lack of regard for an accused having a fair trial. John Bellingham (see page 84) shot the Prime Minister on 11 May 1812 and his trial took place on 15 May. The killers of Thomas Thynne (page 5) were arrested, tried and executed within 26 days of the murder. The Reverend James Hackman (page 104) was executed and dissected 12 days after his murder of Martha Ray. A 17th-century highwayman named Tom Cheney was tried at the Old Bailey Sessions one morning and hanged at Tyburn the same afternoon.

The conduct of trials has also changed. Eighteenth-century trials, of even the most serious crimes, might take only a few minutes or at most an hour or two. The principal reason is that trials lacked several elements that we now consider essential for an accused to have a fair hearing. Although prisoners were often allowed to use lawyers, they had no legal right to representation by a lawyer at their trial until 1836. A prisoner was not permitted to give his own evidence on oath until 1898. The prosecution had power to compel witnesses to attend to give evidence at trial but this right was not granted to the defence until 1867. The evidence of an accomplice was often used by the prosecution against an accused (and was often instrumental in leading to a death sentence). This evidence was often unreliable because it was given by a person who might be trying to save his or her own neck. Even so, it did not have to be corroborated by other evidence until the 19th century.

The methods of punishment of criminals have also changed dramatically. The punishments of Anglo-Saxon times were fines or execution. Whippings and mutilations were also introduced. Surprisingly, William the Conqueror banned executions. However, this was because he favoured mutilation for criminals, often the savage removal of limbs, ears or eyes. Capital punishment soon returned. William II introduced the death penalty for those caught hunting deer in the royal forests. His brother Henry I began to increase the number of offences for which death could be ordered. This process continued until the early 19th century by which time the death penalty could be imposed for over 200 offences that varied in gravity from murder or treason to theft of property worth more than a shilling. Even impersonating a Chelsea Pensioner was a capital offence.

There were many places of punishment in London. Smithfield, Tyburn, Tower Hill and Newgate are the best known, but there were many others. Walter de Stapleton, Treasurer to Edward II, was beheaded in an open area at a fountain in Cheapside known as the Standard in 1326. Pirates were hanged at Execution Dock in Wapping. Executions also took place on Kennington Common, at many London prisons (such as Horsemonger Lane Gaol and Wandsworth Prison) or sometimes at the place where a crime had been committed. New Palace Yard in front of Westminster Hall was also used for punishments; Perkin Warbeck was placed in the stocks there in 1498 and Titus Oates was pilloried there in 1685.

There was an important element of ceremony and display in the criminal justice system. The aim of punishment was deterrence and retribution. That is why the stocks, the pillory and public whippings had such an important role. People could see the offenders being punished. It was also just as important for a criminal to be seen to be executed as it was for the execution to take place at all. Hangings were public ceremonies until 1868 and drew enormous crowds. Until 1783, a condemned man was taken in a procession, headed by the Sheriffs of London or their officers, from Newgate Gaol to the place of execution at Tyburn.

Exhibiting the criminals' remains was also important. Executioners held up the heads of traitors for everyone in the crowd to see. Old London Bridge and its gatehouse (at the southern end of the bridge) were adorned with heads such as those of William Wallace, Jack Cade, Sir Thomas More, Thomas Cromwell and two alleged lovers of Queen Katherine Howard. The heads were dipped in tar to preserve them or in salt to prevent the birds feasting on them. The quarters of those executed might also be displayed. A

German visitor in 1592 noted about 30 heads rotting over the gatehouse of London Bridge. Heads were also placed on Temple Bar. In the 18th century, the bodies of murderers who were hanged at Tyburn and Newgate were dissected and put on public display at Surgeons' Hall in Old Bailey. The corpses of pirates, highwaymen and many murderers might be hung in chains on the highway or near rivers, to warn others of the risks they were taking in committing crime.

The element of display has now gone from the criminal justice system. Capital punishment has, in practice, ceased and any form of corporal punishment is now frowned upon. Imprisonment and fines have taken over as the main types of punishment. London is said to have had more prisons than any other city in the world. The Clink, Newgate, the Fleet, the Marshalsea, Millbank and Pentonville, are all well-known names. The conditions in all of them were atrocious until the late 19th century and often much later, and large numbers of prisoners died of the dreaded gaol fever, a virulent form of typhus. The prison system has gone through dramatic changes. It may still be subject to criticism but prisoners are no longer whipped or placed in dark dungeons. They now have television and table-tennis. An 18th-century prisoner was lucky to have food or bedding.

The reform of criminals is now a key ingredient of the criminal justice system. Whether this results in less crime is still unclear. The protection of society remains a vital aim of the system, at least according to the politicians, but the public today has the same concern that it has had for centuries. The level and horror of crime, as well as the cost of dealing with it, appear ever to increase. The police are short of resources to combat the criminal. More prisons are needed to hold those who ignore the law. If there is one lesson to be learned from a history of crime, it is that we have still not learned how to deal with it effectively.

chapter 1 The Criminal in Action:
Riots, Plots, Murders and Mayhem

THIS SECTION includes some of the crimes that have taken place in London over the centuries. The media sometimes portrays modern London as a hotbed of crime and infested with criminals. However, crime has occurred at all periods and in all cities. The only real changes over the centuries have been the nature of the crimes and the opportunities available to criminals. Some crimes change little. A burglar or thief of the 21st century operates little differently from his 17th- or 18th-century ancestor. Murderers still carry out their horrific deeds but are now more likely to use a gun instead of a sword, knife or poison. Highwaymen used to escape on their horses; today's armed robbers try to get away in cars. Financial crime becomes more complex as the economy and technology develops but an 18th-century forger would probably have had no difficulty in adapting to life as a fraudster using the Internet or a computer.

For centuries the roads around London were very dangerous. Robbers waited there to plunder travellers and if necessary kill them. Many of them worked in gangs. The authorities had no forces to patrol highways and there were no detectives to find offenders after a crime. Parish constables were almost useless as protection against highway robbery or in the detection or pursuit of criminals. Robbers who worked on foot ('footpads') were usually poor and considered as vicious and base criminals by the public. Robbers on horseback became romantic figures known as highwaymen. Footpads watched the inns and taverns on the roads leading out of London, looking for travellers who had fat purses or luggage that might contain valuables. The roads were lined by trees and hedges and therefore perfect for footpads or highwaymen lying in wait for unwary travellers, whether on foot or in slow-moving carriages drawn by horses. These robbers knew that, if caught, they would hang and therefore did not hesitate to kill in order to escape or prevent victims identifying them later. The amount of highway robbery was cut by the creation of the Bow Street Horse Patrol that watched the approaches to London and this type of robbery became almost impossible with the introduction of faster travel on the railways and by car.

The reputation of highwaymen as brave and romantic figures, akin to the Robin Hood of legend, was generally unwarranted. Many highwaymen were gentlemen who already had horses and pistols. Even the poor men who took to the highway generally wore fine clothes and were said to display a chivalrous manner. However, most of the crimes committed by highwaymen were just as sordid and vicious as the crimes of their counterparts on foot. Some highwaymen were brutal killers and rapists. The hanging of a highwayman and the gibbeting of his corpse might be considered a just end, although the public continued to treat highwaymen as daring romantics. Many of them went to the gallows as heroes, despite the robberies (and sometimes murders) that they had committed. Their robberies and exploits were embellished both during their lifetimes and after their deaths. The most notable example of a vicious criminal being immortalised in literature was the highwayman Dick Turpin.

London has always been plagued by thieves. Thieves had different specialities. Some went into shops and filled their pockets or bags with anything valuable or moveable. Others filched food or goods from market stalls and hoped to melt away into the crowds or escape pursuit in the throngs of people. Signs in busy tourist spots or shopping areas of London still warn people of the danger posed by pickpockets. The problem was far worse in previous centuries. At any time, there were thousands of pickpockets working in London. Some operated alone. Some worked in groups, with one perhaps causing a diversion, another bumping into a victim and a third making off with the victim's purse or wallet. Thieves would teach the craft to children (as Fagin and the Artful Dodger did in Charles Dickens' *Oliver Twist*) and the court reports are full of cases where a child was condemned or transported for this theft, often for petty items or amounts of money. A man might suffer from theft at a most embarrassing moment. Many prostitutes entertained their clients in the dark alleys of London and it was not unusual for a girl to take the opportunity of her client's interest in certain parts of her anatomy to relieve him in a rather different way, by taking his watch or wallet.

Burglary remains a serious problem in London. In medieval times, most houses held nothing of value. The few that held valuables (such as plate, furniture and jewellery) were generally guarded or filled with servants. The loot was also difficult to sell. As the population's wealth increased, so more houses contained things worth stealing. A burglar was likely to find bank notes and coins as well as more goods, such as silver, fine clothes and jewellery, that could be sold to fences for cash. The number of house or shop breakers increased throughout the 18th and 19th centuries and some of these burglars, such as Jack Sheppard and Charles Peace, achieved fame or infamy.

Another crime associated with modern life is forgery; that is, the making of a false document or object in order to deceive someone. However, forgers have been at work for centuries. Some 18th- and 19th-century cases, such as the forgeries of Ryland, Dodd, Price, Fauntleroy and the Bidwells, are featured in this book. The number of documents that can be forged has increased as life has become more complex; property deeds, paper money, bills of exchange, guarantees and insurance policies all feature in the records of criminal trials. Forgery was considered a serious offence for which hanging was the usual punishment until 1829. The production of counterfeit currency was seen as a particularly serious crime. It was treated by the courts as treason and therefore a male offender could be punished by being hanged, drawn and quartered and a woman by being burned at the stake. In fact, most male counterfeiters were simply hanged but women were often burned until the late 18th century. Fraudsters such as Robert Maxwell are not exclusively a modern phenomenon, nor are many of the tricks that they employ. Cases that are similar to the frauds of Jabez Balfour (see page 62) and Horatio Bottomley (page 59) are reported regularly in today's media.

Some of the illustrations in this and the following sections are taken from *The Newgate Calendar*. This was not an official publication about criminals held in Newgate Gaol (nor limited to those held there), but the title of a bewildering number of works that described the lives and crimes of offenders, some of whom were hanged and others who were imprisoned, transported or whipped. The information contained in those works was variable. Some include, almost *verbatim*, the evidence presented at trial. Others have only limited information and that of questionable veracity. Some editions borrowed unashamedly from earlier editions, often with mistakes. The point is that all the versions of *The Newgate Calendar* were incredibly successful (and many reprints are still being produced). This shows that the fascination of today's public with crime is not a new phenomenon. In presenting criminals and their crimes in this book, I have borrowed heavily from a number of editions of *The Newgate Calendar* but must also acknowledge the modern research that has improved our knowledge of so many of these criminals.

▼ **The burning of the Priory of St John of Jerusalem near Smithfield by Wat Tyler's rabble**
England was weakened in the late 14th century by the Black Death, famine, increased taxes and unsuccessful wars with France. In 1381, King Richard II was only 14 years old and his ministers, especially John of Gaunt, Duke of Lancaster, were unpopular. A new poll tax was particularly resented. The people hated the collectors (many of whom were corrupt) and the man responsible for the tax, the King's Treasurer Sir Robert Hales (who was also Prior of the Order of Knights Hospitaller). The Peasants' Revolt broke out in Spring 1381; Jack Straw led men from Essex to London and Wat Tyler led men from Kent to Southwark. They attacked and opened the Marshalsea Prison, then crossed London Bridge, aided by London mobs. The rebels attacked the Temple, home of the hated lawyers, burned the Fleet Prison and destroyed most of John of Gaunt's Savoy Palace. They broke into the Tower of London, dragged out the Archbishop of Canterbury and Prior Hales and be-headed them on Tower Hill. The rebels also burned the Priory Church of St John of Jerusalem, which had been built in about 1145 by the Knights Hospitaller as their headquarters. The King met Tyler at Smithfield, offering concessions as well as pardons for the rebels. However, the Lord Mayor of London, Sir William Walworth, stabbed Tyler, who was taken to the hospital at St Bartholomew's Priory but dragged out by the King's men and beheaded. His head was placed on London Bridge. The rebels subsequently dispersed and many of their leaders, including Jack Straw, were executed.

The Gunpowder Plot

▲ The Gunpowder plot conspirators
Fawkes was tortured for three days in the Tower of London and forced to reveal the names of his fellow conspirators.

▼ The execution of the Gunpowder plot conspirators
Catesby, Percy, Christopher Wright and John Wright were killed by the men arresting them. Francis Tresham died in the Tower of London. The eight surviving conspirators were tried in Westminster Hall on 27 January 1606, convicted of treason and sentenced to death. Thomas Bates, Robert Winter, John Grant and Sir Everard Digby were drawn on hurdles to St Paul's Churchyard on 30 January and executed. The next day, Guy Fawkes, Thomas Winter, Ambrose Rookwood and Robert Keyes were drawn on hurdles to Old Palace Yard, to the south of Westminster Hall, and executed. This print of 1795 shows the conspirators being dragged through the streets to Old Palace Yard, then hanged, burned and disembowelled. The mutilated quarters of the plotters were displayed on the gates of the City of London and their heads were placed on spikes on London Bridge. Another alleged conspirator, a Catholic priest named Henry Garnett, was tried at Guildhall in the City of London on 28 March 1606. He was convicted and hanged in St Paul's Churchyard.

▲ The arrest of Guy Fawkes
Guy Fawkes was born of Protestant parents in 1570. He converted to Catholicism and joined with Robert Catesby, Thomas Winter, Robert Winter, Thomas Percy, Christopher Wright, John Wright, Francis Tresham and other Catholic conspirators in a plot to kill the Protestant King James I, his ministers and members of both Houses of Parliament. The conspirators rented a house next to the Palace of Westminster and started digging a tunnel that would have run under Parliament but they were then able to rent a cellar under the House of Lords, where they hid 36 barrels of gunpowder in March 1605. Their plan to blow up Parliament had to be postponed because an outbreak of plague delayed the opening of Parliament until 5 November. Some of the conspirators had second thoughts about the plot, especially about killing hundreds of innocent men. Lord Monteagle received an anonymous letter that warned him not to attend the House of Lords on 5 November because Parliament was about to receive a 'terrible blow'. The letter may have been sent by Francis Tresham, Monteagle's brother-in-law, or possibly from government agents who knew about the plot. Monteagle informed the government, and the Parliament buildings were searched by officers led by Sir Thomas Knyvet. Guy Fawkes had volunteered to light the gunpowder and so he was found in the cellar and was arrested.

► **The murder of Thomas Thynne, 1682**
Thomas Thynne was MP for Wiltshire and the owner of Longleat House. He married Lady Ogle in 1681. She was only 14 years old but a rich heiress, being the only daughter of the Earl of Northumberland. Lady Ogle repented of the match and fled to Holland before she and her husband were bedded. Charles Count Konigsmark, a Swede, had also been a suitor of Lady Ogle. He was so angered at his failure to wed her that he twice challenged Thynne to a duel (which Thynne declined). Konigsmark decided on murder. He had come to England with a soldier and highwayman named Christopher Vratz, who agreed to carry out the murder and engaged John Stern, a Swede, and George Borosky, a Pole, to help him. They attacked Thynne in his coach on Pall Mall on 12 February 1682.

Borosky fired a blunderbuss at Thynne, mortally wounding him with five bullets. Vratz, Borosky and Stern were captured the next day, taken before Magistrates at Hicks Hall and committed to Newgate. Konigsmark was arrested at Gravesend, in disguise, waiting to sail to Sweden. The four men were tried at the Old Bailey Sessions on 28 February. The Count was acquitted of procuring the others to commit murder (probably by bribing the jury) but Vratz, Stern and Borosky were convicted and then hanged on 10 March 1682 in Pall Mall, where they had killed Thynne. Borosky's body was then hung in chains from a gibbet near Mile End. This is a case of swift justice; only 26 days separated the crime, trial and execution. Konigsmark did not survive for long. He died of pleurisy four years later, aged 27.

Stealing the Crown Jewels

◄ **Colonel Thomas Blood**
Thomas Blood stole the Crown from the Tower of London on 9 May 1671. He was born in Ireland in about 1618, the son of a blacksmith. He served in Cromwell's army in Ireland. Following the Restoration of Charles II, Blood was involved in a conspiracy to seize Dublin Castle. This plot was discovered but Blood escaped to Holland, later returning to Ireland and then England. In 1671, he attempted to steal the Crown Jewels from the Tower of London. Blood went to the Tower to see the regalia, in disguise and with a woman pretending to be his wife, and struck up a friendship with Mr Edwards, the keeper of the jewels. Some time later, Blood told Edwards that some friends of his were leaving town early the next day (9 May) but wished to see the regalia. He asked whether they might come before the usual hour. Edwards agreed.

◄ **Blood and his accomplices escaping after stealing the Crown**
Blood engaged three accomplices named Desborough, Kelfy and Perrot. Edwards admitted Blood and his companions but was then knocked down with a wooden mallet carried by one of the conspirators. They hammered the crown and regalia flat but, just as they were leaving, the alarm was raised by Edwards' son. Blood fired two pistols at his pursuers but missed and was captured, together with Perrot. Blood was imprisoned in the Tower and examined in person by King Charles II. Blood's story and demeanour were said to have made such an impression on Charles that he pardoned Blood and granted him a pension until his death in 1680. It is now suspected that Blood may have been working for the King, as Charles was so short of money that he wanted to sell the jewels. Staging a theft could have been the first step in arranging a secret sale.

▼ **Sir Edmund Berry Godfrey strangled by Roman Catholic assassins**

Godfrey was a Justice of the Peace for Westminster and Middlesex. In the summer of 1678, a man named Titus Oates came forward with information about a Catholic conspiracy (called the Popish Plot) to kill King Charles II, and place his Catholic brother, James, on the throne. Godfrey was appointed to review the allegations. He interviewed Oates, who swore his infamous depositions that denounced Catholics for various plots and intrigues. A few days later, Godfrey was heard to suggest that his life was in danger from Catholics who wanted to stop his enquiry into their plots. He left home on 12 October 1678 and disappeared. He was found on 17 October in a ditch on Primrose Hill; he had been strangled and his own sword thrust through his body. This seemed to confirm the fears of many people that there was a Catholic plot to overthrow the Protestant King and government. Another perjurer, Miles Prance, a Catholic who was tortured into his role, came before Parliament in December. He claimed to have acted as lookout for the murderers, Robert Green, Henry Berry and Lawrence Hill, who worked in the Queen's Catholic Chapel in Somerset House, and their accomplices, two Catholic priests named Girald and Kelly. Prance claimed that Godfrey had been strangled and stabbed with his own sword in Somerset House.

His body had been hidden for four days and then carried to Primrose Hill.

Green, Berry and Hill were tried at the Old Bailey Sessions on 10 February 1679 before Lord Chief Justice Scroggs and George Jeffreys, the Recorder of London, both of whom acted unfairly to the defendants and their witnesses throughout the trial. The jury found all three men guilty and were congratulated by the Lord Chief Justice. Green and Hill were hanged at Tyburn on 21 February 1679, and Berry (a Protestant) was hanged there a week later. All three were probably innocent and the truth behind Godfrey's death remains a mystery. Oates paid the price for his lies about Catholic plots. He was convicted of perjury and punished in 1685 (see page 187).

◄ **John Williamson's cruel treatment of his wife**

John Williamson was executed in 1767 for torturing and starving his wife to death. Williamson was a shoemaker who lived in Moorfields. His first wife died after bearing three children. He then proposed to a young woman who had inherited some money but who was said to 'border on idiocy'. Her guardian objected to the marriage but Williamson procured a licence and married her anyway. He then received the money that had been in the guardian's hands. Over the next few weeks, Williamson repeatedly beat his new wife. He then locked her in a closet for weeks, having fastened her hands with handcuffs and drawn them above her head with a rope so that only her toes touched the ground. She was given little food or water. On one of the few occasions when Williamson released her, she was briefly able to sit by the fire and remove some of the vermin that swarmed through her clothes. Williamson returned her to the closet where she died a few days later. He was convicted of murder at the Old Bailey Sessions and sentenced to death. He was hanged in front of a large crowd on 19 January 1767 on gallows opposite Chiswell Street in Moorfields. His body was sent to Surgeons' Hall for dissection and his children were placed in Cripplegate workhouse.

SIR EDMUNDBURY GODFREY *a Zealous* PROTESTANT *Magistrate, who was active in preventing the* Popish *Emissaries from making Converts,* STRANGLED *with a Handkerchief in Somerset House, by five* Roman Catholick Assassins.

▲ **The highwayman, John Cottington, alias Mul-Sack, robbing the Oxford wagon**

Highwaymen and footpads in the 17th, 18th and early 19th centuries haunted many places in and around London, including Hounslow Heath (where gibbets lined the roads to remind highwaymen of their fate if caught), Putney Heath, Norwood and Shooters Hill. In the 17th century, the area around the Holloway Road was 'infested' with highwaymen, including Claude Duval, one of the most famous of them. Indeed, Hornsey Lane was once known as Duval's Lane. Even places now in central London, such as Hyde Park and Belgravia, were known to be dangerous for travellers.

John Cottington, alias Mul-Sack, was a chimney sweep, pickpocket and highwayman. He was born on Cheapside around 1604, the youngest of a haberdasher's 19 children. John was orphaned at the age of eight and apprenticed to a chimney sweep. He ran away after five years but successfully worked as a chimney sweep on his own account. The only liquor he drank was sack, a wine that was usually drunk in a warm or mulled state, sweetened with sugar, so he became known as 'Mul-Sack' or 'Mull'd Sack'. One evening he was drinking at the *Devil Tavern* in Fleet Street, when he saw a beautiful woman, who insisted that they marry before she would respond to his lustful advances. Cottington agreed and they married that evening. Unfortunately, Cottington discovered that he had married a hermaphrodite named Aniseed-Water Robin. This changed his character. He turned to crime as a pickpocket and then took to the highway in the company of Tom Cheney. They set upon Colonel Hewson, who was riding a little ahead of his regiment on a march to Hounslow. Mul-Sack escaped but Cheney was captured. At the Old Bailey Sessions, Cheney argued for a delay to his trial because of his wounds. However, the court did not wish Cheney to escape the penalty of the law by dying in Newgate Gaol and so he was tried immediately, convicted and sentenced to death. His wounds were used as an excuse to

hasten his execution, and he was carried in the cart to Tyburn and hanged that afternoon.

Mul-Sack then worked with a highwayman named Captain Horne, who unfortunately was captured in their very first hold-up and he too was hanged at Tyburn. Mul-Sack then worked alone. He is said to have stolen more money than any highwayman of the period. He held up a wagon carrying £4,000 from London to pay Cromwell's army at Oxford, as shown in this engraving. He also stole £6,000 from the office of the Receiver-General at Reading. Mul-Sack was arrested for this theft but acquitted for lack of evidence. He then had an affair with the wife of John Bridges. Mul-Sack killed Bridges and fled abroad, managing to join the court of King Charles II in exile. He stole silver plate worth £1,500 from Charles and returned home, hoping to obtain a pardon from Cromwell as a reward for information he could provide about the King and his friends. However, no pardon was forthcoming. Mul-Sack was condemned for the murder of John Bridges and hanged at Smithfield in April 1659.

▼ **Thomas Waters robbing a company of Gypsies**

Born at Henley-on-Thames, Oxfordshire, Thomas Waters was orphaned when young and apprenticed to a Notary-Public, near the Royal Exchange in London. Waters left his master before he had completed his term, joined the army but then turned to the highway to earn a better living. His first exploit was against some 25 gypsies near Bromley in Kent, from whom he stole silver spoons, gold rings and other valuables worth about £60. He also held up Sir Ralph Delaval, Vice-Admiral of the English Fleet, stealing a gold watch and about 90 guineas. Waters continued his robberies for over five years, his last one being on Hounslow Heath, where he robbed John Hosey of £1,400 in money and plate. Some of the plate was found on him when he was arrested, so he was sentenced to death, conveyed to Tyburn in a coach on 17 July 1691 and executed, aged 26.

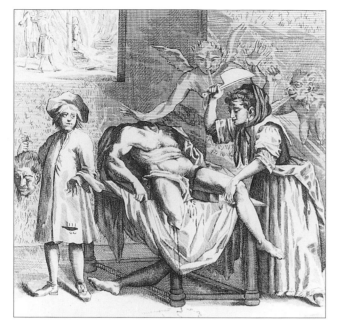

▲ Murder in Long Acre: the murder and dismemberment by Mary Aubrey of her husband

This engraving records a gruesome murder that took place in 1687. Mary Aubrey, a midwife, murdered her husband in Long Acre and chopped off his head and limbs. The murder of a husband by a wife was considered treason under the law. Until 1790, women convicted of treason were burned (a man would be hanged, drawn and quartered). Mary was hanged and then burned at Tyburn (as shown in the inset). Her young son had assisted her but was acquitted because he had acted under his mother's coercion.

◀ Elizabeth Chivers throwing her child into a pond

Elizabeth Chivers lived at Stepney. Her father died when she was young, so she went into service at the age of 14. At the age of 30, she was living with an attorney, Mr Ward and his wife. She became pregnant by Ward and moved into private lodgings for the birth of the child. Mr Ward provided for the mother and child but, three months later, Mrs Ward discovered Elizabeth's whereabouts and 'exposed her shame' in the neighbourhood. In rage and despair, Elizabeth decided to destroy the child and threw it into a pond near Hackney, where the child drowned. Some witnesses took her into custody and she was committed to Newgate. Elizabeth pleaded guilty to murder at the Old Bailey Sessions of July 1712 and was executed on 1 August.

➤ George Price strangling his wife on Hounslow Heath

George Price was born in Hay in Brecknockshire. Moving to London, he met Mary Chambers, a servant at a public house in Hampstead, and two weeks later they married. Price worked as a servant to a gentleman in New Broad Street and his wife lodged in Hampstead. She gave birth to twins but they died soon afterwards. Price was attracted to other women and saw his wife as an obstacle, so he resolved to murder her. He said that he had found her a job as a nursery maid near Putney and drove her by chaise out of town. When they came to Hounslow Heath, it was dark, so he stopped the chaise and strangled his wife with the lash of his whip. He stripped her body, disfigured

it in the hope that it could not be identified, and left it near a gibbet, from which hung the corpses of two criminals. Price brought his wife's clothes to London and disposed of most of them, but returned some that his wife had borrowed from their landlady. This was one cause of his undoing. So many people made enquiries about her that he fled to Portsmouth, terrified of being arrested. He waited for a ship to take him abroad and, whilst drinking in an alehouse, he heard a bellman describing him and calling out his name as a murderer, so he fled to Oxford and then to his father's house in Wales but he was seen by neighbours and fled again. Overtaken by guilt, he returned to London to surrender. He was convicted and condemned at the Old Bailey Sessions, but escaped the hangman by dying of gaol fever in Newgate on 22 October 1738.

▲ A shooting at Stepney Fields

Peter Conway and Michael Richardson were executed in 1770 for murder. They were members of a gang who murdered two men during their first robbery but, terrified at what they had done, fled the scene without stealing anything from the victims. On 26 May 1770, Conway, Richardson, and two men named Jackson and Fox purchased a pair of pistols and made bullets out of old pewter spoons. The next evening, the gang waylaid Mr Venables, a butcher, and Mr Rogers, a carpenter, who were walking from Whitechapel to Stepney. Conway demanded their money but Venables knocked down both Richardson and Fox. Conway and Richardson fired their pistols, killing both Venables and Rogers, and fled to Wapping where they robbed a man of 18 shillings and his watch. A few days later, Jackson was arrested on suspicion of having been involved in the murders. He named his accomplices and was admitted 'an evidence' for the Crown (we now say 'turning Queen's evidence'). Conway was arrested when he tried to pawn the stolen watch and was taken before the magistrate Sir John Fielding at Bow Street and committed to Newgate. Richardson was arrested a few days later. Conway and Richardson were convicted at the next Old Bailey Sessions and sentenced to death. After their execution at Tyburn on 19 July 1770, their bodies were cut down, taken to Bow Common and hung in chains on a gibbet. It is estimated that 50,000 people visited the spot over the next few days.

◄ Richard Noble stabbing John Sayer in the Mint, Southwark

Richard Noble, Attorney at Law of New Inn, was executed in 1713 for murdering John Sayer. Noble was not a successful lawyer and spent much of his time in the company of 'lewd women'. John Sayer had a large estate in Buckinghamshire and married Mary Nevill in 1699, but soon had cause to repent of his choice. Mary told him that she would find a lover as he was unable to satisfy her desires. Sayer bore her contempt with patience and purchased for them a house near Leicester Fields, where they lived at a rate he could not afford in an attempt to please her. Despite this, Mary took lovers and barred Sayer from the marital bed, so he associated with prostitutes and contracted a venereal disease. In time, a surgeon pronounced Sayer cured and Mary admitted him once more to her bed but, within days, both of them had the same disease; perhaps Sayer had not been cured, or perhaps Mary had contracted the disease from one of her lovers and infected her husband. At the time, Mary's widowed mother and her new husband, an army officer named Colonel Salisbury, were living in the Sayers' house. The two women caused many quarrels between their husbands (one almost ended in a duel). Mary Sayer had more affairs, first with a young clergyman and then with an officer in the Guards. Her extravagance so reduced Sayer's fortune that he needed advice to put his affairs in order. He instructed the attorney Richard Noble to help but Noble soon became a lover of both Mary Sayer and her mother. The three of them conspired to steal John Sayer's remaining money. On Noble's advice, Sayer (still in love with his wife) signed an agreement that settled most of his wealth on Mary. Noble also inserted a clause in the settlement by which Sayer agreed not to divorce Mary by reason of 'criminal conversation' (that is adultery) with any person. In 1710, Mary Sayer had a child (probably by Noble), stole £2,000 from John Sayer and went to live with Noble. Noble also procured a court order falsely stating that Sayer owed £400 to Mary's mother. Sayer had to shelter from his creditors in the Fleet Prison because his wife and Noble controlled most of his money. He placed an advert in newspapers cautioning people about Noble and Mary and, publicly exposed, they took lodgings in the Mint in Southwark, which was known as a 'harbour of all manner of vagabonds'. Despite all that had happened, Sayer still wanted his wife to return to him. He decided to seize her by force, procured a warrant from Magistrates and went with constables to the Mint. He entered the rooms in which Noble, Mary and her mother lived. Noble stabbed Sayer with his sword, killing him instantly. Noble and the women were tried at the Surrey Assizes at Kingston; Noble for murder and Mary Sayer and Mrs Salisbury as accessories to murder. The women were acquitted but Noble was convicted and executed at Kingston on 28 March 1713.

▲ The robbery of Dr Trotter in Moorfields

Thieves commonly changed their names to avoid detection and also to claim (if repeatedly brought before a court) that any offence was their first. Anne Holland was a pickpocket who also went by the surnames Andrews, Charlton, Edwards, Goddard and Jackson. Anne's usual method of theft was to hire herself as a servant to a wealthy family and then rob them. She was very attractive and had many lovers. She married a Mr French but gave birth to a child only six months after their wedding. The couple argued and French died soon after his money and goods were seized to settle a court judgment. Anne's second husband, a highwayman named James Wilson, was hanged and she then became associated with Tristram Savage. They visited Dr Trotter, an astrologer in Moorfields, in order to rob him, Savage being disguised as a woman. While Trotter consulted his astrological charts to predict Anne's future, Savage pulled out a pistol. The couple bound Trotter and stole a gold watch, 20 guineas and other valuables. Anne Holland continued her life of theft but was finally caught and executed at Tyburn in 1705.

► George Foster drowning his wife and child in the Paddington Canal

George Foster was executed outside Newgate Gaol in 1803 for drowning his wife and child on 5 December 1802 in the Paddington Canal. Foster lived in North Row, near Grosvenor Square, his two elder children were in the workhouse at Barnet and his wife and youngest child lived with her mother in Old Boswell Court. Foster's wife went to his lodgings every Saturday night. One day, the bodies of the wife and youngest child were found in the canal near the *Mitre Tavern* where Foster had been drinking with his wife. He was tried at the Old Bailey on 14 January 1803. Foster claimed that he and his wife had parted after their drink but he was convicted and sentenced to be hanged and then anatomised. Four days later Foster was brought out to the platform before debtors' door at Newgate. After a short prayer, the cap was pulled over his eyes, the drop fell from under him and he was launched into eternity. His body was cut down and subjected to the galvanic process by Professor Aldini. The object of this experiment was to show

Elizabeth Brownrigg

► The murderess Elizabeth Brownrigg

Elizabeth Brownrigg was executed at Tyburn in 1767 for torturing her female apprentice to death. Elizabeth was married to James Brownrigg, a Greenwich plumber. The couple moved to a house in Fleur-de-Lys Court, Fleet Street, where Mr Brownrigg carried on his business. Mrs Brownrigg had 16 children and had practised midwifery. She was appointed to care for poor women in the workhouse of St Dunstan in the West. She also decided to boost her income by allowing pregnant women to lie-in at her home. Two poor girls, Mary Mitchell of Whitefriars and Mary Jones from the Foundling Hospital, were apprenticed to her as servants in 1765.

►► The cruel treatment of girls by Mrs Brownrigg

Mrs Brownrigg treated the girls with savage barbarity. Mary Jones was frequently whipped until she escaped back to the Foundling Hospital. The Brownriggs ignored the hospital's threats of prosecution. Their treatment of Mary Mitchell was even more cruel, particularly after she made an unsuccessful attempt to escape from the house. The overseers of Whitefriars, unaware of Mrs Brownrigg's cruelty, then apprenticed Mary Clifford to her. Clifford was frequently stripped naked and flogged. She was also put in a cellar with a chain round her neck and given only bread and water. Mrs Brownrigg would whip both girls until she was tired and her eldest son, John, often continued the floggings. She used to bind the girls' hands with a cord and pull it over a pipe near the ceiling. When that gave way, Mr Brownrigg fixed a hook in a beam so that his wife could pull the girls' bound arms up above them. Mary Clifford

that electricity might, in cases of drowning or suffocation, revive the action of the lungs and thereby rekindle life. Electricity was applied to the deceased's face but all that happened was that the jaws quivered, some facial muscles were contorted and one eye opened.

▼ A shooting in court: the turnkey of Newgate shot by William Johnson

William Johnson and Jane Housden were executed in 1714 for the murder of a turnkey (a gaoler) in court. Johnson owned a butcher's shop in Newport Market, London, but this business failed, as did his subsequent businesses as a corn-chandler and victualler. He worked for a surgeon in Gibraltar and saved some money. After his return to England he soon spent his savings and became a highwayman. One of his friends, Jane Housden, was arrested for the offence of coining (she had previously been convicted of coining but pardoned). She was about to be tried at the Old Bailey Sessions when Johnson called in to see her at court. Mr Spurling, the head turnkey of Newgate Gaol, told Johnson that he could not speak to her until her trial had ended. Spurling was known for his cruelty to prisoners and also supplemented his income by dealing in stolen goods. Johnson drew a pistol and shot Spurling dead, in the presence of the court and with shouts of encouragement from Jane Housden. The judges adjourned Housden's trial for coining but immediately tried both her and Johnson for murder. They were convicted, sentenced to death and hanged on 19 September 1714 in the yard of the Sessions House. Johnson's body was then hung in chains near Holloway.

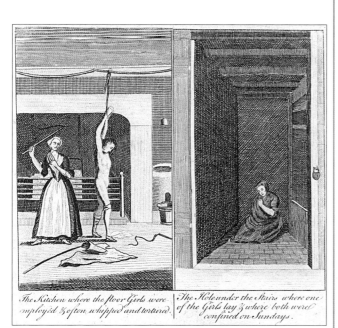

The Kitchen where the poor Girls were employ'd & often whipped and tortured. The Hole under the Stairs where one of the Girls lay & where both were confined on Sundays.

managed to complain of her treatment to a lady who lodged in the house. That lady remonstrated with Mrs Brownrigg who then cut Mary Clifford's tongue with a pair of scissors. The parish authorities were finally persuaded to take action by the Brownriggs' neighbours who had heard the girls' screams. The girls were taken to St Bartholomew's Hospital, but Mary Clifford died a few days later. Mr Brownrigg was taken to Wood Street Compter. Mrs Brownrigg and her son escaped in disguise but were captured in Wandsworth. The Brownriggs were tried at the Old Bailey Sessions. Mr Brownrigg and his son were acquitted of murder but imprisoned for six months for assault, while Mrs Brownrigg was convicted of murder and sentenced to death. After her execution on 14 September 1767, her body was dissected at Surgeons' Hall, where her skeleton was exhibited.

► **The German Princess Mary Carleton with her supposed husband and lawyer**

Mary Carleton was a Kentish adventuress who travelled the Continent, acquired several husbands and was executed in 1673 for returning from transportation. Mary was known as the German Princess because she claimed to be the daughter of the Lord of Holmstein in Germany. She was actually a child of a man from Canterbury, possibly a chorister at the Cathedral or perhaps only a fiddler. Mary was born in 1642. As a child, she loved romantic stories and dreamed of marrying a knight. However, her first husband was a Canterbury shoemaker, Thomas Stedman, who was too poor for Mary's liking so she left him to seek her fortune. She married a surgeon named Day in Dover and, when tried at Maidstone Assizes for bigamy, was fortunate to be acquitted for lack of evidence. Mary went abroad. In Cologne she had an affair with a rich gentleman. She promised to marry him and he gave her many expensive jewels, but she left the city. She returned to London in March 1663, staying at a tavern kept by a Mr King. She told people that she was a daughter of a prince of the Holy Roman Empire but that he had banished her for marrying a noble without his consent (and had executed that noble following a false accusation of treason). From that time, Mary became known as 'the German Princess'. Her third husband was John Carleton, who discovered that she was an imposter and had her arrested. She was committed to Newgate and tried for polygamy on 4 June 1663 at the Old Bailey Sessions, but again acquitted for lack of evidence. Mary then

became an actress, gained many admirers and lived with an elderly gentleman who gave her money and jewellery. One night, she stole all the valuables she could find in his house and left him to take new lodgings. Mary then began cheating tradesmen by taking goods on credit and moving lodgings. On one occasion, she took rooms in Holborn and sent for a young barrister named Mr Justinian. She told him that she was heir to her deceased father and that she wished to arrange her affairs to prevent her extravagant and violent husband, with whom she did not live, benefiting from her fortune, or having any power over it. Whilst the lawyer gave his opinion, a woman entered the room (by prior arrangement) and announced that Mary's husband was about to arrive at her chamber. Mary persuaded the lawyer to get into the closet so that her husband would not find him there. The counterfeit husband entered with a companion and accused Mary of having a lover in the room, whom he would kill. He opened the closet door and found a pale and trembling lawyer. The counterfeit husband drew his sword but Mary held him back and pretended to calm him. Someone suggested reparations for the husband's damaged honour and the lawyer finally agreed to pay £100 for an end to the matter. Not long after, Mary was arrested for stealing a silver tankard in Covent Garden. She was convicted at the Old Bailey Sessions and transported to Jamaica but returned to England after only two years and again set herself up as a rich heiress. She married a rich apothecary of Westminster, robbed him of over £300 and left him for new lodgings. She then stole over £200 and 30 watches from a watchmaker who rented rooms in the same lodging house. Mary was again arrested in December 1672, when she was living near St George's Fields. The Keeper of the Marshalsea Prison recognised her whilst searching her lodging house for some stolen valuables. At the Old Bailey she admitted to being Mary Carleton. Accused of returning from transportation, she pleaded her belly. A jury of matrons found this to be a lie and Carleton was executed at Tyburn on 22 January 1673.

John Hayes' Murder

▼ The murder of John Hayes

Catherine Hayes (née Hall) murdered her husband and was burned alive in 1726. She was born in 1690 in Birmingham. When aged 15, she left home and set off for London but, on the way, was seduced by some army officers. She stayed with them in Worcestershire until they tired of her and dismissed her. Catherine moved to Warwickshire and was hired as a domestic servant by a farmer named Hayes. She married his son John. The elder Mr Hayes set up his son in business as a carpenter and settled property on him to provide the couple with an annual income. He also procured his son's discharge from the army at the cost of £60 after Catherine had persuaded him to enlist. After six years of marriage, Mrs Hayes and her husband moved to London. They took a house, part of which Mr Hayes let as lodgings and from another part of which he operated a chandlery and coal shop. Mrs Hayes spoke about her husband, to others, with contempt (telling one that she would think it no more a sin to murder him than to kill a dog). She also quarrelled with their neighbours, and so the couple moved to Tottenham Court Road and then to Tyburn Road (now Oxford Street). Hayes soon amassed enough money from his business to retire and take lodgings. Thomas Billings lived in the same lodging house and may have been a son of Mrs Hayes (by one of the army officers). After quarrelling with her husband, Mrs Hayes plotted with Billings and another lodger, Thomas Wood, to murder him. She offered them part of the £1,500 that, she said, would come to her on her husband's death. On the night of 1 March 1726, all four of them were drinking. Mr Hayes fell asleep and Billings and Wood then killed him with a hatchet. The murderers discussed the best method of disposing of the body to prevent detection. Mrs Hayes proposed that they cut off his head. Billings supported the head, Wood cut it off with his knife and Mrs Hayes held a bucket to receive the head and blood. They dismembered Hayes' body. Wood and Billings carried the parts, wrapped in a blanket, to Marylebone Fields and threw them in a pond. They also took the head to a wharf near the Horse Ferry, Westminster and threw it into the dock expecting the tide to carry it away. Unfortunately for them, the tide was coming in at the time.

▼ The exhibition of John Hayes' head

A watchman spotted the head in the water the next day. Magistrates ordered that it be set on a pole in the churchyard of St Margaret's, Westminster in case someone could identify it. Thousands went to witness this extraordinary spectacle. The head was then put in a jar of spirits to stop it putrefying and permit continued inspection. In the meantime, Hayes' friends made enquiries after him. At first, Mrs Hayes said that he had left London for a few days but she later claimed that he had killed a man and fled. Two of Mr Hayes' friends were not satisfied with this explanation and soon heard about the exhibited head. They went to a Magistrate who issued warrants for the arrest of Mrs Hayes, Wood and Billings. Mrs Hayes and Wood were taken to Tothill Fields Bridewell and Billings to Clerkenwell New Prison.

◀ The burning of Catherine Hayes

Mr Hayes' body was found at Marylebone and Mrs Hayes was committed to Newgate Gaol. Wood and Billings confessed to the crime and pleaded guilty to murder at their trial. Mrs Hayes denied the murder but was convicted. All three were sentenced to death. Wood cheated the hangman by dying of fever in the condemned hold of Newgate. Mrs Hayes had committed treason by murdering her husband and so her punishment was burning. Hayes and Billings were taken to Tyburn on 9 May 1726. Billings was hanged and his corpse was hung in chains near the pond in Marylebone in to which Mr Hayes' body had been thrown; Mrs Hayes was chained to a stake near the gallows. When women were burned, it was customary for the executioner to strangle them first with a rope so that they were dead before the flames reached them. However, Mrs Hayes was burned alive because the executioner let go of the strangling rope when the flames burned his hands. She survived amidst the flames for a considerable time and it took three hours for her body to be reduced to ashes.

The last burning of a woman took place outside Newgate Gaol in 1789 when Christian Murphy was hanged and then burned for coining (which was also treated as treason).

▲ **The cruel murder of John Steele on Hounslow Heath by Holloway, Haggerty and Hanfield**

John Holloway and Owen Haggerty were hanged for murder before Newgate Gaol in 1807. There were doubts about whether they were truly guilty (a man named Ward was tried in 1813 for the same murder but acquitted). The conviction of Holloway and Haggerty rested on the evidence of a 'wretch as base as themselves' who said he had been their accomplice, but the public indignation against them was so great that their conviction by a jury is hardly surprising. However, they are remembered also because 36 of the spectators at their execution died when panic broke out in the crowd.

John Steele lived in Feltham and had a lavender warehouse in Catherine Street near the Strand. On 6 November 1802, he left home to go to Catherine Street but was never seen again by his family. His body was found in a ditch on Hounslow Heath. He had a fractured skull and many other wounds. His murderers had robbed him of his money, hat and boots. A blood-stained bludgeon, an old pair of shoes and an old felt hat were left near the body. The murderers escaped and, despite the offer of rewards, no-one was arrested. About four years later, Benjamin Hanfield was convicted at the Old Bailey of stealing a pair of shoes and sentenced to transportation to New South Wales. He fell ill on a hulk, awaiting transportation and said that he wanted to confess his part in a murder, which tortured his mind, before he died. He was taken before the Bow Street Magistrates and, promised a pardon, told them about the murder of Mr Steele by Holloway and Haggerty. They were arrested on 9 February 1807 and taken before Mr Moser, the Magistrate at Worship Street Police Office. None of the evidence materially implicated Holloway or Haggerty except that of Hanfield. Holloway and Haggerty denied knowing Hanfield and any knowledge of the crime. However, the information they gave about their whereabouts at the time of the murder turned out to be untrue. Haggerty denied ever having been at Hounslow but a constable overheard the prisoners talking about being at Hounslow on the night of the murder. They were tried at the Old Bailey Sessions on 20 February 1807, when Hanfield gave evidence. He admitted that he had led a 'vicious' life, committing many robberies, and enlisting, then deserting from several army regiments. He claimed to have known Holloway and Haggerty for years and was asked by Holloway to help in a robbery on 6 November 1802. After drinking at various public houses, they hid in trees on Hounslow Heath until a man came along. They demanded his money and were searching him for valuables when a coach came by and Holloway was said to have struck the victim with several vicious blows. Hanfield claimed that he fled the scene, believing the man to be dead, but stated that Holloway and Haggerty caught up with him later, carrying the victim's hat. The jury convicted both Holloway and Haggerty. They were sentenced to be hanged on the following Monday, 23 February. On the day of execution, Haggerty and Holloway were brought out of debtor's door at Newgate to the scaffold, wearing white caps and with their arms pinioned. They were joined on the scaffold by the murderess Elizabeth Godfrey (see page 15). All three were hanged at about 8.15am. The crowd was so large – estimated at 40,000 – that many people were trying to escape from it. The pressure in the crowd became so great that some people were pushed to the ground and trampled. The stall of a man selling pies was overturned. Panic ensued. The condemned hanged for one hour and it was only then that the marshals and constables were able to clear the street. Almost 100 people were killed or injured; 27 bodies were taken to St Bartholomew's Hospital and there were at least nine other deaths.

▲ **Elizabeth Godfrey stabbing Richard Prince on Christmas Day 1806**

Elizabeth Godfrey was executed with Holloway and Haggerty on the gallows at Newgate on 23 February 1807. Elizabeth was a prostitute. She was tried at the Old Bailey on 20 February for the murder on 25 December 1806 of Richard Prince. She rented a room in the same lodging house in Marylebone as Prince and his girlfriend Emily Bisset. Elizabeth moved in on 21 December 1806. On 23 December, she brought a man back to her room. He accused her of robbing him of 18 shillings. As a result of the altercation, Prince called the watch and Elizabeth was detained all night in a watch-house. At 5pm on Christmas Day, Elizabeth knocked on the door of Prince and Bisset's room, asking to speak to Prince. She then stabbed him in the left eye with a knife. Prince died at the Middlesex Hospital. The landlord, William Scott, asked Elizabeth why she had stabbed Prince. She answered 'it served him right'. She was convicted, condemned and hanged. Emily Bisset probably thought that it served her right.

▲ **William Duncan murdering William Chivers**

Duncan murdered his master William Chivers and was transported in March 1807. Duncan was a Scot aged 22 and employed by the elderly Mr Chivers as a gardener near Clapham. On the morning of 24 January 1807, Chivers took his customary walk in the garden, inspecting the gardener's work. A little later, Duncan ran into the house in dismay, shouting to the servants 'Lord, What have I done? I have struck my master and he has fallen'. He then fled. Chivers' body was found in the garden. His face was a shocking spectacle. It appeared that Duncan had struck him with a spade, the blow having entered the lower part of his nose, broken both his jawbones and almost separated his head into two. Duncan was captured and committed to Horsemonger Lane Gaol. At his trial, Duncan stated that Chivers had been angry that he had taken a refreshment break and tried to strike him with his cane. Duncan claimed that, in defending himself with his spade, he had accidentally struck his master. Duncan was convicted of murder and sentenced to death. However, the Privy Council decided that the murder had not been premeditated. Duncan was therefore reprieved but sentenced to transportation for the rest of his life.

Prostitution

▲ The Harlot's progress: greeted by the Madam

Prostitution features in the oldest records of London. Although prostitution is not itself a crime, there are related offences such as soliciting in a public place, and crime has also always had close links to prostitution. Pimps and madams could be prosecuted for living off immoral earnings, operating brothels or for procuring women to become prostitutes. A great part of the proceeds of criminal conduct (for example the loot taken by the burglar Jack Sheppard) was also spent on prostitutes.

Love Lane in the City was a haunt of prostitutes in medieval times. The City authorities made efforts to force prostitution outside the City walls and so, for centuries, Southwark became the abode of prostitutes (as well as criminals and debtors). The 'Stewes' were notorious brothels in buildings on Bankside in Southwark owned by the Bishops of Winchester. Bankside remained notorious until the 19th century for prostitution, which also flourished in the expanding areas to the west of the City. In the 18th century, the area around Drury Lane was notorious for its gin shops and prostitutes. The arcaded piazza of Covent Garden had so many lodging houses, bagnios and Turkish baths that were really brothels that it was described as the great square of Venus. The windows of the bagnios

were filled every night with women, inviting men inside. A list of about 170 women, with their physical descriptions and anecdotes about them, was published annually from 1760 to 1793 and sold openly in the square. Prostitutes patrolled the pavements outside the theatres around Covent Garden and

there were still many brothels in the area in the 19th century. The alleys running off the Strand and St James's Park were also known haunts of prostitutes in the 18th century. James Boswell records that he picked up several girls there. This illustration is the first in a series of engravings from 1732 by Hogarth entitled *The Harlot's Progress*. It shows a young country girl, Kate Hackabout, arriving in London and met by a procuress or madam, said to represent Mother Needham. Hogarth named his main character after a real prostitute. She had been brought before Magistrates in 1730 and used the name Hackabout (the name described her trade since a Hackabout was a vehicle that plied for public hire). Elizabeth Needham was a notorious procuress who had been sentenced to stand in the pillory in 1731 and died a few days later from the injuries she received there. The male figure in the doorway portrayed one of her main customers, Colonel Francis Charteris. He was a notorious fornicator who had been convicted of rape but managed to obtain a pardon through his influential connections. Hogarth's series of plates ended with the Harlot in Bridewell (see page 191) and her death.

◀ **'One shilling a time'**
Gentlemen passed cards such as this around Covent Garden and Soho in the 18th century, with the price of prostitutes and their likenesses. This girl's price is at the top right of the card.

▼ **Prostitutes on the Haymarket**
Haymarket was named after a cattle and sheep market that was held there. In the 18th century it was a street full of inns and houses of entertainment, and a well-known resort of prostitutes. By Victorian times it had become notorious as the 'great parade ground of abandoned women' and many gentlemen made regular visits there. Some of the women on the Haymarket had furnished apartments in Soho, Chelsea and Pimlico and others were domestic servants trying to earn a little extra money. Mayhew included this illustration in his work *London Labour and the London Poor* in 1851.

Prostitution flourished in many other areas of Victorian London and Mayhew estimated that there were 80,000 prostitutes working in London. Bow Street was notorious for brothels, despite the proximity of a police station and London's most famous Magistrates Court. Soho also became known as an area of vice and a haunt of prostitutes. Ratcliff Highway in the East End of London abounded with brothels and prostitutes ready to relieve sailors of their earnings. Notorious for cheaper prostitutes were Spitalfields and Whitechapel, where Jack the Ripper killed at least five prostitutes in 1888.

▲ **An attempt on the life of King George III**
George III was King of Great Britain and Ireland from 1760 until 1820. He suffered from bouts of insanity and was permanently deranged from 1811. George was generally popular with his subjects but was the target of assassination attempts, by Margaret Nicholson in 1786 and James Hadfield in 1800. Hadfield was a private in the 15th Regiment of Dragoons, was wounded in the head in 1794 and then suffered from delusions. He imagined that he was Jesus Christ and therefore had to die, but did not wish to commit the horrible crime of suicide, so he decided to kill the King since that would lead to his execution. He fired a pistol at the King in Drury Lane Theatre on 15 May 1800 but missed his head by a few inches. Hadfield's relatives and fellow soldiers gave evidence of his insane behaviour and he was found not guilty by reason of insanity. He was detained in Bedlam and died there 39 years later.

▼ **Mrs Margaret Nicholson**
Margaret Nicholson was a housemaid who attempted to stab George III with a dessert-knife in 1786. She was certified insane, sent to Bedlam, and died there in 1828.

The Hospital Call'd Bedlam

▲ Bedlam Hospital

Bethlehem Royal Hospital, commonly known as Bedlam, developed from the Priory of St Mary Bethlehem which was founded near Bishopsgate in 1247. Patients with mental disorders were looked after from the late 14th century, but the care in this institution included keeping patients chained, whipping them and ducking them in water. The priory was dissolved in 1547 and the site was purchased by the Mayor and Corporation of London and re-established as a lunatic asylum. The hospital moved to the building pictured here, in Moorfields, in 1675. The entrance was adorned by two statues, named 'Madness' and 'Melancholy', which were modelled on inmates. Patients at Bedlam were chained and held in cells or galleries, while whippings were commonplace until the end of the 18th century. Visitors could pay to enter and view patients until the 19th century, just as we might visit a zoo today. In 1815, a doctor reported that, in one room at Bedlam, he found about ten patients each chained by one arm or leg to the wall, each wearing a sort of dressing gown with nothing to fasten it. Some were sensible and accomplished, some imbeciles. Many women were locked up naked with only one blanket.

The hospital moved to a new site, in Lambeth, in 1815 (now the Imperial War Museum) and to Monks Orchard, Beckenham in Kent in 1930, while criminal lunatics had been transferred to Broadmoor in 1864.

Daniel McNaghton was held in Bedlam after his attempt in 1843 to shoot Sir Robert Peel outside 10 Downing Street. He missed but killed Peel's secretary, Edward Drummond. McNaghton was manifestly mad, believing that he was being spied on by government agents. The three judges at his trial directed the jury to return a verdict of not guilty on the ground of his insanity. There was no practical definition of insanity in law at this time and so the House of Lords sent a series of questions to the judiciary. Their answers became known as the McNaghton Rules. In brief, a man was to be presumed sane and responsible for his actions unless the contrary was proved. In order to establish a defence of insanity, it had to be proved that the accused was labouring under such a defect of reason, from disease of the mind, that he did not know what he was doing or did not know that what he was doing was wrong. These rules were modified by the Homicide Act of 1957, which introduced the concept of diminished responsibility and provided for a person to be convicted of manslaughter, rather than murder, if he was suffering from such abnormality of the mind, at the time of the crime, as to impair substantially his mental responsibility for his act.

➤ John Maycock assisted by John Pope in the murder of Mrs Pooley

Mrs Ann Pooley lived alone in Horseleydown. Her house was robbed in 1806 and her body was found in the kitchen. The murderers had entered the house by pulling out some bricks under a window. A reward was offered for information leading to the arrest of the murderers and a man named John Pope confessed to having committed the burglary with John Maycock. Pope was admitted evidence for the Crown. They were both tried at Kingston on 20 March 1807 and, as Pope's confession was given under promise of a pardon, the court ruled that he had to be acquitted of any charges. Maycock was therefore tried alone. Pope gave evidence that Maycock had asked him to assist in a robbery of an old woman. They broke into the house on 9 August 1806 and hid in the cellar. At about 8pm, Maycock attacked Mrs Pooley and killed her by kneeling on her and holding his arm on her neck. The two men then stole about £90 from the house. Maycock was found guilty and sentenced to be hanged and then dissected. He was executed at Horsemonger Lane Gaol on 23 March 1807.

➤ Samuel Mitchell murdering his own child

Mitchell was executed for the murder of his daughter, Sarah, aged 12. Mitchell was a spinner in Spitalfields. He would have violent outbursts after arguments with his wife, who left him, taking their daughter Sarah to live with her, although the child returned each day to work as an apprentice for her father. One day, Mitchell attacked her (probably maddened by the fact that she lived with his estranged wife) and cut her throat with a razor. He fled but was arrested and tried at the Old Bailey Sessions on 11 January 1807. Mitchell pleaded guilty, was condemned to death and hanged before Newgate on 14 January. His body was dissected at St Bartholomew's Hospital.

➤ Thomas Millwood, the supposed Hammersmith ghost, shot by Francis Smith

Francis Smith was condemned to death in 1804 for the murder of Thomas Millwood. The inhabitants of Hammersmith believed that a ghost haunted their village, but it appears that someone was pretending to be a ghost and scaring local people. Smith, an excise officer, was angry that someone was frightening the superstitious inhabitants, especially women and children, and went out on the night of 3 January 1804 to capture him. He shot an innocent bricklayer, Thomas Millwood, who was wearing white trousers and a white bricklayer's apron. It appears to have been an accident since, after the shooting, Smith asked to be taken into custody. He was tried at the Old Bailey Sessions on 13 January, when he claimed that he thought he was shooting at a ghost. One of the judges noted that he had deliberately carried a loaded gun and so this appeared to be a case of murder. The jury returned a verdict of murder but added their opinion that Smith should only have been charged with manslaughter. The judges took note of this, passing on a request for Royal Mercy and Smith was pardoned on condition of his being imprisoned for one year.

The Cato Street Conspiracy

◄ Arthur Thistlewood and the hay-loft

Economic difficulties and high unemployment in Britain after the Napoleonic wars created a breeding ground for radical agitation. Arthur Thistlewood was a militia officer who developed revolutionary sympathies when visiting America and Paris. He organised a demonstration at Spa Fields on 15 November 1816, intending to seize the Tower of London and Bank of England. The large crowds were peaceful at first but were incited to riot by speeches from Dr James Watson and John Hooper. Some rioters broke into a gunshop and then headed towards the Tower of London. The military were called in and many rioters were arrested, Thistlewood, Watson, Hooper and Thomas Preston being committed to the Tower and tried before the Court of King's Bench at Westminster on 9 June 1817. The jury acquitted them, probably because they did not trust the Crown's main witness, a government spy named Castle.

Thistlewood then became involved in another plot, which became known as the Cato Street conspiracy because the conspirators met in a loft above a stable at 6 Cato Street, near the Edgware Road. They planned to murder Lord Liverpool, the Prime Minister, and his cabinet on 23 February 1820. There were about 25 conspirators, including a government spy named George Edwards. Another conspirator, Thomas Hiden, had qualms about the proposed killing and warned the government of the assassination plan. A detachment of soldiers, constables and Bow Street officers went to the loft. Thistlewood killed one of the officers, Richard Smithers, with his sword and escaped with some other conspirators. James Ings, William Davidson, Richard Tidd, James Wilson, Richard Bradburn, James Gilchrist, Charles Cooper, John Monument and John Shaw Strange were captured and taken to Bow Street, together with many weapons found in the loft. Thistlewood was caught the next day and examined at Bow Street and before the Privy Council, while John Thomas Brunt, John Harrison and others were arrested over the next few days. The spy George Edwards escaped and probably went abroad with government help. Some of the conspirators (including Thistlewood) were held in the Tower, others in Coldbath Fields Prison.

► Four of the condemned conspirators: Richard Tidd, William Davidson, John Thomas Brunt and James Ings

The conspirators were tried at the Old Bailey. Thistlewood's trial, for treason and for the murder of Smithers, started on 17 April 1820, and after four days he was convicted. The trials of Ings, Davidson, Brunt and Tidd (for treason and for being accessories to the murder of Smithers) took six days and they were also found guilty. The other six prisoners then pleaded guilty.

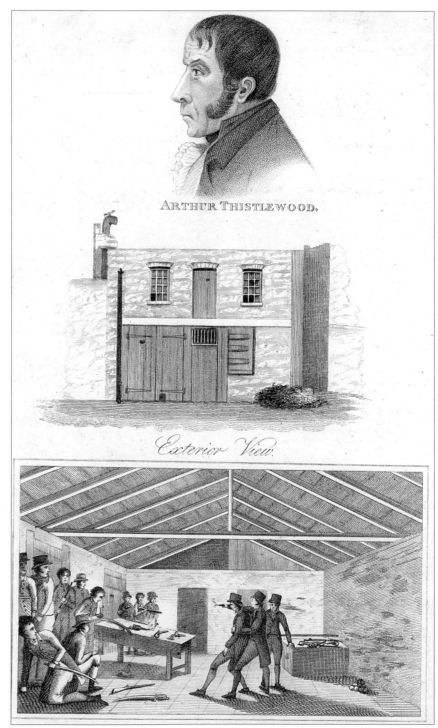

ARTHUR THISTLEWOOD.

Exterior View

RICHARD TIDD.   WILLIAM DAVIDSON

THOMAS BRUNT   JAMES INGS

➤ **Execution of the Cato Street conspirators**
Thistlewood, Ings, Davidson, Brunt and Tidd were hanged
outside Newgate Gaol on 1 May 1820. They were spared being
drawn and quartered but the law still required traitors to be
decapitated. Each man was therefore hanged and then, after
death, his head was severed by a masked man wielding a
surgeon's knife. Their bodies were buried inside Newgate (see
page 149). The conspirators who pleaded guilty escaped
execution: Wilson, Harrison, Cooper, Strange and Bradburn
were transported, and Gilchrist was pardoned.

➤ **Outrage on the Queen**
Victoria, born in 1819, was Queen of
Great Britain and Ireland from 1837 and
Empress of India from 1876 until her
death in 1901. A number of attempts
were made on her life, the first on 10
June 1840 by Edward Oxford, a labourer,
who shot at her as she was being driven
with Prince Albert along Constitution
Hill. Oxford was tried at the Central
Criminal Court (which had replaced the
Old Bailey Sessions in 1834), declared
insane and sent to Bedlam to be held at
Her Majesty's pleasure. The second and
third attempts on Victoria's life were on
30 May and 3 July 1842, by John Francis
(who was transported for life) and John
William Bean, who had merely pointed a
pistol at Victoria (and so was imprisoned
for only 18 months). This illustration,

from *The Illustrated London News* of 26 May 1849, shows a
further attempt. John Hamilton was an unemployed labourer
who fired a pistol (with a blank charge) at Victoria when she
was being driven in a carriage with the Prince of Wales and two
of her daughters near Hyde Park. Hamilton was sentenced to
transportation for seven years. In 1850, a former army officer,
Robert Pate, struck Victoria on the head with a stick in
Piccadilly. His plea of insanity was rejected and he was
sentenced to transportation for seven years. In 1882, Roderick
McLean fired a gun at Victoria at Windsor railway station. He
was found to be insane and committed to a lunatic asylum.

ripped open their bodies (except in one case when he was probably disturbed). He killed at least five prostitutes between August and November 1888 but was never caught. The five victims, all killed within a relatively small area, were:

Mary Ann Nichols, aged 42, on
    31 August in Bucks Row.
Annie Chapman, aged 47, on
    8 September in the back yard of
    29 Hanbury Street.
Elizabeth Stride, aged 44, on
    30 September in Berner Street.
Catherine Eddowes, aged 43, on
    30 September in Mitre Square.
Mary Jane Kelly, aged 25, on 9 November
    at 13 Miller's Court, Dorset Street
    (the only one of the murders
    committed indoors).

The killings became a sensation at the time because of the two murders on 30 September (within ten minutes' walk of each other), the killer's mutilation of the bodies, the ease with which the murderer seemed to escape and the inability of the police to identify or catch him. The police and newspapers received many letters and postcards that were purportedly from the killer. One of these, probably sent by a journalist as a prank, was signed 'Jack the Ripper'. One letter enclosed part of a kidney allegedly taken from one of the victims. Newspaper reports raised awareness among the better-off as to the appalling poverty in the East End and even Queen Victoria took an interest in the case, urging lighting for the courts and alleyways of the East End and improvements in the detective force. The victims were not attractive young women, except perhaps the last victim Kelly. Four were middle-aged mothers

▲ **The Whitechapel horrors: when will the murderer be captured?**

Spitalfields and Whitechapel in the East End of London were areas of great poverty in the late 19th century. Thousands of people lived in overcrowded, filthy rooms, with whole families sharing one room and others paying a few pennies to share a bed (perhaps just a floor and dirty blanket) in squalid lodging-houses. The poorest lived from day to day, in and out of workhouses, earning or stealing what they could to eat and stay alive. Drunkenness and prostitution were rampant. This area was the scene of the activities of an unknown killer, referred to by the police as the Whitechapel murderer, who became known as Jack the Ripper because he cut the throats of his victims and

who were separated from their husbands and who had gradually sunk into the abyss of drink, cheap lodging houses and prostitution in some of the worst areas of London.

Although there were possibly 80,000 prostitutes in London, the killer murdered five who lived within a few hundred yards of each other. Chapman and Kelly lived in lodging houses in Dorset Street. Nichols, Stride and Eddowes lodged, at times, in nearby Flower and Dean Street. The victims may have known each other, at least by sight. Another key point is that the fourth victim, Catherine Eddowes, had been married to a man named John Kelly and so was known as Kate Kelly. After her death, there was a gap of five weeks before the murder of the last victim, also named Kelly. It is therefore possible that

Eddowes was killed by mistake and, when the killer discovered his error, he returned to the area to finish his work. If this is correct, the killer was not a maniac who killed at random, but someone who was hunting specific women and perhaps making the killings look like the work of a madman.

▼ A suspicious character

The horrible murders and mutilations by Jack the Ripper, and the failure of the police to catch the murderer or prevent the killings, alarmed people throughout London and caused panic in the East End. Members of the public assisted in patrolling the streets or joined Vigilance Committees and reported strangers to the police, as well as many men who simply looked suspicious, as shown in this sketch from *The Illustrated London News* of 13 October 1888. Men carrying doctors' bags were likely to be mobbed by crowds or threatened with lynching.

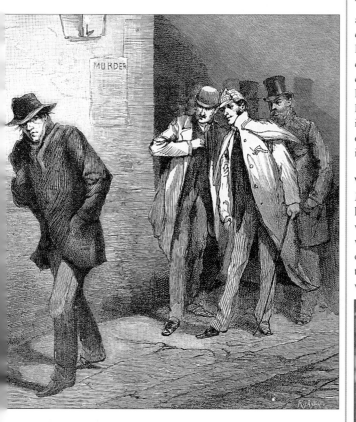

The panic in the East End gradually subsided as weeks and then months passed with no more Ripper-style murders taking place. The career of Jack the Ripper was over as suddenly as it had begun.

More has been written about Jack the Ripper than any other British murderer. The suspects include known murderers (such as George Chapman), butchers, slaughtermen, doctors (including the American Francis Tumblety who fled back to America in December 1888), a schoolmaster and barrister, freemasons and even the Duke of Clarence and Sir William Gull, one of the foremost medical men of the day. The identity of the killer remains a mystery.

▲ An opium den

Today's problems of drugs and drug dealers are not new, but on a vastly greater scale than ever before. It is estimated that 50 per cent of assaults and robberies in London are now drug-related. It was not an offence to take or possess narcotics until the 20th century; fighting the trade in drugs and solving drug-related crimes were only small parts of police work until about 1960. However, the danger of drugs was known for many years: Limehouse in the East End was an area inhabited by Chinese immigrants from about 1890 and the activities of a few Chinese opium smokers and dealers were portrayed, as in this drawing, in a sensational manner by the xenophobic British press.

▼ Police remove a corpse in Leyton

Murder has remained the most serious crime that the police have to deal with. There are sometimes very few clues from which to start an investigation, other than the body of the victim and the circumstances of the killing. In this photograph of 1934, two policemen are using a hand ambulance to move the corpse of Mr Moore, a tobacconist. His badly-burned body was found in a garage in Leyton.

chapter 2 Law and Order:
Thief-takers and the Police

FROM MEDIEVAL TIMES, responsibility for apprehending offenders and guarding citizens and property from crime in the City of London lay with unpaid constables and the watchmen of each of the 26 Wards of the City, under the authority of the Sheriffs and City Marshals. In the City of Westminster and county of Middlesex, these responsibilities lay with the parish constables. The law was administered by Justices of the Peace or Magistrates, and by justices sitting at superior courts, such as the Sessions House in Old Bailey. Prisons were meant to be self-supporting; a governor had to buy his position and was expected to recoup this cost and the expenses of running the prison from fees that were extorted from prisoners. This system was wholly inadequate.

Many areas were dangerous for law enforcement officers: that between Fleet Street and the Thames to the east of the Temple, known as Alsatia, was a hotbed of crime in the 17th and 18th centuries. Attempts to arrest criminals there resulted in armed groups of other criminals fighting the law officers. Much of Southwark, especially an area known as the Mint, and Thieving Lane in Westminster were also known as sanctuaries for criminals. These had been areas of sanctuary in medieval times and criminals resided there in the belief that the ancient privileges remained in force. The populations often warned any wanted men of the arrival of officers of the law and it was said that a warrant of arrest could only be executed in Alsatia with the support of a company of musketeers. In Victorian times, there were still many areas in London where policemen were advised to walk only in pairs. These criminal slums, known as rookeries, such as those of St Giles and Saffron Hill, featured in the novels of Charles Dickens. The most notorious rookery was that of St Giles, the area around modern-day Tottenham Court Road underground station. Constables chasing suspects into the area were likely to be attacked and savagely beaten. In 1840, a number of officers entered St Giles to arrest a gang of coiners who operated there and a pitched battle between police and groups of criminals lasted for several hours.

In the 17th and 18th centuries, many officers of the criminal justice system were corrupt. Magistrates kept the fines paid by criminals and the problems were compounded by the rise of the reward system in the early 18th century. For years, many prosecutions were undertaken not by the state, but by private persons, either those who had suffered as a result of a crime or those men, known as common informers, who worked as private policemen. They could prosecute a wide range of minor offences, such as offences by traders (for example, selling short weight) and were entitled to a share of any fine imposed on the offender. Public rewards also became available: the government offered money for the arrest or conviction of a particular criminal or for anyone who committed a particular type of crime in an area. The Highwaymen Act of 1692 offered a reward of £40 to anyone who arrested, prosecuted and secured the conviction of a highwayman who had committed a capital crime. This was known as a 'parliamentary reward' or sometimes 'blood-money'. Legislation extended this reward system to other types of criminals, including burglars, forgers and some thieves, and led to the rise of private thief-catchers or thief-takers, who were really bounty hunters, paid by results. The government also offered free pardons to offenders who surrendered, confessed and secured the conviction of their accomplices. 'Tyburn tickets' were also offered as rewards for those securing the conviction of thieves, burglars and some other criminals. A ticket exempted the holder for life from serving in all parish or ward offices (some of them onerous, such as the office of constable) and might be sold for between £10 and £40 or even more until their abolition in 1818.

The most famous thief-taker was also London's most famous criminal of the time, Jonathan Wild. He was known (and advertised himself) as the Thief-Taker General of Great Britain and Ireland. He controlled gangs of thieves and burglars from his house in Old Bailey, whilst pocketing rewards for capturing some criminals and for returning some of the loot that his gangs stole.

Henry Fielding, a Magistrate at Bow Street, and Sir John Fielding, his half-brother, instigated reforms to the system of fighting crime. They appointed their own thief-takers, who became known as the Bow Street Runners, and also established foot patrols and, later, horse patrols. These were the model for the Metropolitan and City Police Forces established in London in the 19th century.

Sir Robert Peel was responsible for the foundation of the Metropolitan Police Force in 1829 and so policemen became known as 'Peelers' or 'Bobbies'. For the first 21 years, the force was headed by two joint Commissioners and Magistrates, Richard Mayne (a barrister) and Colonel Charles Rowan (a retired army officer). The force originally consisted of just over 1,000 officers with ten Police Offices including Bow Street, Marlborough Street, Hatton Garden, Worship Street, Whitechapel and 4 Whitehall Place (Scotland Yard). The Metropolitan Police Force had grown to about 3,300 officers by 1839, almost 16,000 officers by 1900 and over 28,000 by 1989, with almost 200 police stations. The force was originally intended to prevent crime and ensure the security of persons and property. The public and media had concerns about a force of men with powers that seemed to threaten a citizen's privacy or liberty and who might be used to spy on opponents of the government. Policemen's powers were therefore limited: they could arrest anyone they saw committing or attempting certain crimes and in some cases search a person or his property, but most property searches required the issue of a warrant by a Magistrate.

The police had to develop during the 19th century in order to counter new problems. More resources had to be applied to the detection of those committing murder and other serious crimes. As a result, a Detective Branch was established in 1842, although by 1868 it had only 15 officers. The police also had to deal with the growing menace of a particularly nasty type of criminal: the bomber. London in the later 19th century was the scene of a series of bomb attacks by anarchists and by the Irish Fenians. The Special Irish Branch was established in 1885 in response to the Fenian bombing campaign, and was later renamed Special Branch.

The City of London Police Force has always been separate from the Metropolitan Police. The City Day Police was formed in 1784 as a response to the Gordon riots of 1780. By 1824, it acted as a Night Police as well. The City was excluded from the jurisdiction of the Metropolitan Police when it was founded in 1829. However, in 1838 the City's system of constables and watchmen was reorganised to form a Day Police and Nightly Watch of 500 men, commanded by a Superintendent. The following year, a Commissioner was appointed to the force, the name of which was changed to The City of London Police Force. This force still has jurisdiction over the Square Mile and is particularly busy fighting financial crime. The force's headquarters are at 26 Old Jewry, with divisions at Snow Hill and Bishopsgate and a mounted branch at Wood Street.

The Thames Police Force was established in 1798 at 259 Wapping New Stairs to fight the enormous amount of theft of cargoes from ships, smuggling and other crime on the river. It was merged into the Metropolitan Police Force in 1839.

➤ Jonathan Wild: Thief-Taker General

Jonathan Wild led a double life. He was a thief-taker who recovered stolen property, sent many criminals to the gallows and became known as the Thief-Taker General. However, he also received stolen goods and controlled informants, pickpockets, prostitutes and gangs of thieves and burglars. This 'Prince of Thieves' was executed at Tyburn in 1725.

Jonathan Wild was born in Wolverhampton in about 1682. He worked as a buckle-maker in Birmingham, Wolverhampton and then (after deserting his wife and child) in London. He fell into debt and was thrown into the Wood Street Compter, where he was held for two years, becoming a 'trusty' of the turnkeys, learning much about the criminal world and forming a liaison with Mary Molyneux (or Milliner), a prostitute and pickpocket. When released, probably as a result of a statute (the Relief of Insolvent Debtors' Act of 1712), Wild and Molyneux lived together and operated a small brothel in Lewkenor's Lane, Covent Garden. Wild also worked for a year for an Under Marshal in the City of London named Charles Hitchen. They acted as thief-takers, living off the rewards they obtained for catching offenders. They also accepted bribes from criminals, prostitutes and keepers of brothels or taverns for not arresting them or searching their premises. Hitchen also worked as a receiver (or fence) of stolen goods and took Wild with him when he went to taverns in Moorfields to meet gangs of thieves and prostitutes who gave him some of the valuables that they had stolen to avoid being locked up. Hitchen and Wild also trained boys as thieves. It was said that 'had Hell itself been ransacked, two greater villains could not have been found'. After about one year, Wild argued with Hitchen and so went into business on his own. The training that he had received from Hitchen was invaluable as he established his criminal empire.

The subsequent career of the Under Marshal Hitchen is of interest. He was removed from his post for receiving stolen goods and other malpractices. He was also known to frequent a house of male prostitutes, in Field Lane near Old Bailey, kept by the aptly named Mother Clap. Hitchen was found guilty in April 1727 of what *The Newgate Calendar* calls 'a crime too loathsome to be named' but was in fact attempted sodomy (he was acquitted of actually committing sodomy). Hitchen was fined £20, pilloried and imprisoned for six months. He died in poverty a few months later. Hitchen got off lightly: the punishment for sodomy in the 18th century was hanging.

Whilst working for Hitchen, Wild had taken a house in Cock Alley from which he ran a brandy shop. He had met many thieves, robbers and highwaymen through Hitchen and Mary Molyneux and realised that Hitchen had been a clumsy and greedy receiver of stolen goods. Wild therefore became a receiver on his own account but continued working as a thief-taker. His two businesses were dependent on each other. Acting as a receiver was punishable by a fine, whipping, imprisonment or transportation but Wild arranged his operation carefully. Stolen goods were never taken to his house but deposited in a safe place. Criminals would tell him the name or address of the victim who had been robbed or burgled. Wild then sold the

The City authorities turned a blind eye to Wild's practices because he was so useful to them. He was a clever detective who brought many violent criminals to justice and received many rewards for this work. For example, in 1716, a gang attacked James Knap and his widowed mother at Sadler's Wells. Knap was injured and his mother died. Wild tracked down the five gang members and organised their arrest. He also betrayed or captured and prosecuted many other offenders (perhaps over 100) although many of them were those who displeased him, perhaps by refusing to share their booty with him, or those thieves for whom he had no further use (such as Joseph Blake, alias 'Blueskin'). Blueskin (see page 28) tried to kill Wild for betraying him.

Wild acquired an ascendancy over almost all the thieves of London. He no longer waited for crimes to occur. He appointed gangs of criminals to operate in different areas and to specialise in different crimes, as pickpockets, burglars or highwaymen. He controlled warehouses in which stolen watches, rings and other valuables could be hidden or from which they could be sent to the Continent for sale.

Wild's private life was also interesting. He lived with Mary Molyneux and then a succession of other women – Judith Nun, Sarah Grigson (alias Perrin), Elizabeth Man and Mary Dean – over the next few years. Wild also had a number of mistresses at any one time.

goods (purporting to act on behalf of others) back to their rightful owners. He therefore obtained better prices than other receivers, was able to pay the thieves more and so became the criminals' favourite fence. His profit was the difference between what he charged the victim and what he paid the criminal. He also acquired a reputation for helping victims. As Wild's fame spread, he was able to move to larger rooms, rented from Mrs Seagoe, at the *Blue Boar Tavern* in Old Bailey. He also ceased approaching victims but merely waited for them to request his help in recovering their stolen goods. Wild would help if the victims paid him a reward or fee for recovery of the goods or for providing information about them.

Wild protected thieves from prosecution (if they brought him stolen goods) by corrupting court officials or prosecution witnesses and by paying people to give false testimony. He employed as his agents many felons who had returned from transportation before their sentence had expired so that he could betray them to the authorities if they did not carry out his wishes.

The Fall of Jonathan Wild

▼ Wild's house in Old Bailey

Wild became richer and more powerful. He left his apartments at Mrs Seagoe's in 1716 and rented a house next to the *Coopers' Arms* tavern, on the opposite side of Old Bailey. Sir William Thompson, the Recorder of London and Solicitor-General, attempted to curb Wild's business. He was responsible for a statute of 1719 that made it a felony for any person to take a reward under the pretence of restoring stolen goods (which means they probably knew the thief's identity) unless they prosecuted or gave evidence against the thief. Wild simply altered his method of business. He instructed victims that, to recover their stolen goods, they had to pay a reward to a street porter (who would be instructed by Wild to go to an appointed place). An assistant of Wild would then pass the goods to the porter in exchange for the money. Wild's business continued to prosper and he moved to a larger house, the King's Head in Old Bailey. This engraving shows that house, as it was in 1813, just before it was demolished (the shop front was added after Wild's death).

Wild was finally arrested on 15 February 1725, as a result of a bitter quarrel between a thief named Edwards and a highwayman, Roger Johnson, who had both worked for him. Wild sided with Johnson and so Edwards, wanting revenge on both Johnson and Wild, informed on them and managed to have Wild arrested for assisting Johnson to escape from a constable. Wild was committed to Newgate Gaol but, having money, was able to live on the Master's side of the gaol, in some comfort and with the benefit of visitors. Once he was in prison, Wild was charged with other offences, primarily receiving stolen goods and being in confederacy with highwaymen, housebreakers and thieves. Two of Wild's thieves, Henry Kelly and his lover Margaret Murphy, had been condemned to death and were awaiting execution. They were pardoned in exchange for giving evidence against Wild, claiming that Wild had sent them to steal from Mrs Stetham's shop on Holborn. They stole a box of lace for which Wild paid them six guineas.

Before his trial commenced, Wild issued a pamphlet naming 67 highwaymen, burglars and other criminals, including Jack Sheppard and Joseph Blake, whom he had apprehended and prosecuted to conviction. The pamphlet was distributed to the jurymen and the public at the Old Bailey Sessions on 13 May 1725 and Wild was then acquitted of being an accessory to the theft from Mrs Stetham. However, Wild was then charged with an offence that he had committed when awaiting trial in Newgate. Mrs Stetham had visited Wild before he was arrested and offered 25 guineas to get her lace back. Wild asked her to call back a few days later, but he was then imprisoned in Newgate, so he wrote to her from the gaol, asking her to bring him 10 guineas, for which he would help her recover the lace. In Newgate, Wild told Stetham to give the money to a porter so that he could pay the people who had her goods. The porter left and later returned to the prison with the lace. However, following Wild's first trial, the authorities knew that the thieves had been Kelly and Murphy, who had given evidence that Wild had known this, yet he took no action nor gave evidence against them. Wild was therefore tried under the Act of 1719 for taking a reward, convicted and sentenced to death. The night before his execution, he tried but failed to take his own life by taking laudanum. Wild was put in the cart, still groggy from the laudanum, and taken to Tyburn on 24 May 1725. He was cursed by the mob during the procession and pelted with dirt and stones. After hanging, his body was buried in St Pancras churchyard but it was dug up a few nights later (probably for use by surgeons) and disappeared. A skeleton that is said to be Wild's was found in a private collection in 1847, presented to the Royal College of Surgeons, and is now in the College museum.

◄ Joseph Blake attempting the life of Jonathan Wild

Joseph Blake, known as 'Blueskin' because of his dark features, was a thief and highwayman who attempted to kill Jonathan Wild. He was born in London and worked as a pickpocket from an early age. By the age of 17 he had spent time in most of London's prisons. He then joined one of Jonathan Wild's gangs and carried out many robberies around London. When one of the gang leaders was arrested (probably double-crossed by Wild), he named his confederates, including Blueskin. He in turn was captured and gave evidence against the other gang members. Blueskin was not freed in exchange for this information because he had not surrendered but had only given evidence after he had been arrested. The court ordered Blueskin to find sureties for his future good

behaviour or be transported. He remained a prisoner for about a year in Wood Street Compter. Jonathan Wild visited him, gave him some money and promised to help him but did not do so. Blueskin finally obtained his own release by arranging sureties and he then worked with Jack Sheppard (see pages 144-5). Blueskin was captured by Wild and his men following his burglary with Sheppard of the house of William Kneebone. Blueskin was brought to the Old Bailey for trial. Wild was going to give evidence against him and was in the bail dock, speaking to some of the prisoners awaiting trial. Blueskin believed that he was going to hang in any event. He therefore took revenge on Wild by seizing him round the neck and cutting his throat, in front of the court, with a penknife. A turnkey pulled Blueskin off Wild before he could finish him off. Wild was unable to give evidence (although he recovered from the wound) but Blueskin was convicted of burglary and executed at Tyburn on 11 November 1724, aged 28.

▲ Jonathan Wild on the road to Tyburn

Condemned prisoners were taken in processions from Newgate Gaol to the place of execution at Tyburn until 1783. In 1605, Robert Dowe gave £50 to St Sepulchre's Church (shown in this engraving) which was on Holborn opposite Newgate Gaol. Dowe requested that the sexton go to Newgate on the eve of executions, ring his bell outside the condemned cell and cry out this cheery little verse:

> All you that in the condemned hold do lie,
> Prepare you, for tomorrow you shall die,
> Watch all, and pray, the hour is drawing near
> That you before the Almighty must appear;

Examine well yourselves, in time repent,
That you may not to eternal flames be sent,
And when St Sepulchre's bell tomorrow tolls,
The Lord above have mercy on your souls.

The following morning, the condemned would be taken to Newgate's Press Yard (which was principally an exercise yard), where their irons were struck off. Their arms were bound and a halter was placed about their necks. Traitors were drawn to Tyburn on a sledge but other condemned criminals were placed in carts, usually two or three in each. The chaplain of Newgate Gaol would ride in one of these or in a separate carriage. They were escorted by the City Marshal, the Under Marshal, constables and javelin men to control the crowds, protect unpopular offenders from lynching and prevent the rescue of popular criminals. Dowe's money also paid for the ringing of the bells of St Sepulchre and a further admonition to be pronounced by the bellman as the condemned prisoners left Newgate in the execution procession. It was also the custom (until 1744) to present a nosegay to each prisoner.

▲ Wild in the cart and pelted by the mob

Hanging days were public holidays. The procession often had to force its way through enormous drunk and rowdy crowds along Holborn and Tyburn Road (now Oxford Street). Some criminals were cheered on their last journey, others were abused and pelted with stones, rotten food, dead animals and ex-crement. The journey to Tyburn might take as much as three hours and it was customary for the procession to stop at a tavern along the way, usually at St Giles-in-the-Fields, so that the condemned could have a last drink.

▲ Stephen Macdaniel, thief-taker

Jonathan Wild was not the only criminal who worked as a thief-taker. Stephen Macdaniel kept a public house in Holborn and worked as a thief-taker, but died in Newgate Gaol as a result of his crimes. Macdaniel formed a gang with the thief-takers John Berry, James Egan and James Salmon to accuse innocent people of crimes and then pocket the rewards. They induced men to commit thefts or robberies and one of the gang would act as a receiver for the stolen goods. Another gang member would act as the informant to the authorities and the gang member who played the receiver would give evidence about the crime. The thieves or robbers would be hanged and Macdaniel and his gang collected the reward.

Macdaniel and his cronies were finally brought to justice. The inhabitants of Greenwich had advertised a reward of £20, in addition to any reward permitted by Act of Parliament, for the arrest of any highwayman or footpad. The gang employed Thomas Blee, who had worked for Berry as an assistant thief-taker, to lead a fake robbery. Blee persuaded two pickpockets named John Ellis and Peter Kelly to help him. James Salmon was to carry valuables near Greenwich and be robbed by Blee and the two men. Blee took Ellis and Kelly to the *Ship* alehouse in Deptford on 23 July 1754. Salmon came in, pretending to be drunk, telling people that he was going to London. Blee, Ellis and Kelly followed Salmon and robbed him near Greenwich. The next day, Blee took Ellis and Kelly to the *Spread Eagle* tavern in Borough Market. Egan was there and Blee told Ellis and Kelly that Egan might buy the stolen goods, which he did. Blee and Egan then left but Egan returned a little later with the 'victim' Salmon and Macdaniel, who arrested Ellis and Kelly. They were taken before a Greenwich Magistrate who committed them to Maidstone Gaol. On the way there, they told a constable how Blee had seduced them into the crime. The constable repeated this to Mr Cox, the High-Constable, who knew that Blee and Macdaniel were acquainted.

◄ Thomas Blee, thief-taker

Blee was arrested and confessed. Cox then went to the Maidstone Assizes, waited until Ellis and Kelly were convicted of robbery and then arrested Macdaniel, Berry, Salmon and Egan, who were attending court to give evidence and receive their reward. On hearing that Blee would give evidence against them, each gang member asked to be admitted as evidences for the Crown against their accomplices. They were all refused since the evidence of Blee was considered sufficient to convict them. The four men were tried at the Old Bailey Sessions and convicted of conspiracy to obtain rewards unjustly. Each of them was sentenced to seven years' imprisonment in Newgate. In addition, each was to stand in the pillory twice. Macdaniel and Berry were pilloried at Hatton Garden on 5 March 1756 and treated severely by the crowd. An enormous crowd gathered when Egan and Salmon were pilloried at Smithfield on 8 March. They were pelted with stones, potatoes and dead dogs and cats. Egan was killed when a stone struck him on the head. The sheriffs feared that the others would die if they were pilloried again and so they were all left in Newgate where they died.

▲ 'Thou shalt steal': the thief-taker Dick Swift
This 18th-century engraving shows a thief-taker named Dick Swift teaching his son the Ten Commandments as including 'Thou shalt steal'. It sums up the contemporary view of the public, having been made aware of the true careers of Jonathan Wild and Stephen Macdaniel, that thief-takers were no better than criminals.

▲ Conducting the night charges to Marlborough Street Police Court
Metropolitan policemen wore black top hats until 1863 and uniforms of blue cloth, their tunics having tails until 1864. A constable carried a rattle (replaced by a whistle in 1880) to call for help and a baton. This drawing shows policemen of about 1840 escorting suspects and offenders who had been arrested overnight to the morning session of the Magistrates sitting at Marlborough Street Police Court.

◄ St Marylebone watch house
Until the Metropolitan Police Force was established in 1829, law and order were the responsibility of local constables and the watch. The watch was instituted by King Edward I to patrol streets at night and keep the peace. It was considerably expanded by Charles II and so watchmen were nicknamed 'Charlies'. Watchmen were based at local watch houses and wore greatcoats and leather helmets (and carried lanterns, bludgeons and rattles). The Marylebone Watch House was established in 1753 at a time when highwaymen regularly attacked travellers who were passing over Marylebone Fields. This hand-coloured aquatint of 1809 and those illustrations on pages 65 (bottom), 148-9 (centre), 155 (bottom), 157 (top), 160 (bottom), 169 (bottom) and 188 (top) are from *The Microcosm of London*, published in three volumes between 1808 and 1810 by Rudolph Ackermann with original drawings by Augustus Pugin and Thomas Rowlandson.

◄ Sir Robert Peel
Sir Robert Peel (1788-1850) was Conservative Home Secretary (1822-7 and 1828-30) and Prime Minister (1834-5 and 1841-6). He was responsible for the creation of the Metropolitan Police Force in 1829 and also for legislation that gradually reduced the number of offences carrying the death penalty to cases of murder, treason, piracy and arson in the Royal Dockyards.

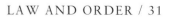

➤ Scotland Yard

A Metropolitan Police Office was established in 1829 at 4 Whitehall Place in Westminster, the house at the left of this photograph, which remained the headquarters of the Metropolitan Police until 1891. The houses in Whitehall Place had been built over two alleys named Middle Scotland Yard and Little Scotland Yard and they backed onto the alley named Great Scotland Yard. Policemen entered the building through the back entrance, in Great Scotland Yard, and so the office soon became known as Scotland Yard (the word 'Great' became redundant when Middle and Little Scotland Yards vanished). The building in the centre of this photograph housed the Criminal Investigation Department and the Special Irish Branch in the 1880s. It was badly damaged by a Fenian bomb on 30 May 1884.

▼ Metropolitan Police officers in about 1900

This postcard shows a sergeant and a mounted officer of the Metropolitan Police in about 1900. The Mounted Branch of the Metropolitan Police had its origins in the Bow Street Horse Patrols founded by Sir John Fielding. Mounted officers were armed with two pistols until 1866 and a sabre until 1925. They are now employed primarily to assist in crime prevention and to control demonstrations.

◄ Metropolitan Police officers at Tonypandy in 1910

This postcard shows Metropolitan Police officers in 1910 wearing greatcoats and helmets (introduced in 1863). These officers were sent to Tonypandy in Wales to help local police during the coalminers' strike.

▲ A woman police officer

The recruitment of women by the Metropolitan Police was preceded by the foundation of two voluntary women's organisations. After the outbreak of war in 1914, thousands of men joined the army and women took many jobs, on a temporary basis, which had previously been a male preserve. Women proved their value in many of these roles which led to their continued employment after the war. The Women Police Service was formed in 1914. The women wore uniforms, patrolled the streets, and were particularly concerned with discouraging girls from becoming prostitutes. Another group, named the Women Special Patrols, also began work in 1914. They did not wear uniforms but had similar objectives in addition to a concern for the welfare of children. Their successful work persuaded the authorities that women should be allowed to join the Metropolitan Police. In November 1918, Mrs Stanley was appointed as Superintendent of the Metropolitan Women Police Patrols, a new branch of the Metropolitan Police, which then recruited 25 policewomen from the ranks of the Women Special Patrols. The Metropolitan Women Police Patrols were gradually expanded and in 1922 given certain powers of arrest. The patrols were reorganised into the Women's Branch of the Metropolitan Police in 1930 (the approximate date of this photograph). Women were integrated directly into the various branches of the force in 1973, the City of London Police Force having recruited its first policewoman in 1949.

◄ Sir Edmund Henderson

Sir Edmund Yeamans Walcott Henderson (1821-96) served as Commissioner of the Metropolitan Police from 1869 until 1886, having previously served in the Royal Engineers, as Comptroller of Convicts in Western Australia, and as Director of Prisons and Inspector-General of military prisons. One of the major achievements during his period of office was the establishment of the Criminal Investigation Department following the discovery of corruption in the Detective Branch at the 'Trial of the Detectives' (see page 85) in 1877. Another important change introduced by Henderson concerned the system of police beats, which had been introduced in 1829. Each officer patrolled a small number of streets so that he would see every spot on his beat every 10 or 15 minutes and there should therefore be a police officer within easy walking distance of any point in London. This system of visible policing – reassuring the public by their presence and guarding people and property from mugging, vandalism or other crimes – is still desired today, even though patrol cars, radio and the availability of back-up arguably constitute a better system. However, the beat system had become impractical by the 1870s; there were not enough policemen to cover the expanding number of London streets (and their denser population), and a constable might have to walk up to 20 miles a night. Henderson therefore introduced the fixed point system and by the end of 1871 there were 270 fixed points manned night and day by a constable, so that a member of the public could find a policeman with ease. Henderson was successful as Commissioner but had a continuing struggle to increase police salaries. He resigned following criticism of the police arrangements for dealing with riots in Trafalgar Square in 1886 – insufficient officers were available to guard property or maintain order and no senior officer was available to direct operations.

➤ Sir Charles Warren

Sir Charles Warren (1840-1927) was an army officer who had served in the Middle East and Africa. He was appointed Commissioner of the Metropolitan Police after Henderson resigned in 1886, when the press called for the appointment of a soldier to ensure that order was restored to London's streets. However, Warren was then criticised by the press for introducing what was seen as excessive militarism into the police and for using police and soldiers to break up a socialist demonstration in Trafalgar Square on Sunday 13 November 1887. It was called Bloody Sunday because two demonstrators were killed. Warren argued with the Home Secretary, Henry Matthews, and with the Receiver of the Metropolitan Police, who exercised stringent financial control over the force. He was also criticised by the press, unfairly, for his officers' failure to catch Jack the Ripper in 1888. For example, he was blamed for refusing to offer a reward when in fact the Home Office prevented him doing so. He was also criticised for not putting sufficient reliance on detective work. Warren published an article noting that he did not have complete control over the CID but was then reprimanded by the Home Office for discussing such matters in public. He decided to resign and return to the army. As his resignation was announced on the day of the last Whitechapel murder, many believed that he had been dismissed for failing to catch the murderer.

James Monro (1838-1920) was Commissioner of the Metropolitan Police from 1888 to 1890. He trained as a lawyer and then worked as a Magistrate and policeman in India. He joined the Metropolitan Police in 1884 as Assistant Commissioner and worked closely with Robert Anderson of the Home Office (later an Assistant Commissioner of the Metropolitan Police), who controlled spies infiltrating the Fenians. They succeeded in bringing the Fenian bombing campaign under control by 1887, putting many of the bombers behind bars. When Henderson resigned as Commissioner in 1886, Monro was expected to succeed him but Sir Charles Warren was brought in over Monro's head. Monro argued with Warren and resigned as Assistant Commissioner, although he was given a post in the Home Office with the title Head of Detectives and he continued as director of Special Branch. Senior CID officers were permitted to consult Monro, behind Warren's back, at the time of the Whitechapel murders in 1888. Warren resigned in November and was replaced by Monro. However, Monro argued with the Home Office over his demands for better uniforms and boots for policemen and over some senior police appointments. He resigned as Commissioner in June 1890 and returned to India as a missionary.

➤ **The Director of Criminal Investigations: Mr C.E. Howard Vincent**

Charles Edward Howard Vincent (1849-1908) was the first Director of Criminal Investigations of the Metropolitan Police. He served in the army and practised as a barrister. Vincent studied continental police systems and, following the 'Trial of the Detectives' (see page 85) in 1877, he was appointed director of the newly formed Criminal Investigation Department in 1878. Vincent expanded the department to 800 detectives, with higher salaries. All Metropolitan Police detectives, whether based at Scotland Yard or with the divisions around London, were brought into a single reporting structure, headed by Vincent. He was responsible directly to the Home Office rather than to the Commissioner (although his successors were responsible to the Commissioner). Vincent improved the *Police Gazette* as a source of information about wanted criminals and he also established the Convict Supervision Office with records of habitual offenders. He founded the Special Irish Branch (renamed Special Branch in 1888) in order to gather intelligence and carry out covert surveillance on Fenian terrorists and, later, anarchists and other left-wing revolutionaries. Vincent served until 1884 and then became a Conservative MP.

▲ New Scotland Yard

The Metropolitan Police headquarters were moved in 1891 to a new building close to Westminster Bridge, photographed here in about 1897. It was named Scotland House but known as New Scotland Yard. During the construction of the building, workers found the torso of a woman, without head or limbs, hidden in the foundations. The victim was never identified. This building was used as the force's headquarters until 1967, when they were transferred to Broadway, near Victoria Street.

▼ The Metropolitan Police Crime Museum, Scotland Yard

This museum was established in 1874 and became known as the Black Museum. It is now located in New Scotland Yard and has been modelled to look as it did in the 19th century, as portrayed in this drawing from *The Illustrated London News* of 13 October 1883. The museum was the idea of Inspector Neame, the officer in charge of the Prisoners' Property Store (which held the belongings of many prisoners until they were released). An Act of 1869 gave the police authority to retain objects used in criminal activities for instructional purposes, so Neame began to collect the tools used by burglars and thieves and to display them for the instruction of police officers in the methods used by criminals. The museum contains a vast array of pictures, weapons and relics from London crimes, including guns, knives, burglars' tools and pictures of criminals and victims. The ingenuity of criminals adds to the horror of their crimes. There is a gun disguised as an umbrella and a flick-knife that doubles as a pistol. The museum also holds items such as ropes that were used for hangings, the bath in which one murderer cut up his victims and the stove on which he boiled a victim's head. Plaster casts of the heads of some murderers and other criminals who were hanged are kept on a shelf. These casts were taken after criminals' executions and include Franz Muller (see page 87). Many of the casts were on display at

Newgate Gaol until its demolition. The museum is not open to the public because of the ferocious weapons on display which are used for lectures on criminal methods. I must therefore thank the Metropolitan Police for allowing me to visit the museum before completing this book.

➤ **City Road Police Station**
Four policemen stand at the door of this police station, photographed in about 1900.

▼ **The Police Station, Hyde Park**
Most of Hyde Park was originally a royal hunting ground. It was opened to the public in the early 17th century, soon became a fashionable place to visit and is now the largest of the Royal Parks. However, the park had a darker side. Highwaymen were active in Hyde Park during the late 17th and 18th centuries. It was also well known as a duelling ground and as the haunt of prostitutes. Many people walking across the park at night in the 19th century were assaulted or robbed by thieves, drunkards or vagrants. There were also public demonstrations and disturbances there in 1866. The park was guarded by only a few park-keepers and so a police station was built in 1867 within the barracks near the centre of the park. The Royal Parks are now the responsibility of the Royal Parks Police Force.

The Thames Police

▼ **The *Royalist*: the Thames Police station at Greenwich**
At the end of the 18th century, London was the greatest port in
the world. Over 1,700 ships might be there at a time, many of
them waiting for a berth where they could unload their cargo.
However, theft and smuggling were rife. Pilfering occurred at

▲ **Retrieving a body from the Thames**
This drawing, also from *The Illustrated London News* in 1888,
shows officers in a patrol boat known as a galley, which was
used by the river police from 1798 to 1925, retrieving a body
from the Thames (the police reported 25 suicides in the river in
1887). These boats were simple rowing boats but the police now
use very sophisticated motor boats, particularly important in
the fight against drugs. On average over 40 bodies are found in
the Thames each year.

docks and wharves or from the ships in port and river pirates
attacked the ships that waited to be unloaded. Hundreds of
Customs officers were corrupt. There were even specialised
thieves, known as mud-larks, who worked with accomplices
among the sailors. They would tip goods overboard into the
Thames so that the mud-larks could retrieve them from the
mud at low tide. The Marine Police Force was founded as a
result of the efforts of Patrick Colquhoun and John Harriott.
Colquhoun was a merchant who served as a London Magistrate
from 1792 until 1818 while Harriott had served in the navy and
in the merchant service. In 1797, Harriott proposed the
formation of a river police for the Thames and such a force, the
first fully organised police force in Britain, was established in
1798. It consisted of 220 constables and 30 quay guards,
commanded by a chief constable, with a
resident Magistrate at Thames Police
Court and headquarters at 259 Wapping
New Stairs on the banks of the Thames.
Harriott was appointed in 1798 as the first
Thames Magistrate and served until 1816.
It is estimated that theft from ships,
wharves and warehouses was cut by 98 per
cent in the first year of operations of the
Marine Police when they obtained 2,200
convictions. The force became the Thames
Division of the Metropolitan Police in
1839. This drawing from *The Illustrated
London News* of 26 May 1888 shows one
of the vessels used as a police station. The
ship, HMS *Royalist*, was a former Royal
Navy survey ship.

▼ **A patrol boat passing the Thames Police station at Waterloo**
The Thames Division had a number of floating police stations.
The *Port Mahon* was used until 1836 when it was replaced by
the *Investigator*. The brig *Scorpion*, moored near the hulks at
Blackwell, was used from 1840 until
replaced in 1864 by the *Royalist*, which
was in turn replaced in 1894 by
Blackwall Police station. Another old
warship, moored near Somerset House,
was used until 1873, when it was
replaced by an office built on Waterloo
Pier (to which was moored a barge).
The Thames Division was unable to
eradicate criminal activity in the docks.
Two further improvements were the
building of enclosed docks and the
creation, by each dock company, of its
own police units (united under the Port
of London Authority in 1909) that co-
operated with the Thames Division.

chapter 3 The Police in Action:
Riot, Bombings and Anarchy

RIOTING has been a constant theme in London's history since the Peasants' Revolt of 1381. For example, during the 18th century, there were regular riots by apprentices, riots at the time of elections, as well as the anti-Catholic Gordon riots of 1780. There were more anti-Catholic riots in 1850 (caused by the building of a Catholic church) and socialist demonstrations and riots in 1866, 1886 and 1887. The marches of Mosley's fascists in the East End in the 1930s, chanting anti-Jewish slogans, led to much violence. In particular Mosley organised a rally of his uniformed blackshirts on Sunday 4 October 1936. This led to street fighting and the 'Battle of Cable Street' (Mosley and about 1,000 members of the British Union of Fascists were imprisoned at the start of the Second World War).

Rioting is a regular occurrence in more modern times; for example, the poll tax riots of 1990, anti-capitalist riots of the last few years and also race or anti-police riots in Notting Hill in the 1950s, Lewisham (1976), Brixton (1981) and Tottenham (1985).

London suffered from a series of bomb attacks in the later 19th century, principally by the nationalist Irish Republican Brotherhood, or Fenian Society, an Irish-American organisation formed in 1858 to overthrow British rule in Ireland. Centuries of neglect and exploitation had resulted in great poverty and discontent in Victorian Ireland. The problems of absentee landlords, high rents and evicted tenants were exacerbated in 1845 by an attack of potato blight, resulting in starvation, disease and mass emigration to England and North America. The rise of violent Irish militants in America and England is, with hindsight, hardly surprising. The Fenians committed many outrages in London over the next 30 years and this led to the creation of the Special Irish Branch (later Special Branch) as part of the Criminal Investigation Department of the Metropolitan Police.

Many police officers have died or been injured in the fight against crime. Some particular cases are noted in this book and a list of policemen who died on duty is contained in *The Official Encyclopedia of Scotland Yard* by Martin Fido and Keith Skinner. Two cases are noted here, to show that the murder of policemen is not a new phenomenon. The first officer of the Metropolitan Police to be murdered on duty was Police Constable Grantham. He was dealing with a domestic dispute in Somers Town on 27 June 1830 but was knocked to the ground and kicked repeatedly in the head by Michael Duggan. Grantham's wife gave birth to twins on the day that her husband died. The same year, Police Constable John Long was stabbed to death when he challenged three suspects on the Gray's Inn Road.

➤ 'A fine body of men': Special Constables in 1887

A depression in the 1880s led to unemployment and poverty for many workers. Mass demonstrations, strikes and street fighting flared up as a result. In 1886, 2,000 unemployed people marched through the West End carrying red flags and throwing stones. Many shops were looted. Their leader, John Burns, was arrested for incitement but acquitted at his trial. A larger demonstration took place the following year when crowds of the destitute and unemployed were camping in Trafalgar Square. Many political meetings and demonstrations took place, but meetings in and around the square were then prohibited and so a mass meeting to challenge this order was called for Sunday 13 November 1887. About 100,000 people took part, marching from different parts of London and converging on Trafalgar Square. The dispersal of these demonstrators by police and soldiers resulted in the deaths of two demonstrators, with many others injured. Seventy-seven policemen were injured on the day that became known as Bloody Sunday. Eleanor Marx, daughter of Karl Marx, was in the crowd at Parliament Square and later complained of police brutality. This drawing, from *The Graphic* of 26 November 1887, shows Special Constables (known as Specials) in Trafalgar Square, before the fighting, being instructed in their duties. About 6,000 Specials, created by a statute of 1831, were sworn on this occasion. The law permitted magistrates to appoint any number of Special Constables to control crowds and prevent riots. They were unpaid volunteers who were given powers of arrest and a uniform. The rioting of 1887 was the third occasion upon which Specials had been called out in London to assist the police; the previous occasions were at the time of the Chartist demonstrations of 1848 and during the Fenian terror campaign of 1867. In all these cases, the Specials were called out for a particular event and then disbanded. A permanent Metropolitan Special Constabulary was established in 1914.

➤ The riot in Trafalgar Square, 1887

One group of demonstrators, including William Morris and Bernard Shaw, marched from Clerkenwell towards Parliament Square. They were met by 4,000 police and soldiers in St Martin's Lane and dispersed. This drawing shows the red flag being taken from their socialist leader, Helen Taylor.

◄ The Hyde Park riot, 1866

Political agitation in London has a long history but it took a militant turn in 1866. During the summer, there were some peaceful demonstrations in Trafalgar Square but the authorities then tried to stop a mass demonstration in Hyde Park, organised by the Reform League, which was pressing for an extension of the electoral franchise. Over 3,200 policemen were present to keep order and the park gates were closed against the demonstrators. Many of the respectable people among them left and went to Trafalgar Square to hear a speech by John Bright. However, a mob tore down the railings on the Park Lane side of Hyde Park and fought the police. This drawing shows that episode, which became known as the 'Battle of the Railings'. Twenty-eight policemen were seriously hurt and many others, including Commissioner Mayne, were injured. Mayne realised that he had lost control of the situation and, for the first time since the founding of the Metropolitan Police, troops had to be called in to restore order. The demonstrators were forced back by mounted police and cavalry with drawn sabres.

Robert Bontine Cunninghame Graham (1852-1936) was a Scottish nationalist and socialist, who was elected as a Liberal MP in 1886. John Elliot Burns (1858-1943) was a trade union leader and socialist politician. He joined the Social Democratic Federation in 1884, and became a well known speaker in London, being arrested twice. Graham and Burns were tried at the Old Bailey in January 1888 and convicted of participating in an unlawful assembly on Bloody Sunday but acquitted of assaulting the police. Each was sentenced to six weeks' imprisonment in Holloway Gaol. Burns continued to work for the unemployed and poor workers of London, using his powers of oratory to assist the London dockworkers when in August 1889 they went on strike for better wages and working conditions. He later joined the Liberal party.

▲ The red flag falls

Bloody Sunday was not the first violent demonstration in London in 1887. The authorities were prepared on 13 November because demonstrations in previous weeks by the unemployed and socialists had also turned to violence. In October, the police had tried to prevent demonstrators marching from Hyde Park into the West End because so much damage had been caused there by demonstrations the previous year. Demonstrators fought with the police in Hyde Park, Berkeley Square and Dover Street, some managing to get to Pall Mall, Trafalgar Square and the Embankment, where they were charged by mounted police. There were further meetings and violence in and around Hyde Park and Green Park over the next few days. Later that month, there was a march from Clerkenwell Green to Trafalgar Square and then to Westminster, where the demonstrators demanded jobs and the replacement of Sir Charles Warren as Commissioner by a civilian. The march was generally peaceful but a few hundred demonstrators entered Westminster Abbey and caused a disturbance during the Sunday afternoon service.

▲ Cutlass exercise

In the mid-19th century the police were armed only with lanterns, rattles and truncheons. However, cutlasses and pistols were kept in reserve at police stations. Part of the response to the Fenian outrages, threatened from 1865, was to train police officers in the use of the cutlass. This drawing from *The Illustrated London News* in 1867 shows policemen training with cutlasses at Wellington Barracks in St James' Park.

The Fenian Outrage, 1867

➤ **The Fenian outrage in Clerkenwell, 1867**

Two leading members of the Fenians, Richard Burke and Joseph Casey, were arrested in London and held on remand at the House of Detention in Clerkenwell in 1867. Some other Fenians attempted to free them. The plan was that, while Burke and Casey were exercising in the prison yard, a wagon filled with explosives would be used to blow a hole in the prison wall. The explosion on 13 December 1867 blew a hole, 60 feet wide, in the wall and demolished nearby houses. Twelve people were killed and 120 were injured. Burke and Casey did not escape because the prison governor had been warned about an escape attempt and so suspended prisoners' exercise in the yard, keeping Burke and Casey locked in their cells. This drawing from *The Illustrated London News* shows the damage to the prison walls and the houses opposite.

➤ **The Fenian prisoners at Bow Street Police Court**

The police arrested three suspects as they fled the scene of the crime. Three others were arrested later. Timothy and William Desmond, Michael Barrett, Jeremiah Allen, Nicholas English and Ann Justice were tried at the Old Bailey. Charges were also laid against John O'Keefe and Patrick Mullany, who had not been captured. Michael Barrett was accused of actually lighting the fuse, convicted and became the last man to be hanged in public outside Newgate Gaol. The other five suspects were acquitted.

➤ **The prisoners in the Black Maria**
The suspects charged with involvement in the Clerkenwell bombing were held at Millbank Prison and regularly taken before the Bow Street Magistrates, in a horse-drawn prison van, escorted by mounted police who were armed with cutlasses and revolvers.

The Dynamite Plot, 1883

➤ **The dynamite plot of 1883: three prisoners and their captors**
The Fenian bombings in London continued for many years. A new series of Fenian outrages began in late 1882, many of them the work of Irish-American terrorists later known as the Dynamiters. Two explosions in Glasgow in early 1883 were followed by an explosion at the offices of *The Times* and, on 15 March 1883, an explosion outside the Local Government Office in Whitehall. These explosions only caused slight damage. These portraits are from *The Graphic* of 28 April 1883, which featured eight men involved in the London and Glasgow explosions and 11 officers of the Metropolitan and Birmingham Police who were involved in the bombers' arrests. This was one of the successful operations of the Special Irish Branch, headed by Chief Inspector Adolphus Williams and Inspector John Littlechild.

INSPECTOR JOHN GEORGE LITTLECHILD, CRIMINAL INVESTIGATION DEPARTMENT
Who Arrested Henry Hayward Wilson and Dr. Thomas Gallagher (alias Fletcher) at 17, Nelson Square, Blackfriars Road, April 5

INSPECTOR JOHN LANGRISH
Who Arrested William Joseph Lynch (alias Norman) at the Beaufort Hotel, Southampton Street, Strand, April 5

JOHN O'CONNOR (ALIAS HENRY DALTON)
Arrested April 5, at Bowles's American Reading Rooms, Strand. Charged with Treason-Felony

WILLIAM JOSEPH LYNCH (ALIAS NORMAN)
Arrested at the Beaufort Hotel, Southampton Street, Strand, April 5, with Nitro-Glycerine in His Possession. Lynch Has Now Turned Queen's Evidence

BERNARD GALLAGHER
Arrested at Glasgow, Charged with Treason-Felony

▼ **An escort to Millbank**
The Dynamiters who were captured in 1883 were held in high security. This drawing shows them being escorted from Bow Street Police Station to Millbank Prison by armed police.

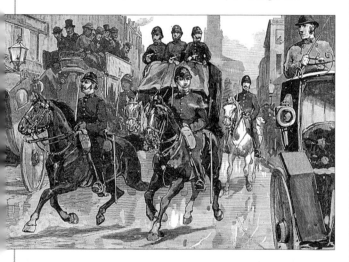

➤ **Bang!**
This drawing from *The Illustrated London News* shows the Fenians' attempt to blow up the Local Government Office on 15 March 1883. The police station in King Street is on the left. The bombers also attacked railways: in October 1883, a bomb went off in a tunnel near Praed Street station on the Metropolitan Line, and over 60 passengers were injured. Explosions continued in 1884: two bombs exploded in St James's Square, one near Nelson's column in Trafalgar Square and one in Scotland Yard, damaging the offices of the CID and the Special Irish Branch. Nearly 30 people were hurt in these explosions. In December 1884, a terrorist dropped a bomb over one of the parapets of London Bridge, which killed him but fortunately no-one else. It caused little damage to the bridge but hundreds of windows were broken in buildings on both sides of the Thames. The terrorists managed to explode three bombs, almost simultaneously, on 24 January 1885, one at the Tower of London and two in the crypt of Westminster Hall. The first bomb in the crypt injured two police constables. The second was removed in a courageous act by one of those officers, William Cole, who was awarded the Albert Medal.

Two of the bombers were captured: James George Gilbert, *alias* Cunningham, *alias* Dalton, an Irishman who had lived in America for some years, was convicted with Harry Burton at the Old Bailey in May 1885 and sentenced to life imprisonment.

Martial Bourdin

▲ Death of an anarchist; the bomber Bourdin

The Fenians were not the only terrorists who exploded bombs in London in the 19th century. In 1894 the police also had to take action against anarchists. A Frenchman named Martial Bourdin was killed on 15 February by the explosion of a bomb he was carrying up Observatory Hill at Greenwich. Bourdin was a tailor working in Great Titchfield Street. It is believed that he had been taking the bomb to Paris but thought that he was being followed, became nervous and got out of the train on which he was travelling at Greenwich, intending to use the bomb on the Observatory instead. As he walked up the hill, he began preparing the bomb for use, but it exploded. Bourdin was badly injured and died soon afterwards in hospital. His papers revealed that he was an anarchist and a member of the Club Autonomie in Windmill Street, near Tottenham Court Road.

▲ Ten pounds reward

Public notices have played a part in the fight against crime since the 18th century. Many posters were printed and distributed privately, usually by the victims of crime, or printed on the authority of local magistrates and the police. This poster, from 1833, offers a reward of £10 for the recovery of property stolen from rooms in Soho.

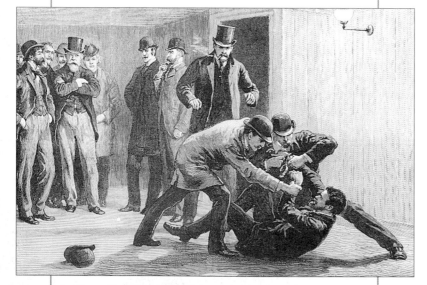

▲ The police raid on the Club Autonomie

The club was raided that night by detectives led by Chief Inspector William Melville and Detective Sergeant Michael Walsh. They searched the club for arms and documents and interrogated its members (who were mostly French and German). One or two put up a struggle and had to be handcuffed, but no arms were found.

The Battle of Stepney

▼ **The battle of Stepney: armed police at the scene**

The anarchist menace continued into the early years of the 20th century. Many Russians, Poles, Latvians and Lithuanians had come to England from Tsarist Russia. Most were peaceful and merely wanted to escape the attentions of the Tsarist police, but some were violent anarchists. In January 1909, two armed Latvians named Paul Hefeldt and Jacob Lepidus (*alias* Meyer) committed a robbery in Tottenham. Police officers and members of the public pursued the two men who fired guns as they fled. They killed a schoolboy (Ralph Joscelyne) and a policeman (Constable William Tyler) and wounded 18 others during the chase that covered six miles on foot, by car and a hijacked tram. Hefeldt was shot and died in hospital. Lepidus killed himself when he was cornered in a house. The press dubbed the events as the Tottenham Outrage and alleged that Hefeldt and Lepidus had been engaged in revolutionary activities. The authorities' distrust of any refugees from Russia seemed to be validated by events the following year. On 16 December 1910, a group of Russian and Latvian anarchists attempted to rob a jeweller's shop in Houndsditch but were discovered by officers of the City of London Police. The anarchists started shooting at the unarmed police officers, killing three (Sergeants Charles Tucker and Robert Bentley and Constable Joseph Choate) and wounding four others. Most of the anarchists escaped but they had accidentally shot their leader, George Gardstein, who died that night. Some of the gang were captured over the next few days. Two others, Fritz Svaars and Josef Vogel, were traced on 3 January 1911 to a house at 100 Sidney Street in Stepney in the East End. They barricaded themselves into the house and kept 400 policemen and a detachment of the Scots Guards at bay with gun shots for five hours, wounding a police sergeant and several onlookers. This photograph shows the Home Secretary, Winston Churchill, who came to witness the battle, surrounded by armed policemen.

▼ **The battle of Stepney: the fire**

The two anarchists died when the house caught fire. All of the men who had been arrested were acquitted because there was no proof that they had been associated with the murders of the police officers. One mystery that has never been solved was the true identity of a leading member of the gang named Peter 'the Painter' Piatkow. He may have been a Tsarist secret agent who was sent to England to provoke the anarchists to violence (in the hope that this would cause the British government to stop giving them asylum). He was never found.

➤ Absconded: William Meyn

This was a fairly typical poster, printed and issued privately in the early 19th century. It offered a reward of 10 guineas for information leading to the apprehension of William Meyn, *alias* Mey, *alias* Phillips, who was alleged by his employers in Bucklersbury to have stolen money from them and absconded.

▼ Murder: £200 reward

This notice was issued from Scotland Yard on 4 July 1881, the first time that the police issued a picture of a wanted man. The notice offered a £200 reward for information leading to the arrest of Percy Lefroy Mapleton, a journalist living in Wallington, who also called himself Percy Lefroy or Arthur Lefroy. On 27 June 1881, he shot and stabbed Mr Gold, a coin dealer, on the London to Brighton train when it entered a

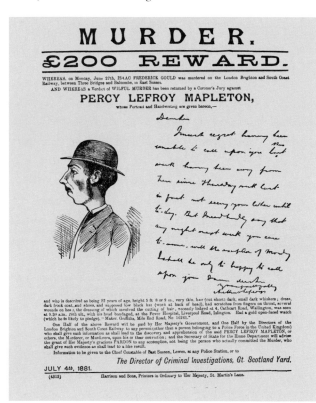

tunnel. Lefroy then threw Gold's body out of a window. When Lefroy got off the train, a ticket collector noticed bloodstains on his clothing and he was questioned but released. After the body was found, Lefroy was arrested and the police found some rare coins in his lodgings. Lefroy escaped out of the back of the house but was located after he, rather stupidly, wrote a letter to his former employer asking for his wages. Lefroy was convicted at Maidstone Assizes and hanged at Lewes Gaol on 29 November 1881.

➤ Murder and mutilation

Dr Hawley Harvey Crippen murdered his wife Cora in 1910 (see page 90). This poster was issued by the Metropolitan Police following the discovery of remains of Mrs Crippen, buried in the cellar of their house in Islington. The police obtained warrants for the arrest of Dr Crippen and his mistress Ethel Le Neve who were captured on a ship on their way to Canada.

chapter 4 The Courts of London:
Trials, Defendants and the Judiciary

LONDON was the home of many courts; those for the trials of its own inhabitants but also courts for many of the most important crimes that took place elsewhere in England and Wales. This section reviews those courts, some of the judges and lawyers who worked in them, and many of the accused who were brought before those courts.

Serious crimes in most of England were tried at Assizes, held in permanent or temporary courtrooms, by justices who travelled on circuits. The Assizes were replaced by a network of Crown Courts in 1971. The Assize circuits did not include the City of London or Middlesex. Offenders in London, Middlesex and parts of the adjoining counties were held until their trial in Newgate Gaol or other prisons, then brought before justices who sat at eight annual sessions of the Commissions of Oyer and Terminer (to hear and determine) and the Commissions of Gaol Delivery from Newgate. The sessions usually lasted three days. Until the 16th century, there was no specific courthouse for these trials, but the Sheriffs and Corporation of the City would hire rooms close to the prison. A special courthouse, the Sessions House, was built in Old Bailey, adjoining Newgate Gaol, in 1539.

Criminal trials at Assizes and at the Old Bailey Sessions House were conducted by one or more justices and a jury. Juries have been a part of the English legal system since the 12th century, consisting of local men who originally assisted justices by bringing alleged offenders before them and telling them what they knew of a case. By the 15th century, there were two types of juries, both of which were meant to be independent and protect individual freedom by deciding on questions of fact. A grand jury had its origins in the concept of a meeting of members of a community to consider the case against a suspected offender. The prosecution presented a bill or written accusation with supporting evidence to the grand jury. It was up to the jurors, by majority vote, to decide whether the charge was supported by the evidence, that is a 'true bill', and thus warranted a trial. Grand juries were abolished in England in 1933 but still survive in the United States. The petit jury still survives. It consisted of 12 men (and now also women) who decided on the guilt or innocence of the accused in a criminal trial. Jury verdicts had to be unanimous until 1967. The judge would rule on matters of law, control the proceedings and direct the jury as to legal points when appropriate. He would also pass sentence on a convicted offender in accordance with the law and the jury's findings of fact.

There has always been the possibility that a jury might be intimidated or corrupted by criminals but in past centuries the authorities might also be to blame. In 1670, the Quakers and many other religious groups were being persecuted for their beliefs. William Penn and another Quaker were tried for preaching to other Quakers. The jury at the Old Bailey Sessions was strongly instructed by the judges to convict the defendants but they did not do so. The jury was therefore locked up overnight without food. The next day they refused to change their verdict and one of the judges shouted, 'We shall have a positive verdict or you shall starve for it!'. The jury held firm for a few days despite being fined by the judges for 'going contrary to plain evidence' and then gaoled in Newgate for failing to pay the fines. Four jurors remained in custody for several months until they won a ruling from another court for damages for their suffering. The right of a jury to bring in a verdict according to their conscience was therefore established.

Less serious offences were tried without juries by Justices of the Peace, later known as Magistrates. They sat at Quarter Sessions (which were held four times a year) in each county. From the 19th century, Magistrates also sat, between the Quarter Sessions, at Petty Sessions. Magistrates also examined defendants and witnesses prior to a trial and later conducted committal hearings to decide whether evidence was sufficient for defendants to face a trial. The City of London and the City of Westminster also had their own sessions at which Magistrates sat to undertake examinations and dispense justice. Crown Courts replaced the Quarter Sessions in 1971.

Justices of the Peace were unpaid (and originally made money from court fees and fines that were levied on offenders). Before the institution of a police force, the system of parish constables and Justices of the Peace was quite insufficient to deal with crime in a major city. However, a change was brought about by the efforts of the first Bow Street Magistrate, Sir Thomas de Veil, and his successors Henry and Sir John Fielding. Sir Thomas de Veil was a Justice of the Peace for Westminster and Middlesex in the early 18th century and, like most Justices, worked from his own home or office. He was very active in the fight against crime, issuing warrants for the arrest of offenders and examining them thoroughly. He was particularly renowned for his efforts to break up the gangs of robbers and other criminals who plagued London. De Veil moved to a house on the west side of Bow Street in 1739, establishing the first court or office known as a Police Office there. De Veil and the Fieldings commanded paid constables and thief-takers, kept registers of known criminals and issued wanted notices to help in the fight against crime.

This concept of a court or office with a Justice of the Peace, commanding professional constables to detect crime and arrest offenders, was very successful. The Bow Street Office became famous and the model for seven new Police Offices in London and Middlesex. These were established by a statute of 1792 at Great Marlborough Street, Queen Square, Worship Street, Shadwell, Hatton Garden, Southwark and at Lambeth Street (in Whitechapel). A further office, at Marylebone, was established in 1821. Each office was staffed by paid (stipendiary) Magistrates and full-time, paid constables to assist them.

A statute of 1839 removed the executive functions of these Magistrates at the Police Offices (for example directing constables in their work), leaving them to examine suspects brought before them, issue warrants for arrests or searches and try minor offences. Metropolitan Police officers were attached to each office to be responsible for the prosecution of offenders in the cases heard by the Magistrates. The statute also renamed the offices as Police Courts. The Police Court was the accepted term until the 1940s. These courts are now known as Magistrates Courts.

The Court of King's Bench (or Queen's Bench when the monarch was a woman) also had jurisdiction in criminal cases. For example, it would consider disputed or important points of law that arose out of a criminal trial. It could also issue a writ of habeas corpus ('that you have the body'). This was a court order requiring that an imprisoned person be brought before a court for the legality of his detention to be tested. This concept existed in English Common Law from medieval times and was enshrined in statute by the Habeas Corpus Act of 1679.

The Sessions House in Old Bailey

▲ The Sessions House in 1720

The Sessions House built in 1539 was burnt down in the Great Fire of London in 1666 but was rebuilt. It was then used until 1774, when it was replaced by a new building. This drawing, from *Old and New London*, shows the Sessions House in about 1720. The court was open to the weather at one end, with a railed enclosure to hold the prisoners brought before it for trial.

The fresh air gave the judges, court officials, witnesses and public some protection from the diseases carried by many of the prisoners who were brought to the Sessions House from Newgate Gaol next door. Despite this, the Lord Mayor, two judges, an alderman and 50 others at the Sessions House in 1750 died of typhus, contracted from a prisoner brought before them from Newgate. The stench emanating from the gaol was sometimes overpowering. This led to the custom of sweet-smelling herbs and flowers, to counter the unpleasant odours, being strewn around the courts or carried in bouquets by judges.

The judges at the Sessions House were the Lord Mayor, the Recorder and the Common Serjeant of London. The Recorder and Serjeant still sit in the Central Criminal Court in Old Bailey that, as noted below, replaced the Sessions House. Trials are also conducted by the Lord Chief Justice and High Court and Circuit Judges. The Recorder is the senior law officer of the City of London and the senior judge at the Central Criminal Court. His office dates from the 13th century (the first known Recorder was Geoffrey de Norton in 1298) and other famous men who served as Recorder include Sir Edward Coke and the notorious Judge Jeffreys, who was Recorder in 1678. The Common Serjeant of London is the deputy to the Recorder. The first known Common Serjeant was Gregory de Norton in 1319, the son of Geoffrey de Norton (the first known Recorder). The Common Serjeant was originally elected by the Lord Mayor, the Aldermen and the Court of Common Council but he has been appointed by the Crown since 1888.

➤ **The trial of Lord William Russell: 1683**
Lord William Russell was a son of the
5th Earl of Bedford who was charged
with complicity in the Rye House Plot of
1683. This conspiracy was led by Sir
Thomas Armstrong and Algernon Sidney
and aimed to secure the Protestant
succession. The conspirators planned to
kill Charles II and his brother, James,
Duke of York (a Catholic) at Rye House,
in order to procure the succession of
Charles' illegitimate (but Protestant) son,
James, Duke of Monmouth. Russell was
alleged to have attended meetings (also
attended by the Duke of Monmouth)
during which the assassination was
discussed and was charged with high
treason. Prosecuting counsel was George
Jeffreys, who was later appointed as a
judge and became known as 'Bloody

Jeffreys'. Russell was convicted and executed on 21 July 1683 in
Lincoln's Inn Fields. Other conspirators were also executed.
Sidney was tried before Judge Jeffreys in November 1683 and
executed on Tower Hill. Sir Thomas Armstrong (see page 116)
escaped to Holland but was captured, brought back to London
and executed in 1684. The Earl of Essex was taken to the Tower
and died there from a cut throat. He probably committed
suicide but some thought that he had been assassinated by
order of the King and his Council.

▼ **'Bloody Jeffreys'**
George Jeffreys (1648-89) was one of the best known, but
severe, judges of the 17th century. He was called to the Bar at
Inner Temple in 1668 and appointed Common Serjeant of
London in 1671, aged only 23, and Recorder in 1678. Jeffreys
acted as prosecuting counsel at the trial of Lord William
Russell in 1683 and was then appointed Lord Chief Justice at

the astonishingly early age of 33. He conducted the trial of Sir
Thomas Armstrong (see page 116) in 1684. Following the
accession of James II in 1685, Jeffreys presided at the trial of
Titus Oates (see page 187). He also held the 'Bloody Assizes' in
the west of England after the suppression of Monmouth's
rebellion and, as a result, became known as 'Bloody Jeffreys'. In
nine days of court hearings, Jeffreys sentenced 300 rebels to
death and 800 to transportation and virtual slavery in the West
Indies or Americas. Many other rebels were whipped. Jeffreys
appeared to take a vindictive pleasure in sentencing the rebels
and, to speed up the proceedings, he made it clear that any
defendant pleading guilty might be shown mercy but anyone
convicted after trial could expect a death sentence. He was
rewarded for his work by appointment as Lord Chancellor.
James II fled England in 1688 and Jeffreys tried to do the same.
He was caught at a tavern in Wapping attempting to escape on
a ship to Hamburg, disguised as a seaman. He was seized by an
angry mob and taken to the Tower where he died in 1689.

◄ **Alderman Cornish**
Henry Cornish was a Presbyterian
Alderman of London who was elected
sheriff in 1680. He was convicted of
inciting riots in 1682 and fined. He was
then tried in 1683 for implication in the
Rye House Plot and executed on
23 October.

The New Sessions House in Old Bailey

➤ The Sessions House in 1812
This engraving shows the Sessions House that was built in 1774 on Old Bailey for sittings of the sessions of Oyer and Terminer and Gaol Delivery. Those sessions were abolished in 1834 and replaced by the Central Criminal Court. The sessions of this court took place 12 times each year in the Sessions House. People therefore continued to talk of someone being tried at the Old Bailey. The building had been constructed, like the previous Sessions House, with only one court but the large amount of business necessitated the construction of a second courtroom, known as the New Court, and two further courts by the mid-19th century. When Newgate Gaol was closed, it was decided to erect a new building on the site of both Newgate and the Sessions House. This building was called the Central Criminal Court and opened in 1907 but it was still known to many as the Old Bailey.

▼ A trial at the Sessions House in Old Bailey
This engraving of 1841 shows a trial at the Sessions House in Old Bailey. The presiding judge sits beneath the sword of justice (a symbol of the authority of the Lord Mayor of London). The 12 men of the jury are to the right of the picture. The Sessions House was always busy; by 1845, over 2,000 people were being tried there each year.

William Palmer

▲ **A trial at the Central Criminal Court: Palmer the poisoner**
This drawing, from *The Illustrated London News*, shows Dr William Palmer, known as the Rugeley poisoner, in the dock at the Central Criminal Court in 1856. Palmer was born in 1824 and worked as an apprentice druggist in Liverpool but was dismissed for stealing money. He then worked for a surgeon in Rugeley in Staffordshire, then at the Stafford Infirmary and later at St Bartholomew's Hospital in London. He returned to Rugeley and set up a medical practice there. However, Palmer was in constant financial difficulties and owed enormous sums to moneylenders as a result of his womanising and gambling on horse races. He had at least one illegitimate child by a servant girl (and some writers have suggested that he had up to 14 illegitimate children by 14 different girls). In November 1855,

Palmer poisoned his friend John Cook. He and Cook had gone to the races together; Palmer lost money but Cook won about £2,000. Cook fell ill after a supper party and Palmer volunteered to collect his winnings for him. Cook died, so Palmer used Cook's winnings to pay off some of his own debts. A post-mortem on Cook's body found traces of the poison antimony and Palmer was arrested.

◄ **William Palmer**
Public hostility to Palmer was so great that an Act of Parliament was passed authorising the move of prisoners' trials if a fair trial at their county Assizes was unlikely. Palmer's trial for Cook's murder was moved to the Central Criminal Court and commenced on 14 May 1856 before three judges – Lord Chief Justice Campbell, Mr Justice Cresswell and Baron Alderson. The prosecution was led by the Attorney-General, Sir Alexander Cockburn (who later presided at the perjury trial of the Tichborne claimant). The trial lasted 11 days – one of the longest of the century – and the press and public took great interest in the case. It was discovered that Palmer had probably poisoned his mother-in-law so that her property would pass to his wife (and therefore to his control). He also poisoned his wife in 1854 and his brother Walter in 1855 after he had insured each of their lives for £13,000. Two men to whom Palmer owed money and an uncle from whom he expected a legacy also died within a few days of staying at his home. Palmer was convicted of Cook's murder (so it was unnecessary to try him for the other murders) and he was hanged in front of a large crowd outside Stafford Gaol on 14 June 1856.

◄ **Dr Lamson at the Central Criminal Court**
Dr George Henry Lamson was executed in 1882 for murder. Lamson had a medical practice at Bournemouth but turned to murder to solve his financial difficulties, which were in part due to his addiction to morphia. His wife and her brothers had each inherited a share of their parents' wealth. One of the brothers, Percy John, was aged 18, disabled and lived at Blenheim House School in Wimbledon. Lamson visited Percy on 3 December 1881, where they took refreshment with the principal of the school and Lamson handed out some pieces of Dundee cake, already cut, that he had brought with him. He also gave Percy a capsule that he claimed was medicine. He then left for Paris but Percy was taken ill ten minutes later and died that night. Lamson was arrested on his return from Paris and tried at the Central Criminal Court over six days in March 1882. It was discovered that Lamson had purchased some aconitine (or wolf's-bane), a little-known poison, from a chemist and that he had fed it to Percy in the piece of Dundee cake (rather than the medicine capsule). Lamson was convicted of murder. He confessed his crime to the chaplain at Wandsworth Prison and was executed there on 28 April 1882.

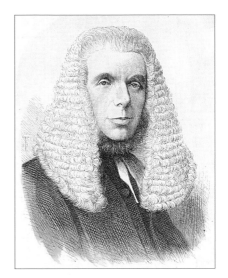

▲ **Sir Thomas Chambers QC, MP: Common Serjeant of the City of London**
Thomas Chambers (1814-91) was called to the Bar at Middle Temple in 1840. He was appointed Common Serjeant of the City of London in 1857 and Recorder of London in 1878. He also served as a Liberal Party MP.

▼ **The interior of a court in the Sessions House in Old Bailey in 1897**
This photograph shows the interior of a courtroom in the Sessions House in about 1897, shortly before it was demolished. The dock, with a glass screen, is on the left. The jurors' box is under the windows and faced by the barristers' pews. The low table in the centre of the court is for the solicitors. To the right is the judge's seat and the Old Bailey sword, the symbol of the Lord Mayor's authority, hangs below the canopy.

➤ **Waiting to enter the dock**
This drawing from *The Graphic* in 1873 shows prisoners waiting to be taken into the dock at the Central Criminal Court.

Patrick O'Donnell

◄ **Patrick O'Donnell: the committal**
Patrick O'Donnell was hanged in 1883 for the murder at sea of James Carey, a town councillor of Dublin. Carey had joined the Fenians and organised the assassination in Phoenix Park, Dublin in 1882 of Lord Frederick Cavendish, the Chief Secretary for Ireland, and Harry Burke, the Permanent Under-Secretary. Carey was arrested in January 1883. He appeared at Kilmainham Court House in February and then turned Queen's evidence, sending five men to the gallows. The authorities then tried to smuggle Carey to South Africa and he was escorted from Capetown to Port Elizabeth on board the ship *Melrose*. O'Donnell boarded the ship and shot Carey (as punishment for informing on his Fenian colleagues) whilst at sea on 29 July 1883. O'Donnell was brought to London in September 1883 and held in Millbank Prison. He was taken before Bow Street Police Court, where this portrait was drawn, and was committed for trial to the Central Criminal Court.

◄ **The trial of Patrick O'Donnell**
O'Donnell was convicted of Carey's murder at the Central Criminal Court in November 1883. This courtroom scene shows the cross-examination of Mrs Carey. O'Donnell is pictured in the inset numbered 5. The man in the inset numbered 3 was Nathan Marks of Cape Town, who had witnessed Carey's murder on the ship. O'Donnell was convicted and hanged in Newgate Gaol on 17 December.

▲ The Pimlico poisoning case: Adelaide Bartlett

Adelaide Bartlett (pictured at the top left of this drawing) was a pretty woman who was tried at the Central Criminal Court in 1886, accused of murdering her husband with liquid chloroform, the only recorded case of its use in a British homicide. Adelaide Blanche de la Tremouille was born in France, the illegitimate daughter of a rich Englishman whose identity remains a mystery. She was brought to England as a child and in 1875, aged 19, she married Edwin Bartlett, who was 11 years her senior. Edwin agreed to complete Adelaide's education and not to consummate the marriage until she was 21. He had eccentric views on marriage, believing that a man should have two wives: one for intellectual companionship and one for what he described as 'use', that is sexual pleasure. Adelaide was to fulfill the first function. She was unhappy within a year of the marriage and became intimate with a Methodist minister, George Dyson (pictured at the top right). Edwin seems to have approved of this liaison, even of their kissing in his presence. Adelaide later told a doctor that she had only had sex with Edwin once (and that this led to pregnancy and a miscarriage) and that Edwin 'gave' her to Dyson. Edwin made a will in 1885 leaving all his property to Adelaide and appointing Dyson as one of his executors. Edwin and Adelaide then moved to 85 Claverton Street, Pimlico. Dyson's visits to Adelaide became more frequent and Edwin fell ill, a doctor diagnosing acute gastritis but it is now thought that Edwin was being poisoned with lead. His condition worsened and he died on 1 January 1886. A post-mortem revealed that Edwin's death was caused by a large amount of chloroform that was found in his stomach. The question was how it got there. Suicide was ruled out because drinking chloroform would cause a burning sensation to the throat and internal organs. If the chloroform had been administered to Edwin (perhaps when he was unconscious), it would have left traces in his mouth and throat (and there were none). Dyson had purchased chloroform from some chemists at Adelaide's request, which she admitted using for Edwin, but only sprinkled on a handkerchief to help him sleep and to avoid his sexual advances (which he had decided to resume). Adelaide and Dyson had suspiciously disposed of the chloroform bottles, and the verdict of an inquest was that Adelaide had poisoned Edwin and that Dyson was an accessory before the fact.

Adelaide was charged with murder and Dyson was charged as an accessory. At the commencement of the trial at the Central Criminal Court, the prosecution offered no evidence against Dyson (and so he was discharged) because they wanted Dyson to give evidence against Adelaide (at the time, a defendant could not give any evidence), particularly about his purchase of chloroform at her request. The media and public took great interest in the trial and particularly Dyson's evidence as to the immoral goings on in the Bartlett household. However, the prosecution could not prove how chloroform had got into Edwin's stomach nor who had administered it. Adelaide was acquitted. A surgeon at St Bartholomew's Hospital stated, 'Now that it is all over she should tell us, in the interests of science, how she did it'. Adelaide disappeared after her trial and probably went to France or America.

The Central Criminal Court

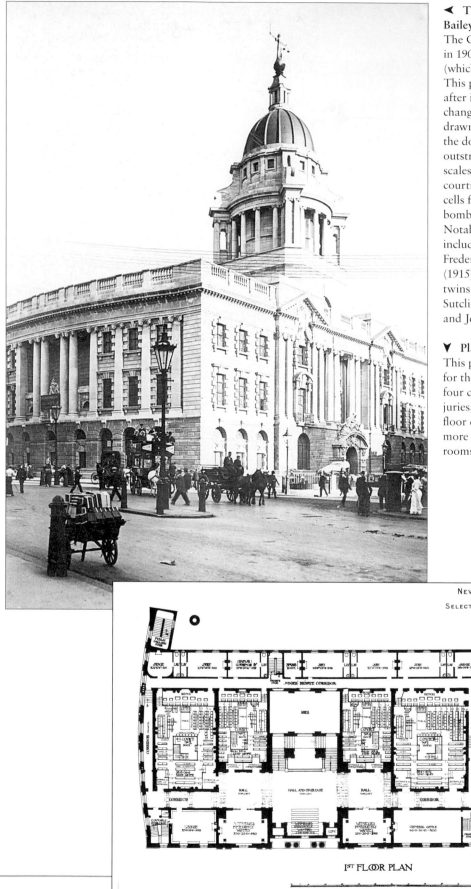

◄ **The Central Criminal Court in Old Bailey**

The Central Criminal Court was opened in 1907 on the site of Newgate Gaol (which had been demolished in 1902). This postcard shows the building soon after its completion, a view that is little changed today, except for the horse-drawn vehicles in the street. On top of the dome is the figure of Justice with outstretched arms holding a sword and scales. The building contained four courtrooms (but now has 19), with 70 cells for defendants. It was damaged by bombs in 1940 and 1941 but restored. Notable trials that have taken place here include those of Dr Crippen in 1910, Frederick Seddon (1912), George Smith (1915), William Joyce (1945), the Kray twins (1969), Donald Nilsen (1976), Peter Sutcliffe, the 'Yorkshire Ripper' (1981) and Jeffrey Archer (2001).

▼ **Plan of the Central Criminal Court**

This plan of June 1900 shows the design for the first floor of the building, with four courtrooms and rooms for the juries, witnesses and judges. The ground floor contained the prisoners' cells and more rooms for witnesses, including two rooms for 'better-class' witnesses.

NEW SESSIONS HOUSE. OLD BAILEY. E.C.

SELECTED DESIGN, E. W. MOUNTFORD. F.R.I.B.A. ARCHITECT

1ST FLOOR PLAN

▲ Mr Justice Day
Sir John Charles Frederic Sigismund Day (1826-1908) was called to the Bar in 1849, knighted in 1882 and was a judge of the Queen's Bench Division from 1882 to 1901. He was known as a stern judge in trials at the Central Criminal Court.

➤ The hanging judge: Mr Justice Avory
Sir Horace Edmund Avory (1851-1935) was called to the Bar at Inner Temple in 1875 and became one of the official prosecuting counsel at the Central Criminal Court in 1889. Avory was one of the prosecution counsel at the trials of Jabez Balfour (see page 62), Adolf Beck (page 92) and Oscar Wilde (page 91). He was appointed as a judge of the King's Bench Division in 1910 and became known as a hanging judge with a very cold manner. He was one of the three judges at the trial of Sir Roger Casement. He also presided at the trial of Browne and Kennedy (see page 93) and sentenced them both to death. Avory worked as a judge until his death in 1935.

➤ Sir Edward Marshall Hall
Sir Edward Marshall Hall (1858-1927) was called to the Bar at Inner Temple in 1883. His knowledge of forensic medicine was unequalled by any barrister at the time and he became one of the best known barristers for defending prisoners on capital charges. One of his greatest successes was in defending Robert Wood in 1907. Wood was accused of killing a prostitute named Phyllis Dimmock in Camden Town. Marshall Hall successfully cast doubt on the evidence of some Crown witnesses and also put the accused in the witness box (this had only been permitted since the Criminal Evidence Act of 1898). Wood was the first man accused of murder to be acquitted after giving evidence at his own trial. This tactic backfired when Marshall Hall defended Frederick Seddon (see page 58) in 1912. The jury convicted him, probably influenced by his arrogance and cold manner. In 1922, Marshall Hall defended Madame Fahmy, who had shot her brutal Egyptian husband at point blank range in a room at the *Savoy Hotel*. While presenting the defence, Marshall Hall acted the part of the husband, portraying him as a villain from the East, and crouched and snarled so convincingly that the jury acquitted his client.

The Trial of the Seddons

▼ Mr and Mrs Seddon in the dock at the Old Bailey

Photography in the courts was banned in 1925 and so photographs of the accused in the dock are rare. Frederick Seddon was hanged for murder in 1912. He had a mean and grasping nature, worked for an insurance company and lived with his wife Margaret and children at 63 Tollington Park, Islington. In July 1910, the Seddons took in a lodger, a wealthy spinster named Eliza Barrow, aged 49. She was rather strange, dressed badly and spent only about £1 a week on food and lodgings, yet owned assets worth about £4,000 (including gold, stocks and leasehold properties). She had argued with all her friends and quarrelled with (and spat at) her former landlords. Over the next few months, Seddon acquired all her stocks and property in exchange for paying her an annuity of £3 a week. Miss Barrow began suffering from vomiting and diarrhoea on 1 September 1911. She made a will that appointed Seddon as her executor and as a trustee to hold her estate until the beneficiaries (two young orphans) came of age. Mrs Seddon cared for Miss Barrow for 14 days and cooked her meals. A doctor visited regularly and diagnosed Miss Barrow's illness as epidemic diarrhoea. She died on 14 September.

▶▶ Frederick Seddon

Seddon benefited from Miss Barrow's death because he no longer had to pay the annuity. He arranged a cheap burial for her and received a commission from the undertakers. None of her relatives were told about her death, but a cousin called to see her and was informed that she had been buried. He asked about her stocks and property and Seddon said that they had been transferred to him. The cousin went to the police, Miss Barrow's body was exhumed and she was found to have died of arsenic poisoning.

▶ Miss Eliza Barrow

Mr and Mrs Seddon were arrested and tried for murder at the Old Bailey in March 1912. The prosecution alleged that the Seddons had extracted arsenic from fly-papers (used to kill flies) by boiling them in water. Each paper was said to contain enough arsenic to kill a person. The Seddons' daughter had allegedly bought a pack of papers a few days before Miss Barrow became ill. However, Mrs Seddon claimed that it was she who had purchased the fly-papers and that she had done so at Miss Barrow's request, after she became ill, because so many flies were being attracted by the smell of the sick woman's room. Frederick Seddon went into the witness box. He was unshaken during cross-examination but his cold, mean and arrogant manner probably swayed the jury against him, and he was convicted even though there was no evidence that he had handled arsenic or had any knowledge as to its toxic effects. The prime evidence against him was his financial motive to murder Miss Barrow. Mrs Seddon was acquitted by the jury, after a performance in the witness box as a meek, downtrodden wife, even though the prosecution alleged that she had actually administered the arsenic in Miss Barrow's meals. Many people were uneasy that Seddon had been convicted on circumstantial and scientific evidence, which was not then generally trusted. About 250,000 people signed a petition for his reprieve but it was of no avail and Seddon was executed on 18 April 1912 at Pentonville Prison, where about 7,000 people gathered outside the prison gates on the morning of his execution.

◄ **Penal servitude for a fraudster: Horatio Bottomley**

Horatio William Bottomley was a journalist, financier, fraudster and Member of Parliament. Bottomley worked first as a journalist and founded a number of publications. He was made bankrupt in 1891 but acquitted of fraud in 1893. He became Liberal MP for South Hackney in 1906 and promoted a number of companies, most of which collapsed. He was again acquitted of fraud in 1909, bankrupted a second time in 1911 and forced to resign as an MP. He re-established his reputation by use of his talents as a journalist and speaker on patriotic issues during the First World War. He then set up the Victory Bond Club, an investment scheme for poorer members of the public, investors' money being used to buy government bonds. However, Bottomley took most of the £900,000 that was invested for his mistresses, gambling and luxurious lifestyle. He was tried for fraud at the Central Criminal Court in 1922, where, during his final speech, Bottomley told the jury that the sword of justice (hanging from the wall behind the judge) would drop from its scabbard if they found him guilty. The jury convicted him and he was sentenced to seven years' penal servitude. This drawing shows warders about to lead Bottomley to the cells. He was released in 1927, bankrupted a third time in 1930 and died in poverty in 1933.

▲ **Westminster Hall**

The Palace of Westminster was the principal royal residence in London from the reign of Edward the Confessor until the reign of Henry VII. Westminster Hall was built in about 1097 by William Rufus and rebuilt by Richard II. It is the only surviving part of the original Palace. This print of 1808 shows the hall's exterior. It was used for banquets and, from the 13th century, to accommodate the Royal Courts: both civil, such as the Court of Chancery, and those with criminal jurisdiction, such as the Court of King's Bench. Many trials before the House of Lords were also heard here, such as the treason trial of Lord Lovat (in 1747) and the trial in 1776 of Elizabeth Chudleigh, Duchess of Kingston for bigamy. Other famous trials that took place here include those of William Wallace in 1305, Sir Thomas More (1535), Guy Fawkes and his confederates (1606), the Earl of Strafford (1641), King Charles I (1649) and Warren Hastings (which lasted seven years, from 1788 to 1795).

◤ **The Court of King's Bench in the reign of Henry VI**

The Court of King's Bench sat in Westminster Hall from the 13th until the 19th centuries. The courts sitting in the hall were originally only separated by low partitions until proper courtrooms were constructed within the hall in 1740. In the 15th century, the Court of King's Bench had jurisdiction over all crimes that involved a breach of the King's peace. This illustration, from a manuscript of the reign of Henry VI, shows five judges sitting in this court. A prisoner in fetters, guarded by a tipstaff, stands at the bar of the court while six other prisoners, with their legs chained together, wait at the back of the court.

▲ Lord Lovat

Simon Fraser, 12th Baron Lovat (1667-1747), was a Jacobite intriguer outlawed for treason in 1698. He obtained a pardon and assumed the title Baron Lovat in 1699, securing his inheritance of the Lovat estates by violence. He forcibly married the widow of his uncle, the previous Lord Lovat, and is said to have torn off her clothes and consummated the marriage with many members of his clan present as witnesses. Lovat was again outlawed in 1701 for this outrage and fled to France. He returned to Scotland and, during the rebellion of 1715, rallied his clan to the Crown and was then pardoned. Lovat gave only lukewarm support to Prince Charles in 1745, but was held hostage by government forces for the fidelity of his clan. Lovat escaped but was captured, brought to London and tried for treason.

► The trial of Lord Lovat in Westminster Hall, 1747

Lovat was tried by the House of Lords in Westminster Hall. This drawing shows the magnificent roof that was added to the hall by Richard II. Lovat is in the foreground, standing behind five rows of Earls, Barons and Viscounts, while the galleries were filled with hundreds of spectators including members of the House of Commons and nobles' families. The trial started on 9 March 1747. Lovat was convicted of treason on 19 March and executed on Tower Hill on 9 April, aged 80. An immense crowd gathered to watch his execution and one of the stands collapsed, killing 20 spectators.

Printed for & Sold by CARINGTON BOWLES   No. 69 St Pauls Church Yard

A Perspective View of Westminster Hall, with both Houses of Parliament assembled on the Tryal of SIMON LORD LOVAT.

Also a View of the Peeresses their Daughters the Foreign Embassadors & the rest of y nu Company as they were ranged on the Scaffolding erected on that Solemn Occasion.

1. The Kings Chair on the Throne.
2. Prince of Wales Seat.
3. Duke of Cumberlands Seat.
4. A Chair for the Ld High Steward.
5. Ld High Steward remov'd from his Chair, nearer the Bar for conveniency of hearing.
6. The two Arch Bishops.
7. Bishops on Two Benches.

8. The great Officers of State Dukes and Marquisses on the front Seat.
9. The Barons seated behind the Dukes.
10. Earls & Viscounts.
11. The remainder of the Barons Seated behind the Earls & Viscounts.
12. The Master of the Rolls.
13. The Head Master in Chancery.
14. The Judges Sitting on the inside of

Woolpacks, and the Masters in siting on the outside.
15. The Serjeant at Mace.
16. Lord High Stewards Purse be
17. Clerks belonging to y House of y
18. Four Mace Bearers & two Horn behind them Peers Sons all of t
19. Four Mace Bearers & Ld High Gentlemen, all of them Standi

REFERENCES to the Scaffolding round the HOUSE of LORDS

A. The Speaker of the House of Commons.
B. The Members of the House of Commons on the side seats.
C. Other Members of the House of Commons in front Seats.
D. The Manage as for y House of Commons.
E. The Solicitors & Clerks belonging to the Managers.
F. Lord Lovat at the Bar with the Gentleman of the Tower on his Right hand, & the Gentleman Jailers with y Axe on his left.
G. The Witness giving Evidence.

H. The Prisoners Council.
I. Writer taking the Trial.
K. The Kings Box with a Velvet Chair, and Ladies on 6 Rows of Benches.
L. The Prince of Wales Box, with Ladies Seated on 6 Benches.
M. A Box with Benches for the D. of Cumberld. Princesses & their Attendants, behind this Box was 3 Benches for the use of the Lord High Stewards Family, & 1 Bench for the Ld Chief Justice.
N. The Box where Princ Amelia Sat during y Trial

O. The Box for Foreign Embassa
P. Peeresses & their Daughters on 4 B
Q. Seats for Peers Tickets, besides the Side, there were 9 seats in front for
R. The D. of Ancasters Gallery at y You Hall, containing 17 Rows of Sea 860 People. At the Northend wa Gallery belonging to the same y whole space behind y Commons Benches for Peers Tickets.
S. Gallery belonging to y Board of Works.
T. The Earl of Orfords Gallery.

N.B. All the Seats were Cover'd & Scaffolding hung with Red Bays, excepting where the House of Commons Sat, & that was cover'd with Green

Begun on Monday the 9th Day of March, and continued on Tuesday the 10th Wednesday 11th Friday 13th Monday 16th Wednesday 18th and Thurs Days of March 1747, on the last of which Days Judgement of HIGH TREASON was given against him.

► John Wilkes before the Court of King's Bench

John Wilkes (1727-97) was born in Clerkenwell. He was a member of the infamous Hell Fire Club and squandered the money he inherited from his rich father (and his wife's fortune) on gambling and other vices. Wilkes was elected as MP for Aylesbury in 1757 and tried to obtain a lucrative post from the government. He was rebuffed and so attacked the government instead. He was the co-founder of the paper *North Briton* and was arrested in 1763 for libel on George III's minister, Lord Bute. He was released because of his privilege as a member of the House of Commons and because he had been arrested illegally. The warrant had not named him but was a general warrant, ordering the arrest of the (unnamed) authors, printers and publishers of the *North Briton*. The courts pronounced such warrants to be illegal. Wilkes was expelled from the Commons in 1764 and outlawed for libel and fighting a duel. He was elected as MP for Middlesex in 1768, then surrendered himself and was held in the King's Bench Prison. Although the Court of King's Bench reversed his outlawry, Wilkes was again expelled from the Commons for publishing libels. He was re-elected as MP for Middlesex three times but, each time, the authorities annulled the elections. Wilkes was elected a fourth time in 1774 and finally took his seat (holding it until 1790). He was also elected as an Alderman of the City of London (and as Lord Mayor in 1774) and assisted in defending the Bank of England during the Gordon riots of 1780.

◄ William Murray, Earl of Mansfield, Lord Chief Justice

William Murray (1705-93) was called to the Bar at Lincoln's Inn in 1730. He was appointed Solicitor-General in 1742, Attorney-General in 1754 and Lord Chief Justice in 1756. Murray reversed Wilkes' outlawry on a technical point. He was created Earl of Mansfield in 1776 but he became very unpopular as a result of his judgments in certain cases of the period (even though he merely applied the law) and his house was sacked and burned during the Gordon riots.

► Abraham Thornton, who claimed trial by battle in 1817

Abraham Thornton was a bricklayer who was tried at Warwick Assizes in 1817 for the murder of Mary Ashford. She had gone on 26 May 1817 to a dance at Tyburn, near Birmingham, where

Thornton was heard to say, 'I will have connection with her though it cost me my life'. They danced and then left together at 3am. Mary was murdered on her way home. Footprints of a man and woman were found in a field near the path Mary would have taken, which showed that the couple had struggled near a spot where the ground had been indented by a man's knees and toes. From that spot, only a man's footprints could be seen, with blood marks, leading to a pit. It seemed that the man had carried a body dripping blood, and Mary's body was found at the bottom of the pit, where it appeared she had been thrown after a man had violated her. She drowned. Thornton admitted having sex with Mary but claimed that she had consented (and that they had then parted to go to their homes). However, the marks of the man's shoes fitted his own and blood was found on his clothes. Thornton remained silent at his trial but some witnesses said that he had returned home before the murder could have occurred. He was acquitted. The outraged public collected money to pay for a new prosecution, by way of appeal, by the victim's young brother, William Ashford (such prosecution appeals were permitted until 1819). The appeal was to be heard by the Court of King's Bench in Westminster Hall and so Thornton was taken to London. On 17 November 1817, Thornton demanded trial of that appeal by 'wager of battle'. The judges ruled that the law permitting trial by battle was still in force. William Ashford was much smaller than the athletic Thornton and so he declined the challenge to combat. Thornton was discharged and probably emigrated to America. Trial by battle was abolished by statute in 1819.

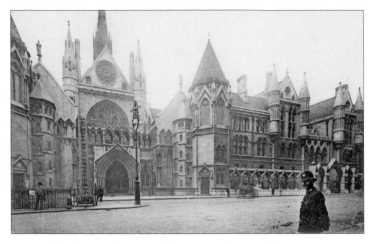

▲ The Royal Courts of Justice on the Strand

The Royal Courts of Justice are housed in buildings on the Strand, opened in 1882 to replace the courtrooms at Westminster. The buildings originally had 19 courts but many more have been added. There are over 1,000 rooms and three miles of corridors. The courts here deal predominantly with civil actions, bankruptcy and companies' affairs but the courtrooms of the Court of Appeal, Criminal Division, including the Lord Chief Justice's Court, are also here. High Court Judges, sitting in Chambers, also hear applications relating to criminal prosecutions and the custody of prisoners. The basement has cells for prisoners whose cases are being heard.

▼ Guildhall in the City of London

The Corporation of the City of London, consisting of the Lord Mayor, Sheriffs, Aldermen and Court of Common Council, has governed the Square Mile since medieval times. Guildhall was the City's administrative centre from the 15th century but the building also had a judicial function. Guildhall was used for some important trials, such as that of the Earl of Surrey (in 1547), Lady Jane Grey, her husband Lord Guildford Dudley and Archbishop Cranmer (1554). Dr Lopez, a Spanish Jew and physician to Queen Elizabeth, was tried here in 1594, accused of attempting to poison the Queen. He was hanged at Tyburn. Henry Garnett, the Superior of the Order of Jesuits in England, was tried here in 1606 for his role in the Gunpowder plot and hanged. Some of the City of London's own courts also sat in

Guildhall. The City had two Magistrates Courts (one at Guildhall and one at Mansion House) and each Sheriff held a court until 1867, originally at his Compter (prison) and then at Guildhall. Guildhall was badly damaged in the Second World War but part of the Great Hall survives. The building on the left in this postcard of 1913 was the Justice Room, built in the 18th century and demolished in 1972.

▼ The trial of Jabez Balfour and his co-directors of the Liberator Society

Jabez Spencer Balfour was a respectable, teetotal businessman, a Justice of the Peace and Liberal MP for Burnley. However, his business empire collapsed in 1892 and it was discovered that he had been committing frauds for 20 years. Balfour formed his first company, the Liberator Permanent Benefit Building Society, in 1868. He then established many other investment and property companies and financed each company by the process of 'snow-balling', whereby each company financed another. Balfour had to pay dividends to investors in the first company but he paid them from money subscribed by investors in his second company. Dividends for investors in his second company were paid out of the subscriptions of investors in his third company and so on. Balfour made a fortune for himself but he was cooking the books of his companies as properties were traded between them at inflated prices and the companies also made loans to each other at high interest rates to produce paper profits. Published accounts of each company portrayed flourishing businesses, so investors were willing to invest more and more money. However, one of Balfour's companies failed in 1892 with liabilities of over £5 million and other companies followed. Thousands of investors were ruined. Balfour fled to Argentina but was extradited and tried for fraud (with some of his co-directors) in 1895 before the Court of Queen's Bench, sitting at the Royal Courts of Justice. Balfour was sentenced to 14 years' penal servitude.

MR. W. H. HARRIS
Sheriff of the City of London

ALDERMAN SIR HENRY ISAACS
Lord Mayor

MR. ALDERMAN STUART KNILL
Sheriff of the City of London

▲ **A trial at Guildhall**
The Court of King's (or Queen's) Bench
sometimes sat at Guildhall. For example,
the trial of the British Bank directors
took place before this court, sitting at
Guildhall, in February 1858.

▲ **The Lord Mayor and Sheriffs in November 1889**
The Lord Mayor is the head of the Corporation of the City of
London. The first known holder of the office was Henry
Fitzailwyn who served from 1192 until his death in 1212. The
Lord Mayor is elected by Aldermen. He is also the City's chief
Magistrate (the right of London citizens to elect their own
Magistrate was granted by King John's charter of 1215). Each
Alderman is elected for a City ward and may sit as a Justice of
the Peace in the Magistrates Courts at Mansion House and
Guildhall. The office of Sheriff of the City of London and
Middlesex dates from the 11th century. Two Sheriffs are elected
annually by Liverymen of the City livery companies. They
ceased to represent Middlesex in 1888. The Sheriffs attend on
the Lord Mayor at official functions and attend sessions of the
Central Criminal Court. They also controlled and supervised
the City prisons known as Compters (see pages 140-1) and
appointed the hangmen at Tyburn and Newgate. *The Graphic*
of 9 November 1889 announced who was taking office as Lord
Mayor and the Sheriffs for the following year, the new Lord
Mayor being Sir Henry Aaron Isaacs (1830-1909). He had been
elected as an Alderman in 1883 and appointed as a Sheriff in
1886. The two new Sheriffs in 1889 were Sir Walter Henry
Harris and Sir Stuart Knill. Harris was a member of the
London Stock Exchange and a senior officer of three London
livery companies. Knill had been elected as an Alderman in
1885 and was elected Lord Mayor in 1892.

▲ **Slingsby Bethel, Sheriff of London
and Middlesex 1680**
Slingsby Bethel (1617-97) was a
republican who worked in Hamburg
from 1637 to 1649. He was elected as MP
for Knaresborough in 1659 and as a
Sheriff of the City of London and
Middlesex in 1680. He was unable to
serve at first because he refused to take
oaths to the monarch and church that
were required by law. However, Bethel
subsequently took the oaths and was
elected.

◄ **Mansion House**
Lord Mayors originally used their own houses or hired rooms for their official duties. Mansion House was the first official home for the Lord Mayor. It was completed in 1752 and included a Justice Room for one of the City's Magistrates Courts. This court dealt with offences committed in the south part of the City. There were cells below the court to hold prisoners awaiting the hearing of their cases.

▼ The great City forgeries

Four Americans – George Bidwell, his brother Austin, Edwin Noyes and George Macdonnell – came to London in 1872 and attempted an audacious fraud upon the Bank of England. The fraud relied on bills of exchange and promissory notes (written promises to pay money in the future) that were issued by banks or companies. Banks would accept these bills and notes from the holders, paying out a discounted amount of cash (and become entitled to receive the full amount of the future payments). Austin opened a bank account at the Bank of England in the name 'Frederick Warren' and paid in some cash and a genuine bill of exchange from Rothschilds. Having gained the Bank's confidence, Austin obtained the Bank's agreement that they would discount more bills (that is pay him a discounted amount of cash immediately and wait for the full payment due on the bills). Austin then deposited many bills, purportedly drawn by Rothschilds but in fact forged by Macdonnell. Austin also opened an account in the name of Warren at the Continental Bank. The Bank of England paid out over £100,000 to Austin, who transferred it to the Continental Bank account (and used it to purchase gold or US Treasury bonds). The Bank of England then noticed that the date was missing from two bills and its enquiries revealed that the bills were forged. Noyes was arrested but the others fled: Austin Bidwell was arrested in Cuba, George Bidwell in Scotland and Macdonnell on a ship as it arrived in New York. This drawing from *The Graphic* shows the examination of George Bidwell and Edwin Noyes before the Lord Mayor and Aldermen of the City of London, sitting as Magistrates in Mansion House in April 1873. Noyes is standing in the dock at the left of the picture and George Bidwell is sitting next to him (he was permitted to sit because he had been injured while attempting to escape). Bidwell's landlady is in the witness box and counsel for the prosecution is addressing the Lord Mayor. The four fraudsters were convicted at the Old Bailey in August 1873 and sentenced to penal servitude for life. George Bidwell was released due to illness after 14 years but suddenly recovered and made money by giving lectures. The other three men each served about 17 years in prison.

Sessions House, Clerkenwell Green

▲ **The Sessions House, Clerkenwell Green**
A new Sessions House was built in 1779 on Clerkenwell Green to replace Hicks' Hall as the venue for the Middlesex Quarter Sessions, Sessions of the Peace and sessions of Oyer and Terminer. This Sessions House became notorious for the severe sentences imposed by the judges and Magistrates who sat there. A woman aged 78 was sentenced to seven years' imprisonment for stealing some mutton and a man was sentenced to 20 years' penal servitude for stealing two pairs of boots. The county of London was established in 1888 out of parts of Middlesex, Surrey and Kent. The Middlesex Sessions were moved to Westminster Guildhall in 1892 but sessions for the county of London continued at Clerkenwell until 1921, when they were moved to a new Sessions House at Newington Butts.

▲ **Hicks' Hall**
Hicks' Hall was a Sessions House built in about 1612 in St John Street at his own expense by Sir Baptist Hicks, a Justice of the Peace for Middlesex, for holding the Sessions of the Peace and sessions of Oyer and Terminer for Middlesex. The building included a dissecting room, where criminals were dissected in public, and the skeletons of some criminals adorned the walls of the room. Hicks' Hall was demolished in 1777.

➤ **Interior of the Sessions House, Clerkenwell Green**
This aquatint by Pugin and Rowlandson of 1809 shows the hall inside the Sessions House, the dome above it, and the staircase leading up to the court.

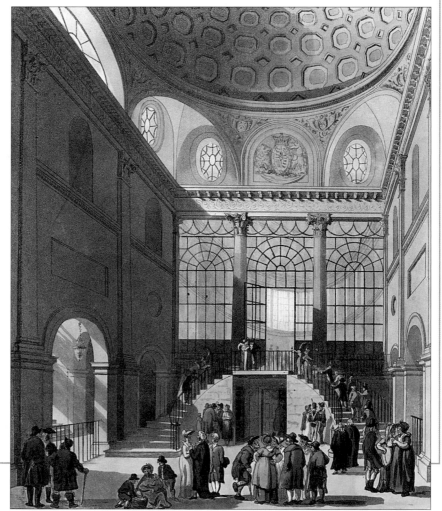

Middlesex Sessions

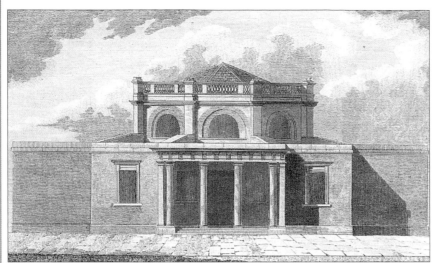

◄ **The Westminster Sessions, Middlesex Guildhall**
The Sessions for the City of Westminster were held from the 17th century in rooms in the Gate House, a building near Westminster Abbey that actually consisted of two adjoining gates. Other rooms in the Gate House (see page 162) were used as a prison until its demolition in 1776. The sessions were subsequently held in the Guildhall of the City of Westminster (shown here in 1813) that was built in 1805 on the west of Parliament Square.

◄ **Sir William Bodkin, Assistant Judge of the Middlesex Quarter Sessions**
William Henry Bodkin (1791-1874) was called to the Bar at Gray's Inn in 1826. He was one of the prosecution counsel at the trial of William Palmer, the poisoner, at the Old Bailey in 1856. He was appointed an Assistant Judge of the Middlesex Quarter Sessions in 1859 and knighted in 1867.

▼ **Middlesex Guildhall, Westminster in about 1920**
The building of 1805 was enlarged in 1893 and rebuilt in 1913, as shown in this photograph. The building now houses Middlesex Crown Court.

Bow Street Magistrates

LONDON MAGISTRATES of the 17th and 18th centuries dispensed justice and directed constables to locate offenders. However, they were also corrupt. They were not paid salaries and until 1792 they kept for themselves fines or bail money from offenders and fees from parish officials or complainants appearing before them. They also received bribes from criminals. Magistrates were described as 'mean, ignorant and rapacious' people who 'acted from the most scandalous principles of selfish avarice'. However, Sir Thomas de Veil was very different, a former soldier who was appointed as a Justice of the Peace for Westminster and Middlesex. His house on Leicester Fields was his court, office and an early type of police station. De Veil received a fortune in fees, like other Magistrates, and had mistresses and illegitimate children. However, he took his responsibilities to enforce law and order seriously and had a reputation for impartiality. He ordered the arrest of many suspects and made particular efforts to break up the gangs of robbers and thieves who plagued London. De Veil moved to a house on Bow Street in 1739, established the first Police Office there and became the first Bow Street Magistrate. (Bow Street is now the most famous of London's Magistrates Courts.) De Veil died in 1746 but his successors at Bow Street, Henry and Sir John Fielding, continued his work. De Veil's courthouse was used until 1881 when it was replaced by the present court (see pages 68-9) on the other side of Bow Street.

▼ Henry Fielding

Henry Fielding (1707-54) was a lawyer and author, most famous for his novel *Tom Jones*. He was called to the bar at Middle Temple in 1740 and appointed as a Justice of the Peace for Westminster in 1748. Fielding fought the problem of robbery in London by paying informers from a special fund and also employed the first professional detectives. Parish constables and watchmen were inadequate for finding and arresting criminals. Constables were only appointed for one year and, since the post was unpaid, most were unwilling to act for longer and so build up any experience. Fielding proposed that the government should pay salaries to those who enforced the law. In the meantime, he used a small government grant to establish a group of seven conscientious householders as volunteer constables to find and arrest criminals. They did not wear uniforms but were the first London detectives. They also undertook investigations outside London when requested and became known as thief-takers or 'Mr Fielding's people'. The government grant was sufficient to pay only small salaries and the expenses of investigations and so it was intended that they should receive rewards for convictions they obtained. Unfortunately, Londoners distrusted thief-takers (many remembered Jonathan Wild) and courts refused to allow Fielding's men to collect rewards. The force was disbanded.

▼ The blind Magistrate: Sir John Fielding

Sir John Fielding was the blind half-brother of Henry Fielding. He was appointed as a Westminster Magistrate in 1750 and as the Bow Street Magistrate on Henry's death in 1754. Until his death in 1780, Sir John continued the work of de Veil and Henry Fielding in breaking up the robber gangs that worked in London. He kept records of criminals who came before him and published lists of wanted offenders. He also revived his brother's force of detectives, who pursued suspects, used information from informers in the criminal world and became known as the Bow Street Runners. Fielding persuaded the government to grant £4,000 a year which enabled him to establish foot patrols of officers, stationed at Bow Street, to make the streets safer, particularly from footpads. He also established horse patrols but this experiment failed because the government would not provide funds to pay them (uniformed horse patrols were again formed in 1805 and absorbed into the Metropolitan Police in 1836). The Bow Street Runners remained under the control of Bow Street Magistrates until they were disbanded in 1839 when Magistrates lost responsibility for police work. Some of the Runners joined the Metropolitan Police.

Bow Street

▲ **The examination of Dr Bernard before the Bow Street Magistrate**
The examination of suspects and witnesses, to establish whether someone should be committed to trial, was an important function of Magistrates. This drawing shows the examination of Dr Simon Bernard, a French exile living in London, before the Magistrate Mr Jardine in February 1858. Two bombs were thrown by Italian revolutionaries at the coach of the French Emperor Napoleon III in Paris in January 1858. Eight people died and 156 were injured. The leader of the plot, Felice Orsini, was arrested and later guillotined. He had carried a British passport in the name of Thomas Allsop and it was discovered that planning of the assassination attempt had taken place in London. Dr Simon Bernard was an explosives expert, who was arrested in Bayswater where he made a living by teaching languages. He was tried at the Old Bailey but acquitted after a rousing speech to the jury in which he accused Napoleon of trying to destroy Britain as an asylum for those opposed to his rule.

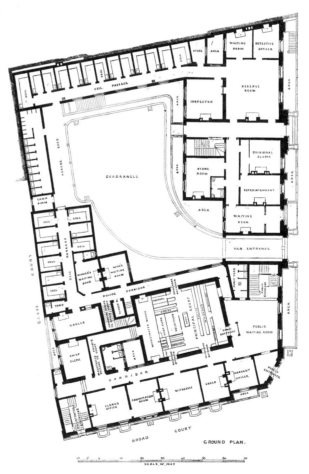

➤ **Plan of the new Bow Street Police Station and Court in 1881**
The building contained four courtrooms because of the increasing amount of work for the Magistrates. Passages connected the courts to the police station, on the ground floor of which were prisoners' cells and a courtyard where prisoners could be placed in, or discharged from, police carriages and vans that entered from Bow Street.

➤ **Interior of the Police Court at Bow Street in 1897**
The interior of Bow Street today is little different from that in 1897 when this photograph was taken.

▲ Bow Street Police Station and Magistrates Court
From 1797, a room in a tavern opposite Bow Street Police Office
was used to hold prisoners due to appear before a Magistrate.
A police station was built on this site when the Metropolitan
Police was formed in 1829. A new police station and
Magistrates Court were completed in 1881. The police station
has been replaced by that at Charing Cross but the court is still
in operation and the view is little changed from this photograph
of about 1910.

▲ 'Remanded': Mrs Osborne leaving the dock
This drawing, from *The Graphic* of 13 February 1892, shows a
lady leaving the dock at Bow Street Magistrates Court, having
been remanded in custody until her trial. This was an episode
in the Great Pearl Mystery that started with the purchase of
jewels from Messrs Spink in February 1891 and a civil action in
December 1891. Mrs Osborne was then charged with obtaining
money under false pretences and returned from abroad to
surrender to a warrant for her arrest. She was taken before the
Lord Mayor but discharged when the prosecution offered no
evidence against her. However, she was immediately re-arrested
on a charge of perjury relating to the civil trial. Mrs Osborne
was taken before the Magistrate Sir John Bridge at Bow Street
and remanded in custody in Holloway Prison.

A consultation with his solicitor
The Graphic published many sketches from inside the London Police Courts. This drawing of 1887 shows a prisoner in his cell at Bow Street consulting his solicitor about his case.

Mr Greenwood at Clerkenwell Police Court
Although not as famous as Bow Street, the other Police Courts of London were busy dealing with a continual flow of offenders. This drawing shows Mr Greenwood, a Magistrate at Clerkenwell Police Court in 1847, examining a woman.

Seven convictions for drunkenness
Many hearings at Magistrates Courts were for petty offences, drunkenness or vagrancy. This drawing from *The Sphere* in January 1903 shows Donovan Ross in the dock at Marylebone Magistrates Court. He had been arrested for being intoxicated and he admitted seven convictions for drunkenness that year. The Magistrate, Mr Plowden, did not send Ross to prison but fined him a shilling and banned him from drinking at public houses for three years.

Mr Ballantine, senior Magistrate at Thames Police Court
Many of the cases at Thames Police Court involved offences in the docks or on the River Thames. John Harriott (one of the founders of the Marine Police) was the first Magistrate at this court. He took a leading part in the investigation of the Ratcliff Highway murders in 1811 (see page 127). This drawing shows the senior Magistrate, Mr Ballantine, in 1846, when had served at the court for 25 years.

▲ The night charges at Marlborough Street
Night charges were offenders or suspects who were arrested
overnight, held in police cells and taken before Magistrates in
the morning. Night charges were usually petty offenders, many
of them drunk, who were arrested after street or tavern brawls,
or prostitutes who were arrested for soliciting. This drawing of
1887 shows night charges being taken into Marlborough Street
Magistrates Court.

► Inside the Black Maria
A carriage or van, known as a Black Maria, was used from 1858
to transport criminals between courts and prisons. They were
nine feet long, and five feet wide and high. Up to thirty
prisoners might be crammed into them,
both male and female, respectable and
clean or poor and filthy. Later carriages
had a central passage with small boxes
on each side to hold individual prisoners,
as shown in this drawing from *The
Graphic* in 1887. The doors of the boxes
had hatches so that an officer could see
prisoners at all times. From 1914 the
horse-drawn carriages were gradually
replaced by motorised vans.

► The identification parade
In the 19th century, identification
parades might be quite informal and
were commonly held at Magistrates
Courts. They are now subject to
legislation and codes of conduct and
generally take place at police stations.
This drawing, from *The Graphic*, shows
an identification parade at Marlborough
Street Magistrates Court in 1887.

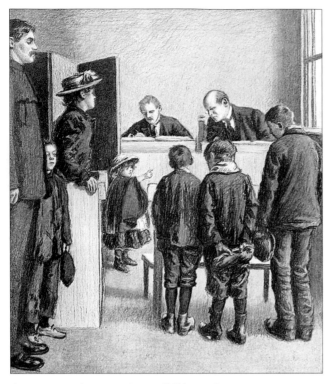

A scene at the Westminster Children's Court

By the late 19th century, the authorities admitted that the criminal justice system should not treat children and young persons in the same way as adults. The Children Act of 1908 established children's courts in which selected Magistrates dealt with cases against anyone under 16 years of age. Capital punishment was also abolished for that age group. Tuesday and Friday afternoons were set aside at Westminster, Bow Street, Clerkenwell, Tower Bridge, Old Street and Greenwich Magistrates Courts for the Children's Court hearings, to which the public were not admitted. In this drawing of 1910, the Westminster Magistrate Mr Francis asks a young girl which of the boys before her stole her money.

▼ **The Bravo mystery: the cross-examination of Sir William Gull at the inquest**

The Bravo mystery was a *cause célèbre* of the Victorian period that was avidly followed by the media and public. It involved a mysterious death by poison and an affair between a married woman and an older man. No criminal trial was held but the principal suspect, Florence Bravo, faced the equivalent of a public trial over her adultery and husband's death but without any of the protections of the criminal justice system or law of evidence. Florence Ricardo was a wealthy young widow, living in The Priory, a large house in Balham. Her new husband, a barrister named Charles Delauney Turner Bravo, joined her there in January 1876. Bravo had little money of his own. Florence had a miscarriage in April and 12 days later Charles was taken ill with severe vomiting. He told doctors that he might have swallowed some laudanum that he had been rubbing on his gums (he was suffering from neuralgia). Charles did not ask any questions about his illness or why he was in such agony, and showed no suspicion against his wife or Mrs Cox, Florence's companion and housekeeper. He even made a will leaving the little he owned to Florence. Charles died after several days. A post-mortem revealed that he died of a single dose of the poison antimony. Many people believed that he had committed suicide but two public inquests, held at the nearby *Bedford Arms*, threw suspicion on Mrs Cox and on Florence who had (before her marriage to Charles) an elderly lover named Dr James Gully (and an earlier miscarriage as a result). Mrs Cox was said to have quarrelled with Charles because he wanted her to leave but this is now doubted. The first inquest returned an open verdict but a second inquest, over 23 days in July and August 1876, developed into a trial of Florence and Mrs Cox. A verdict of murder was returned but with a rider that there was insufficient evidence as to the guilt of any person. Neither woman was charged in respect of Charles' death and it remains uncertain whether this was murder, suicide or an accident. Some writers claim that Florence poisoned Charles to escape from an unhappy marriage. Another writer has suggested that Charles was in fact slowly poisoning Florence with antimony (in order to get rid of her but keep her money) and that he accidentally took a fatal dose of antimony himself. One of the doctors who had tended Charles Bravo and gave evidence at the inquest was Sir William Gull, the physician to the Prince of Wales and Queen Victoria and probably the most famous medical man of his time. Some writers claim that he was involved in the Jack the Ripper murders but there is little evidence for these theories.

chapter 5 Criminal Portraits

IN THE 19TH CENTURY some scientists known as phrenologists put forward theories that character traits could be identified from the lumps and bumps on a person's head. Two Germans developed these ideas and claimed that there was a relationship between the shape of a person's head and his or her mental abilities. They claimed that the mind could be divided into 37 characteristics, such as possessiveness, avarice and conscientiousness, each of which could be identified with certain parts of the brain and located by examination of the skull. This was one of the reasons for making plaster casts of the heads of hanged criminals, many of which are now held in the Metropolitan Police Crime Museum. The casts could be shown to police officers as representing the faces or skulls of classic criminal types and thus assist officers to find such criminals and arrest them.

The ideas of phrenologists and other scientists who believed that criminals could be detected by physical or psychological characteristics were widely accepted for years. You may still hear someone say something along the lines of 'I wouldn't trust him, his eyes are too close together'. A book entitled *The Criminal* by Havelock Ellis, published in 1901, has many photographs and drawings of the heads of criminals and the mentally ill, with a text of which the following are merely examples:

> The average size of criminals' heads is probably about the same as that of ordinary people's heads; but both small and large heads are found [in criminals] in greater proportion … thieves more frequently have small heads; the large heads are usually found among murderers ….
>
> Even non-scientific observers have noted the frequency among criminals of projecting or of long and voluminous ears …. The hearing of criminals is relatively obtuse [dull of perception] and they are prone to disease of the ear ….
>
> The stupidity and the cunning of the criminal are in reality closely related, they approximate him to savages and lower animals. Like the savage, the criminal is lacking in curiosity, the foundation of science, and one of the very highest acquisitions of the highly-developed man.

The words 'spurious science' (or 'rubbish') spring to mind. It is now generally accepted that there are no areas of the brain that can be identified with particular human characteristics. The shape of a person's skull and ears (or other features) has no relationship to specific character or personality traits. There is really no way to tell if someone is going to commit crime. The most important factors, in my opinion, are probably opportunity, economic circumstances, instability in a person's family when a child, and the influences during a person's adolescence.

Portraits of criminals confirm that criminals come from all classes and sections of society. Criminals can be male or female, fat or thin, rich or poor, handsome or ugly and clever or stupid. Some criminals do have eyes that are close together, but I suspect that a few of the saints did as well.

➤ John Selman
Selman stole a purse on Christmas Day from Leonard Barry, servant to Lord Harrington, but, rather stupidly, he did so during a service in the King's Chapel at Whitehall in the presence of the King and many of the nobility. He was executed near Charing Cross on 7 January 1612.

▲ Moll Cut-Purse
Mary Markham, alias Frith, was a notorious thief and fence. She was born in Aldersgate Street in about 1584 and was commonly known as Moll Cut-Purse, from her original profession of cutting purses. She dressed like a man (as in this illustration) and was said to have been so ugly as never to be wooed by a man. She was often arrested for cutting purses or picking pockets (and held in Bridewell, Newgate or the Compters) and she was burned in the hand four times. Transvestism was an offence in ecclesiastical law and, in 1612, Moll was convicted in the Bishop of London's Court for wearing 'indecent and manly apparel' and sentenced to stand in penance in a white sheet at St Paul's Cross. Nevertheless, she continued to dress in men's clothes and continued thieving. Moll also committed some highway robberies but was captured after a robbery on Hounslow Heath, taken to Newgate, tried and condemned. She obtained a pardon and, frightened by her narrow escape from the gallows, ceased going on the highway and took a house on Fleet Street. From there she operated as a fence – a buyer of stolen goods – operating a brokerage for watches, rings and other jewellery from which victims could, upon payment, obtain the return of their possessions. She made a small fortune and had three maids by the time of her death in 1659.

◄ James Whitney, the notorious highwayman
James Whitney was a highwayman who believed in dressing well. He was born in Stevenage, Hertfordshire and apprenticed to a butcher. He then ran the *George Inn* at Cheshunt where he entertained many criminals, but his business failed and he moved to London and became a highwayman. After committing many robberies, he was betrayed by Mother Cosens who kept a brothel in Milford Lane, near the Strand, and arrested. Whitney was convicted and sentenced to death at the Old Bailey Sessions, then executed at Smithfield on 19 December 1694.

◀ Imagining the death of the King: James Sheppard

James Sheppard was born in Southwark in 1701 and executed for treason in 1718. He was at school in Salisbury at the time of the Jacobite Rebellion of 1715 and became a supporter of the Pretender after reading Jacobite pamphlets. Sheppard was then apprenticed to a coach-painter in Bishopsgate Street and decided that King George I should be killed. He wrote a letter to this effect (offering to kill the King) to a clergyman named Heath, who had refused to acknowledge George I as King. However, Sheppard sent the letter by mistake to a Reverend Leake who passed it to the authorities. Sheppard was tried before the Recorder of London, convicted of treason and executed at Tyburn on 17 March 1718.

◥ Execution of an attorney: Thomas Carr

Thomas Carr, an attorney-at-law in the Temple, and his lover Elizabeth Adams were executed in 1738 for robbery. On 15 October 1737, Carr and Adams were tried at the Old Bailey Sessions for robbing William Quarrington of 93 guineas and a gold ring at the *Angel & Crown Tavern* near Temple Bar. They were found guilty and condemned. Carr petitioned for the Royal Mercy but the Privy Council replied that 'The flagrant breach of the law was greatly aggravated by being committed by a man professing the law'.

▼ The accomplice: Elizabeth Adams

Thirteen people were carried from Newgate to Tyburn on 18 January 1738, including Carr and Adams, each in a coach. They were placed in the cart and, just before it drew away, they kissed each other, joined hands and thus were launched into eternity.

➤ Dick Turpin

Richard or Dick Turpin is perhaps the most famous British highwayman, but many of the stories about him, such as his horse being named 'Black Bess' and his ride from London to York in one night, are fiction. Turpin was not a hero but a desperate criminal. He killed two men and was hanged at York in 1739 for horse-stealing. Turpin was born in 1706 in Hempstead, Essex. He was apprenticed to a butcher in Whitechapel but was frequently convicted of minor crimes. He married and then worked as a butcher in Essex but some of the meat that he sold came from animals that he stole from local farmers. A warrant was issued for his arrest but he escaped and joined a gang of men named Gregory, Fielder, Rose and Wheeler. They carried out robberies and burglaries at houses at Charlton, Croydon and many other places around London. For example, on 4 February 1735, they stole £26 and silver plate from Mr Lawrence, near Edgware in Middlesex, and a housemaid was raped by one of the gang. On 7 February, the gang robbed Mr Francis, a farmer near Marylebone. Mr Francis, his family and servants, were bound and beaten during the robbery. The public was so alarmed that the King offered a reward of £100 for the gang's arrest. The gang carried out robberies near Putney, Blackheath and Hackney but were then surprised by constables at an ale-house in Westminster. Fielder, Rose and Wheeler were captured (and Gregory was arrested later) but Turpin escaped through a window. Wheeler gave evidence against his companions who were hanged at Tyburn. Over the next three years, Turpin committed many robberies with the highwayman Tom King. They became well known and therefore unable to stay in inns or houses. They built a concealed cave or hide in Epping Forest, where they lived, ate and slept between robberies, and Turpin's wife supplied them with food and drink. Thomas Morris, a servant of one of the keepers of Epping Forest, was eager to collect the £100 reward for Turpin. He and another man found Turpin in the hide on 4 May 1737 but Turpin shot Morris dead and escaped. The reward for Turpin's capture was increased to £200, but Turpin and King continued their lives as highwaymen until Turpin stole a traveller's thoroughbred horse. Handbills describing the horse were issued and Mr Bayes, the landlord of the *Green Man* in Epping Forest, decided to earn the reward for Turpin. He heard that a horse fitting the description had been left in a stable at the *Red Lion Inn* in Whitechapel, and with some other men he tried to seize Turpin and King when they came to collect the horse. Turpin shot at Bayes but missed and killed King. Turpin fled to Lincolnshire, where he assumed the name John Palmer and stole some horses, and then to Yorkshire. He was arrested there for a minor offence but then also charged with stealing the horses in Lincolnshire. Turpin was held in York Castle and wrote to his brother in Essex, stating that he was held under the name Palmer and asking that a character witness be found for him. The brother could not

afford the postage due on the letter, so it was returned to the local post office, where it was seen by Turpin's old schoolmaster, Mr Smith, who recognised his pupil's handwriting. The letter was opened and revealed the highwayman's whereabouts. The local Magistrates sent Smith to York and he identified Palmer as Turpin. He was convicted at York Assizes on 22 March 1739 of horse-stealing and executed at York on 7 April 1739.

◀ Sally Salisbury

Sarah Priddon, also known as Mrs Sally Salisbury, was a prostitute who was born in about 1690. By the age of 14, she had already been abandoned by her first rich lover, the notorious rake Colonel Charteris (see page 16). Sally then worked from Mother Wisebourne's brothel in Covent Garden, having affairs with a number of government ministers, and became one of the most famous prostitutes of the period. In 1723, she was still working and said to be 'well acquainted' with the Hon. J. — F. — (he is not named in the various editions of *The Newgate Calendar* but was in fact Mr Finch, the son of the Countess of Winchelsea). Sally went with Finch one night to the *Three Tuns Tavern* in Chandos Street. A tavern servant went to the room in which they were staying and heard them argue about an opera ticket that Finch had given to Sally's sister. She stabbed him but, regretting what she had done, sent for a surgeon. Finch forgave Sally but his family prosecuted her. At her trial at the Old Bailey on 24 April 1723, Sally's counsel denied that she had acted with malice. He claimed that her action arose from sudden passion, the consequence of the gift to her sister, whom Mr Finch had wished to seduce. Counsel for the Crown ridiculed this idea, insinuating that a woman of Sally's character would not have any tender regard for her sister's reputation. The jury acquitted her of attempted murder but found her guilty of assault and wounding. Sally was sentenced to a fine of £100 and imprisonment for one year. However, she died after nine months in Newgate Gaol.

▲ James Hall

James Hall, pictured in this engraving in leg irons in Newgate Gaol, was executed for murder in 1741. He was born in Wells, Somerset but came to London and worked as a servant to Mr Penny who had chambers in Clement's Inn. Falling into financial difficulties, Hall decided to murder and rob his master. Late one night, Hall waited for Penny to undress and then struck him from behind with a stick. Hall then cut his victim's throat, holding the head over a chamber pot to collect the blood. He mixed the blood with water and threw it in the sink and the coal hole, and then threw his master's body and bloody clothing into the privy. He stole 36 guineas. A few days later, Hall went to see Mr Wotton, his master's nephew, and asked after Mr Penny, claiming that he had left the chambers and gone away. Wotton made enquiries after his uncle and soon had Hall arrested on suspicion of murder. Hall declared his innocence but then made an unsuccessful attempt to escape and finally confessed to the murder. He was tried at the Old Bailey Sessions in August 1741, pleaded guilty and was sentenced to death. He was hanged at the end of Catherine Street, near the Strand, on 15 September 1741, aged 37. His body was hung in chains at Shepherd's Bush.

▼ Elizabeth Jeffries and John Swan

Elizabeth Jeffries and John Swan were executed in Epping Forest in 1752. Swan is shown in this engraving in a set of leg and hand irons. Elizabeth's wealthy uncle, Mr Jeffries, lived in Walthamstow and had no children, so he therefore adopted his niece and made a will, leaving most of his property to her. However, she behaved badly and then overheard him saying that he would alter his will. Elizabeth decided to murder her uncle to prevent him doing so and her accomplice in the murder was John Swan, her uncle's gardener and possibly her lover. Elizabeth and Swan asked another servant, named Mathews, to help them, promising him £700. Mathews was dismissed by Mr Jeffries and so agreed. Mathews met Swan and Elizabeth at Mr Jeffries' house on 3 July 1751 but decided that he could not commit murder. Swan then went into the house with two pistols and when Mathews heard a shot he fled. Immediately afterwards, Elizabeth shouted for assistance and told neighbours, who arrived and found Mr Jeffries dying, that there had been a burglary during which her uncle had been shot. Suspicions arose and Elizabeth was arrested but she was discharged for lack of evidence and took possession of her uncle's estate under the will. Mathews was then located and became an evidence for the Crown. Elizabeth Jeffries and John Swan were arrested and convicted at Chelmsford on 11 March 1752, Swan for petty treason in killing his master and Elizabeth for aiding and abetting Swan. On the day of execution, Jeffries was placed in a cart and Swan on a sledge. Both were hanged in Epping Forest on 28 March. Elizabeth's body was buried but Swan's body was hung in chains in the forest.

James Maclane

James Maclane was hanged at Tyburn in 1750 for highway robbery. He had become known as the 'gentleman highwayman' because of his lavish lifestyle and fine clothes. Maclane was from a Scottish family that settled in Ireland. He dissipated a fortune left to him by his father, then came to London, married and received £500 as a marriage settlement from his wife's father, with which he started a grocery business in Welbeck Street. His wife died and their children were placed in the care of her parents. Maclane then sold his business and assumed the life of a gentleman in the hope of marrying an heiress. Within six months, he had spent all his money and took to the highway in 1748 with an Irish apothecary named Plunkett. The two men committed many robberies, including one on the Earl of Eglinton. In the daytime, however, they kept up the lifestyle of gentlemen; Maclane spent lavishly on clothes and had lodgings in St James's Street and Chelsea. The men even used some of the stolen money to pay for a suite of rooms at White's Club. During a robbery of a coach in 1750, Maclane stole valuables, some fine clothes and even the lace from a man's waistcoat. The robbery was reported in a newspaper with a list of the stolen items. Unfortunately, Maclane tried to sell the lace to the man who had sold it to the victim and also tried to sell the clothes to a dealer who had seen the list of stolen goods. Maclane was taken before a Magistrate. Many people of rank attended his examination and several even contributed money for his expenses. Maclane was committed to the Gatehouse but then requested a second examination before the Magistrate, at which he confessed to many robberies. At his trial at the Old Bailey, Lady Caroline Petersham spoke on his behalf and many women wept when he was convicted and condemned. Maclane was sent to Newgate Gaol and about 3,000 people paid to see him there on one day alone. He was executed at Tyburn on 3 October 1750.

Thomas Savage returning to Hannah Blay's lodging

Thomas Savage was an apprentice, aged 17, who murdered a fellow servant and was hanged twice on 28 October 1668. Savage was born in St Giles in the Fields and apprenticed to a vintner, at the *Ship* tavern at Ratcliff. Savage led a loose and profligate life. His vices included whoring, drunkenness and theft. He spent many Sundays at a brothel on Ratcliff Highway with Hannah Blay, a 'vile, common strumpet'. She continually asked him for more money and suggested that he rob his master. Savage said that the maid was always home with him but Hannah urged him to murder her. She pressed Savage for money one morning and plied him with drink. Savage returned home and, when his master left for church, he killed the maid with a hammer and stole £60 from his master's chamber. He returned to Blay's lodgings, gave her a small amount of money and then left London. Savage was caught in an ale-house and admitted the murder and theft. He was carried back to Ratcliff, committed to Newgate, then sentenced to death at the Old Bailey. He was taken to the place of execution at Ratcliff Cross and, after a short speech, turned off the cart. He struggled for a while and a friend struck him several blows on his breast to put him out of his pain. Savage hung motionless for a time and, appearing to be dead, was cut down. However, he began to breathe again and opened his eyes (although he could not speak). Within an hour, the Sheriff's officers came to the house in which he lay and carried him back to the place of execution. He was then hanged until he was dead.

➤ **Elizabeth Canning and Mary Squires**

The case of Canning and Squires was the talk of all London in 1753 and 1754. Elizabeth Canning was 18 and worked as a domestic servant in Aldermanbury. She disappeared after visiting relatives on 1 January 1753 but reappeared, emaciated and dirty, one month later. She said that she had been attacked in Moorfields by two men who had stolen her money and taken her to a house, being operated as a brothel, on the Hertford Road near Enfield Wash. There she was threatened by an old woman with a knife who stole her clothes and tried to induce her to become a prostitute. Elizabeth refused and was kept prisoner but escaped on 29 January. She described the house in which she had been held and this appeared to be a house owned by Susannah (or 'Mother') Wells, who was arrested with Mary Squires (a gypsy aged 75) and a girl named Virtue Hall who also resided in the house. Elizabeth Canning identified Squires as the woman who robbed her and claimed that Virtue Hall had been present. Virtue denied any knowledge of the matter but, when examined by the Bow Street Magistrate Henry Fielding, she confessed that Canning had been at the house. Mary Squires was tried at the Old Bailey Sessions before the Lord Mayor, Sir Crisp Gascoyne, and three other judges, for assault and robbery. Wells was tried for harbouring Squires knowing her to have committed a felony. Mary Squires denied the charges, and three men swore that she was in Dorset at the time, but their evidence was discounted and they were later tried for perjury. Squires and Wells were convicted, principally on the evidence of Virtue Hall. Squires was condemned to death and Wells was burned in the hand and sentenced to six months' imprisonment in Newgate. However, Sir Crisp Gascoyne then seems to have changed his mind about the case. Some suggested that this was because he was bedding the beautiful daughter of Mary Squires. In any event, Gascoyne secured the King's pardon for Mary Squires and then procured the prosecution, in May 1754, of Elizabeth Canning for perjury. Virtue Hall went back on her previous evidence and claimed that Canning's story was false and that she had been bullied into her confession by Henry Fielding. About 30 people gave evidence of Canning's good character but she was convicted of perjury and sentenced to transportation for seven years. Her friends collected £100 for her and she went to America and married there. She died in Connecticut in 1773.

People continued to argue about the case. A pamphlet by Dr Hill, who published the *British Magazine*, attacked Canning's story and noted that Henry Fielding had examined Hall for six hours before she made her confession. Fielding denied that he had bullied Hall and argued on behalf of Canning. Some said that Canning had been pregnant and that her disappearance in January had been a story she invented to cover up the fact that she had had an abortion. The case remains a mystery.

The true Pictures of Elizabeth Canning and Mary Squires.

▼ **William Hawke in the Press Yard, Newgate**

William Hawke was executed at Tyburn in 1774 for highway robbery. He worked in a public house in Saffron Hill, then became a highwayman. He committed many robberies with James Field, another notorious highwayman, but they were arrested and transported to America. They both returned to England and again worked together on the highway until their capture. Field was executed but Hawke escaped to France. He again returned to England and worked as a highwayman until arrested at his lodgings in Shoe Lane by Sir John Fielding's officers. Hawke was committed to Newgate, convicted of robbery and executed on 1 July 1774. He is pictured here in the Press Yard, the exercise yard at Newgate Gaol.

▲ Dr Dodd

William Dodd was a Doctor of Divinity and a well known preacher at the Pimlico Chapel, which he built near Buckingham Palace. He was Prebendary of Brecon, tutor and chaplain to the Earl of Chesterfield, a chaplain to King George III and the promoter of many charities, such as the Society for the Relief of Insolvent Debtors. He was executed at Tyburn in 1777 for forgery. Dr Dodd had a good income but an extravagant lifestyle. Dodd or his wife attempted to obtain another lucrative post for him in the church by writing to the wife of the Lord Chancellor (who was responsible for the appointment) offering her £3,000 if the position could be procured. As a result, Dodd's name was removed from the list of the King's Chaplains. He was soon in desperate financial straits and so turned to forgery. He pretended that his patron Philip Stanhope, Earl of Chesterfield, needed to borrow £4,000 secretly and urgently. Dodd took an unsigned bond to a broker named Lewis Robertson, asking him to find someone who would lend the money to Lord Chesterfield. Henry Fletcher and Samuel Peach agreed to do so and Robertson returned the bond to Dodd for Chesterfield to sign it. Dodd returned the bond to Robertson the next day, apparently executed by Chesterfield and witnessed by himself. Robertson knew that Mr Fletcher would require all legal formalities to be complied with (and object to a bond with a signature witnessed by only one person) so Robertson therefore added his signature as a witness. He then obtained the £4,000 and handed it to Dodd. Fletcher's attorney Mr Manly saw the bond, was suspicious and went to see Lord Chesterfield. He denied any knowledge of the bond. Fletcher and Manly laid an information at Guildhall against Dodd and Robertson alleging forgery. Robertson was arrested but later released. Fletcher, Manly and two of the Lord Mayor's officers visited Dr Dodd and told him that repaying the money was the only way to save himself. Dodd effectively admitted his guilt by handing over £4,000 in notes and drafts. He was then taken before the Lord Mayor and charged. He claimed that he had not intended to defraud Chesterfield or Fletcher but had

needed some money to pay tradesmen's bills and would, he claimed, have repaid the money in six months. Dodd was committed to Wood Street Compter and tried at the Old Bailey Sessions on 22 February 1777. The jury found him guilty but recommended him for a pardon. Dodd was held in Newgate Gaol pending the court's consideration of some points of law, then returned to court in May 1777. The judge sentenced him to death. Great efforts were made to save Dodd because of his charitable work and because he had repaid most of the money. Newspapers were filled with articles and letters in his favour. A petition signed by 23,000 people was presented to the King. However, as mercy had recently been denied to the Perreau brothers (see page 103), it seemed inadvisable to grant it to a former Royal Chaplain. Dr Dodd was taken to Tyburn in a coach on 27 June 1777, past immense crowds of people, and executed.

▼ William Ryland cutting his throat on sight of the officers of justice

William Wynne Ryland was an accomplished engraver who was executed in 1783 for forgery. He was appointed as engraver to King George III and was paid £300 a year. He also set up a print shop and engraver's business in Cornhill with a partner, but lost money. Ryland soon fell into debt by gambling and keeping an expensive mistress. He forged some bills of exchange for over £7,000 purportedly drawn on the East India Company and provided them to a bank as security for loans. Suspected of the offence, Ryland disguised himself and hid under a false name, with his wife, in lodgings in Stepney at the house of Richard Freeman, a cobbler. Unfortunately, Mrs Ryland took one of her husband's shoes to her landlord for mending. It had the name Ryland inside, and Freeman informed the authorities to obtain the reward that had been offered for Ryland. When the officers from Bow Street went to arrest Ryland, he cut his throat with a razor. The wound was not mortal and Ryland was convicted of forgery at the Old Bailey Sessions on 26 July 1783. He was executed at Tyburn on 29 August 1783.

James Bolland, a sheriff's officer, executed for forgery

Bailiffs have never enjoyed a good reputation. In the 18th century, many bailiffs (then known as sheriff's officers) took advantage of the deficiencies in the legal system and the draconian laws against debtors to line their own pockets. The most notorious example was James Bolland, a sheriff's officer who was hanged in 1772 for forgery. Bolland was originally a butcher in Southwark, but he sold his business and obtained an appointment as one of the officers of the Sheriff of Surrey (which then included Southwark). He rented a house in Falcon Court, near St George's Church in Southwark, and fitted it up as a sponging-house, that is, a lock-up for newly arrested debtors. He extorted fees from the inmates but these were insufficient to pay for his profligate lifestyle and so he turned to fraud. Many people employed him to pursue their debtors and obtain payment of the debts or arrest the debtors. However, he defrauded them. Bolland often obtained the money and kept it for himself, telling a creditor that the debtor could not be found or had escaped from custody. Bolland also cleared his own debts by a fraudulent bankruptcy, procuring a friend to issue a commission of bankruptcy against him (having first hidden his most valuable effects with friends), then obtaining a certificate of release by forged documents. Bolland returned to his old practices, working as an officer of the Sheriff of Middlesex for some years, despite being caught cheating a creditor and being held in the Fleet Prison for a time. He then hired a large house near Temple Bar and continued to arrest prisoners (and extort fees from them). He also engaged in various frauds. Bolland obtained much work from 'sharp practice' attorneys that he had met, arranging for traders' goods and stock to be seized, or for men to be imprisoned, on the basis of false allegations of debt. He also established a man in an elegant house, with a footman and carriage. This man obtained many goods on credit (the goods being passed to Bolland) and, when the fraud was about to be exposed, Bolland had the man thrown into Newgate as a debtor. Bolland's villainy was at last exposed in newspapers. The Sheriffs suspended him from acting as their officer. Desperate for money, Bolland committed his last crime, forging the endorsement on a bill of exchange for £100 in order to obtain credit. He was tried at the Old Bailey and hanged at Tyburn on 18 March 1772.

▼ Jerry Avershaw

Lewis Jeremiah Avershaw was executed on Kennington Common in 1795, aged 22, for shooting a constable. Jerry Avershaw worked as a highwayman for about five years, particularly on Putney Heath and Wimbledon Common. An informer said that Avershaw was drinking at the *Three Brewers* public house in Southwark and the Southwark Magistrates issued a warrant for his arrest. Two constables, David Price and Bernard Turner, went to the public house. Avershaw took a loaded pistol in each hand, warning the officers to keep back. However, the officers attempted to seize him. Avershaw fired and severely wounded both of them. Price died a few hours later. Avershaw was tried at Croydon on 30 July 1795 for murdering Price and wounding Turner. After hearing the evidence, the jury took three minutes to consult and convict him. The judge put on the cap for sentencing him to death. Avershaw then contemptuously put on his own hat and vented torrents of abuse at the judge and jury, accusing them of his murder. He was hanged on Kennington Common on 3 August 1795 and his body was gibbeted at Putney.

◄ Major Semple

Major James George Semple was sentenced three times to transportation for theft. Semple was born in Scotland and served in the British army during the American Revolution and later in the Prussian and Russian armies. He returned to England but was convicted at the Old Bailey Sessions on 1 September 1785 for stealing a carriage. He had hired a carriage in Whitechapel but sold it rather than return it to the owner. Semple was sentenced to transportation to a penal settlement for seven years but was pardoned on condition that he went abroad. He was in France during the Revolution, denounced as a spy but escaped and again enlisted in the Prussian army. He returned to England and was again tried for theft at the Old Bailey Sessions in 1795, having gone to a shop in Wigmore Street, using the alias Lieutenant Colonel Lisle, and taken away a shirt and material, saying that he needed to consult his sister before ordering a large number of shirts to be made. He did not return to the shop. Semple was again sentenced to transportation for seven years. He was held in Newgate for two years, then put on a transport for New South Wales. Semple was one of the ringleaders of a mutiny on the transport and so he and 28 others were set adrift in an open boat. He survived and spent time in Brazil and Portugal, where he was arrested at the request of the British authorities and taken to Gibraltar. He was brought back to England in April 1799, sent to Tothill Fields Bridewell and again transported. In 1810 he returned from Botany Bay to England and to crime. He was convicted at Middlesex Sessions on 3 December 1814 of obtaining food by deception and, for a third time, transported for seven years.

Charles Price

▲ Charles Price the swindler

Charles Price was a notorious swindler and forger who committed suicide in 1786. He was born in London in about 1730, the son of a clothes salesman. Price committed many frauds, often adopting a disguise. He is even said to have cheated his own father, by wearing a disguise, out of an expensive suit. At one time, Price posed as a Methodist preacher, defrauding several people of large sums of money. Price also worked for a merchant in Holland, under the assumed name of Johnston. He debauched the merchant's daughter, robbed the merchant and returned to England. In 1775, he advertised for a partner to provide capital for a planned brewery. Samuel Foote advanced £500 but the money (and Price) soon disappeared. He also advertised a service to obtain wives for gentlemen and swindled a Mr Wigmore of 50 guineas. Price was arrested for this offence but escaped.

◄ Charles Price in disguise

Price began a series of frauds on the Bank of England in 1780. He disguised himself, wore a patch over his left eye and assumed the name of Brank. He forged many bank-notes, employing an honest man named Samuel to pass them (many in the purchase of lottery tickets). After passing notes worth £1,400, Samuel was arrested and imprisoned but Price escaped and in 1782 began swindling tradesmen by purchasing goods from shops with his counterfeit bank-notes or having them changed at banks by unsuspecting assistants. He was finally arrested on 14 January 1786, using the name Palton, and held in Tothill Fields Bridewell. Price knew that he would be hanged (it was estimated that he had defrauded people of a total of £100,000) and so he hanged himself. A coroner's jury passed a verdict of 'self-murder' and his body was buried in Tothill Fields, with a stake driven through it.

Governor Wall

▼ **A case of delayed justice: Governor Wall in the condemned cell**

Joseph Wall, a Governor of Goree, was executed in 1802 for murder, nearly 20 years after his crime, having caused a soldier to be flogged to death. Wall was born in Ireland in 1737 and joined the army in 1760. He was appointed Governor of the garrison of Goree, an island near the Gambia in Africa in 1779. On 10 July 1782, he ordered that a soldier, Benjamin Armstrong, should receive 800 lashes because he (and some other soldiers) had asked the garrison's paymaster why Wall had stopped their pay. Armstrong was punished without a court-martial or even the chance to say anything in his defence. Wall also ordered that Armstrong should be flogged, not with the usual cat-o'-nine-tails but with a rope of greater thickness. Wall stood by the floggers and encouraged them. He left the island the next day to return to England. Armstrong died five days later. News of the soldier's death reached Britain in 1784 and a warrant was issued for Wall's arrest. Wall evaded the officers executing the warrant and escaped abroad, living in France and Italy under an assumed name. He returned to Britain in 1797 and concealed himself but considered giving himself up to justice. He lived in Lambeth and then near Bedford Square, and was arrested after he wrote a letter to the Secretary of State, saying that he had returned to meet the charges against him. By then, the matter had almost been forgotten and if Wall had not written the letter, it is likely that he would not have been molested.

▼ **The execution of Governor Wall and his cruelty at Goree**

At his trial on 20 January 1802, Wall alleged that Armstrong had been guilty of mutiny and that his death was due to his drinking strong spirits in hospital after the flogging. However, he was not believed because he had not mentioned any mutiny when he had reported to the government on his return to England in 1782. Wall was convicted, sentenced to death and placed in the condemned cell in Newgate Gaol. He was hanged outside Newgate on 28 January 1802. He was suspended in convulsive agony for over 15 minutes. His body was cut down after one hour, taken away for dissection, then buried.

▲ John Bellingham

John Bellingham was executed for the murder of the Prime Minister Spencer Perceval in the House of Commons in May 1812. Bellingham was brought up in London. He worked for merchants in the Russian trade and in Archangel in Russia for many years. Disputes arose there and Bellingham was found to owe 2,000 roubles (about £200) to some Russian merchants. He also faced a criminal suit over a letter in which he alleged that certain ships' insurance were fraudulent transactions. He was held in various prisons and, on release, ordered to stay in Russia until he had repaid the 2,000 roubles. He received some help from the British Ambassador in Russia but felt that it was insufficient. Bellingham finally obtained permission to return to England in May 1809. He brooded on his problems in Russia and decided that they had been the fault of the British Ambassador for failing to protect his rights as a British subject. He became more unbalanced and claimed compensation from the British Government, applying unsuccessfully to the Treasury, the Privy Council and Spencer Perceval (then Chancellor of the Exchequer). Bellingham's MP refused to help him petition the House of Commons and a petition to the Prince Regent was simply referred back to the Treasury. Bellingham decided on a new course of action. He moved to London and began visiting the House of Commons so that he could identify members. He purchased a pair of pistols and on 11 May 1812 he took up position at the doors leading into the Commons chamber. Bellingham shot Perceval (by then Prime Minister) as he walked through the lobby, and he died soon after. Bellingham did not try to escape but was seized and questioned in the prison room of the Serjeant-at-Arms by some members of the Commons who were also Magistrates for Middlesex. When asked about his motives, he answered, 'It was want of redress and denial of justice on the part of the government'. Bellingham was taken to Newgate and four days later, on 15 May, tried at the Old Bailey Sessions. Some witnesses claimed that he was insane. Bellingham's own speech to the jury rambled on for two hours, during which this

drawing was made. He was probably insane but the courts at this time were not equipped to deal with such cases unless the accused was obviously out of his mind. The jury found Bellingham guilty and he was sentenced to death. He was hanged outside Newgate Gaol and his body was dissected at St Bartholomew's Hospital, where the anatomical theatre was crowded with spectators.

◄ Henry Fauntleroy

Henry Fauntleroy was executed in 1824 for forgery. He was the managing partner of the banking-house of Marsh & Co in Berners Street. In 1815, Frances Young had lodged with the bank a power of attorney that authorised it to receive (then pass to her) the dividends on £5,450 of government stock in her name. The dividends were regularly paid to her but Fauntleroy had forged another power of attorney, authorising him to sell the stock, which he did in September 1820. This fraudulent sale was discovered and Fauntleroy was arrested in September 1824 on a warrant issued from Marlborough Street Police Office. It was then discovered that, since 1814, he had sold stock to the value of £400,000 under similar forged powers of attorney. A document was found in his papers, in which he admitted forging the powers of attorney to stave off the bankruptcy of his banking-house. He had sold the stock but kept up payment of the dividends to the true owners so they would not discover the sale of their stock. It was also discovered that Fauntleroy had been separated from his wife for years and had been secretly maintaining some expensive mistresses. He also spent a fortune on his houses in London and Brighton, expensive dinner parties, a library, horses and carriages. Fauntleroy was tried for forgery at the Old Bailey Sessions on 30 October 1824. He was convicted of using the forgery and sentenced to death. About 100,000 people watched him hang outside Newgate on 30 November 1824.

➤ Daniel Good

Good was born in Ireland and worked as a coachman for a gentleman in Roehampton. On 6 April 1842, he purchased a pair of breeches from a pawnbroker in Wandsworth. He was also seen to steal a pair of trousers and so the pawnbroker sent a policeman, the shop boy and a neighbour to the stables where Good lived. He denied the theft but the policeman found a naked female torso (with the head, legs and arms chopped off) under some hay. Good fled. An axe and saw, covered in blood, were also found in the stable and charred bones were found in the remains of a fire in the adjoining coach house. Good had burned the victims' head, legs and arms. After many enquiries, it was discovered that the victim was Jane Jones who had lived with Good as his wife. During the search for Good, his real wife (a woman known as 'Old Molly Good') was located in Spitalfields and Good had visited her a few days before. The police believed that he might return and so watched the house and made enquiries in the area. Unfortunately, they did so in uniform rather than plain clothes. Good spotted them and escaped again. A reward was offered for his arrest and he was found on 16 April in Tunbridge Wells. This sketch of Good was made at Bow Street Police Court on 21 April. He was convicted of murder at the Central Criminal Court and hanged outside Newgate Gaol on 23 May 1842. The crowd was said to have been the largest that ever assembled there. Good's escapes confirmed the need for experienced detectives to catch criminals (London had been without any detectives since the Bow Street Runners were disbanded in 1839) and the need for some police work to be undertaken in plain clothes. This prompted the formation of the Detective Branch of the Metropolitan Police in 1842, initially of only eight men. By 1868, the branch still had only 15 detectives.

◄ Joseph Hunton

Hunton was a Quaker who was hanged for forgery at Newgate in 1828. Hunton had a good reputation in the City, having been a successful sugar-baker, then a partner in Dickson & Co, warehousemen of Ironmonger Lane. However, he speculated unsuccessfully on the Stock Exchange and the Dickson & Co partnership was dissolved. Some forged bills of exchange, purportedly drawn by Dickson & Co, then appeared in circulation. Hunton fled when the forgeries were discovered but he was found on board a ship at Plymouth, destined for New York, using an assumed name. He was taken to London, examined before the Lord Mayor, then convicted of forgery at the Old Bailey Sessions on 28 October 1828. Hunton was sentenced to death and executed on 8 December 1828. Capital punishment was abolished in cases of forgery soon afterwards. Thomas Maynard was the next (and last) man to be hanged for this crime, on 31 December 1829. That must have ruined his family's New Year's Eve celebrations.

◄ The Turf Frauds

The Turf Frauds of 1877 resulted in a trial of Metropolitan Police detectives for corruption and the reorganisation of the Detective Branch into the Criminal Investigation Department (CID). Harry Benson (pictured here) and William Kurr were confidence tricksters who had carried out many frauds involving bets on horse races. They carried out a complex sting in 1877. They printed a dummy racing newspaper, the *Sport*, with false reports of an English gambler whose system of betting on horses was so successful that bookmakers would not accept his bets. He would therefore pay commission to French residents who placed bets for him in their names and, of course, with their money. Benson and Kurr prepared dummy bookmakers' letterheads as receipts for cash bets on non-existent races. They also prepared cheques of the Bank of London (which did not exist) to pay out purported winnings. A rich Parisian, Madame de Goncourt, placed bets totalling about £1,000 and received some cheques as winnings. She then sent £10,000 which the fraudsters could have stolen, but they were greedy and requested £30,000. The lady consulted her lawyer about transferring this money; he was suspicious and alerted the authorities. Benson was arrested in Holland but Chief Inspector Nathaniel Druscovich took a long time to arrange for his extradition. Detectives arrested Kurr but only after he had fled on many occasions just before his arrest was to take place. Benson and Kurr were convicted and then disclosed corruption. Inspector John Meiklejohn had been accepting bribes from bookmakers and swindlers for years and tipped off Kurr when he was about to be arrested. Druscovich had got into debt, borrowed money from Kurr and then also accepted bribes. Chief Inspectors Clarke and Palmer were also implicated. At their trial, Palmer was acquitted but the other three (and a solicitor, Edward Froggett) were each sentenced to two years' hard labour for conspiracy to pervert the course of justice. A Committee of Inquiry found many problems, including lack of supervision, within the Detective Branch and so it was reshaped into the CID under the newly appointed Howard Vincent.

The Mannings

◄ Maria Manning
The Mannings were held in Horsemonger Lane Gaol and tried for murder at the Old Bailey. Chief Baron Pollock was the senior trial judge. Maria wanted to be tried separately from her husband so that his admission could not be used against her. Her counsel argued that she could rely, as a foreigner, on a statute of 1355 that stated that a foreigner was entitled to a jury of six Englishmen and six foreigners. This would have necessitated separate trials for Frederick and Maria. Pollock denied the application on the basis that Maria had married an Englishman and so could not object to an all-English jury. The jury found both Frederick and Maria guilty. Frederick then made a full confession, saying that his wife had shot O'Connor but that he had finished him off with a crowbar.

▲ Frederick George Manning

Frederick Manning and his wife Maria were hanged for murdering her lover for his money. Maria de Roux was a lady's maid who was born in Switzerland. She had an affair with Patrick O'Connor, who worked in the London docks but was also a moneylender. Maria then met and married Manning, a guard on the Great Western Railway, who was dismissed on suspicion of being involved in robberies from two trains. The Mannings moved to Minver Place in Bermondsey, and Maria continued to see O'Connor. They were in financial difficulties and invited O'Connor to dinner on 8 August 1849. He was never seen alive again. His workmates reported him missing and the police made enquiries at the Mannings' house. They denied having seen O'Connor. The police returned a few days later: Frederick and Maria had fled and O'Connor's body was found under the kitchen floor. He had been shot in the head and had other wounds from a blunt instrument. His body had been buried in quicklime to hasten its decomposition. Frederick was arrested in Jersey and Maria in Edinburgh. This drawing of Frederick was made when he and Maria were taken before Southwark Police Court on 6 September 1849. Frederick claimed that Maria had instigated the crime and he also admitted that they had stolen some shares and money from the dead man's lodgings after the murder.

Maria tried to appeal but this was very difficult for a defendant. The Court of Criminal Appeal was not established until 1907. Certain points of law could be appealed to the House of Lords by the issue of a Writ of Error but this required the consent of the Attorney-General, which was not granted. There was a limited right of appeal as to a judge's legal rulings to the Court of Crown Cases Reserved. Maria appealed against Pollock's rejection of her claim to a mixed jury, but Pollock was one of the judges sitting in that appeal court. It is perhaps not very surprising that the court did not overturn his decision. Maria would therefore hang with her husband. Charles Dickens was in the crowd of 50,000 people who attended the execution on the morning of 13 November 1849 at Horsemonger Lane Gaol. The Mannings were then buried in the prison courtyard. Dickens noted that the crowd, that began gathering the night before, included thieves, prostitutes and ruffians, who engaged in fighting and indecent, foul and offensive behaviour. He wrote:

> I believe that a sight so conceivably awful as the wickedness and levity of the immense crowd collected at that execution could be imagined by no man. The horrors of the gibbet and of the crime which brought the wretched murderers to it faded in my mind before the atrocious bearing, looks and language of the assembled spectators.

► Henry Wainwright

Henry Wainwright was executed in 1875 for the murder of his mistress. He was a respectable, married man, with children, who regularly attended church, lectured on literature and owned a brush-making business at 215 Whitechapel Road. However, he led a double life. He set up his mistress Harriet Lane in a house in Mile End and they had two children. Wainwright fell into financial difficulties from running two homes. He reduced the amount that he paid to Harriet and moved her family to cheaper accommodation. Harriet began to

drink heavily and made unpleasant scenes at Wainwright's shop about her lack of money. She then disappeared. Wainwright told Harriet's relatives that she had gone to live with another man and he paid for the children to be cared for by some friends who then received a letter, from a man named Edward Frieake, saying that he and Harriet were going to live on the Continent. Wainwright was still in financial difficulty. He was made bankrupt a year later and had to give up his Whitechapel shop. He asked a workman to help him move some parcels, two of which were heavy and gave off a foul smell. The workman

Franz Muller

➤ Franz Muller, the railway murderer

Muller was born in Germany and committed the first murder on a British train. On 9 July 1864, a bank clerk named Thomas Briggs aged 69 was found, badly injured, on the railway line between Hackney Wick and Bow. He had been beaten with his own walking stick, robbed of his gold watch and thrown out of a train carriage window. He died that night. His blood-stained stick and a black beaver hat that did not belong to him were found in a carriage compartment. The hat was distinctive and identified as the type of hat worn by a German tailor named Franz Muller. A man of Muller's description had also exchanged Brigg's watch chain for a new one at a jewellery shop on Cheapside (appropriately owned by John Death). The police searched Muller's lodgings but he had taken a ship to America. Officers took a faster ship and were waiting for Muller when he arrived in New York. He had the victim's watch and hat, having mistakenly taken the latter instead of his own when he had fled from the train. Muller was extradited and convicted of murder at the Old Bailey in October 1864. There were concerns that Muller had not had a fair trial as newspapers had been publishing many articles about his guilt in the weeks before the trial and the evidence against him was weak. Petitions were submitted on Muller's behalf and the King of Prussia requested mercy for him in a telegram to Queen Victoria. Despite this, Muller was hanged outside Newgate in front of 50,000 people on 14 November 1864. He was buried in Dead Man's Walk.

➘ The Lord Chief Baron, Sir Frederick Pollock

Sir Jonathan Frederick Pollock (1783-1870) was called to the Bar at Middle Temple. He was MP for Huntingdon from 1831 and knighted in 1834. Pollock served in Peel's governments as Attorney-General (1834-35 and 1841-44). He was Chief Baron (the senior judge) of the Court of Exchequer from 1844 to 1866 and created a Baronet in 1866. Pollock was a courteous and scholarly judge but not an impartial one. During a trial in 1846, he implied that a defendant was obviously guilty and said that he could not imagine how the defence 'could be so insane as to examine witnesses'. Pollock was the senior of the judges at the trials of the Mannings and Franz Muller. He summed up the evidence against Muller for the jury, stressing the strength (in his opinion) of the circumstantial evidence against him. His fellow judge (and son-in-law) Baron Martin announced Muller's death sentence.

opened one and saw a decomposing head and arm, but said nothing. Wainwright took the parcels away in a cab. The workman followed, saw Wainwright take the parcels to the house of his brother Thomas and then summoned the police. It appears that Henry Wainwright had taken Harriet to his shop, shot her in the head and buried her under the floor. Thomas Wainwright had written the letter purporting to come from Edward Frieake. He also helped Henry to exhume her body a year later, cut it in pieces and parcel them up. The brothers were tried at the Old Bailey in November 1875 before Lord Chief Justice Cockburn. Henry was executed at Newgate on 21 December and Thomas was sentenced to seven years in prison. Although by

1875 hangings were no longer held in public, the Lord Mayor and Sheriffs of London invited about 60 people into Newgate to witness Wainwright's execution. As he was brought to the scaffold, Wainwright is said to have glanced at the spectators and said 'Come to see a man die, have you, you curs!' It would be interesting to know what Lord Chief Justice Cockburn truly thought of Wainwright. Cockburn was not married but was known for his wild living and fondness for women. When practising at the Bar he had left many inns or hotels by windows to escape creditors or bailiffs. He was also accompanied on circuit by various women and had three illegitimate children by the wife of a Cambridge greengrocer.

▼ The execution of Charles Peace

Charles Frederick Peace was one of Britain's most notorious burglars, who also committed two murders and was hanged in 1879. Peace was born in Sheffield, a small, agile and strong man, perfectly suited for a career as a burglar. He was also a master of disguise. Peace married Hannah Ward and played the violin, but also used an old violin case to carry his housebreaking tools. He committed an enormous number of burglaries but was caught and imprisoned four times, spending 16 years in prisons, including Millbank, Wakefield, Portland, Pentonville and Dartmoor, between 1851 and 1872. Peace then worked as a picture-frame maker in Sheffield but continued a life of burglary. Determined never to return to prison, he began carrying firearms. He was disturbed during a burglary in Manchester in 1876 by PC Nicholas Cock. Peace fired two shots, killed Cock and escaped. Three Irishmen were tried for the murder. One of them, William Habron, was sentenced to death (Peace watched the trial from the public gallery) but this was commuted to life imprisonment. At this time, Peace had fallen for his neighbour's wife, Mrs Dyson, who responded to his advances at first but then rejected him. The night after watching Habron sentenced to death, Peace waylaid her. Mr Dyson intervened and Peace shot him dead, then disappeared. The police issued posters for the wanted man, offering a reward of £100 for information leading to his conviction. Peace assumed the name John Thompson and moved to Nunhead in London. To neighbours, he seemed an upright man of independent means, who hosted musical evenings at his home. However, all was not what it seemed. The woman who lived with him as Mrs Thompson was in fact his mistress. Their lodger, Mrs Ward, was in fact his wife. Peace also continued his career as a burglar. While burgling a house in Blackheath on 10 October 1878, he was challenged by PC Edward Robinson. He fired five shots at Robinson but only wounded him and was arrested. Peace was convicted under the name John Thompson of attempted murder at the Old Bailey in November. He was sentenced to life imprisonment by Mr Justice Hawkins and sent to Pentonville Prison. His true identity was then established, and he was tried at Leeds Assizes for the murder of Mr Dyson, convicted and sentenced to death. He then also confessed to killing PC Cock and was hanged at Armley Gaol in Leeds on 25 February 1879. This drawing of the execution is from a pamphlet, entitled *Life, trial and execution of Charles Peace*, published shortly afterwards and costing one penny.

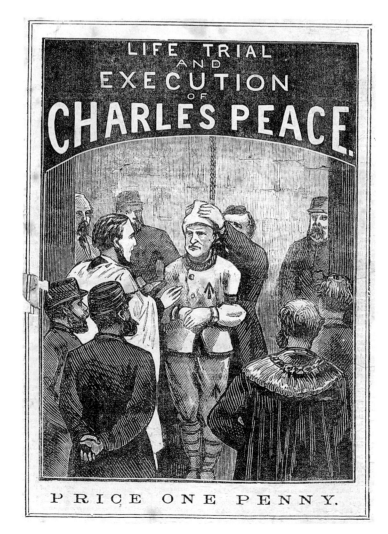

◄ The Lambeth poisoner: Dr Thomas Neill Cream

Cream was born in Scotland in 1850, graduated in medicine in Canada and then went to the United States where he worked as a physician. He was imprisoned for life there in 1881, for murdering the husband of his mistress with strychnine. Cream was released in 1891 and moved to London, lodging at 103 Lambeth Palace Road. From there, dressed in his top hat and silk-lined cloak, he preyed on prostitutes, giving them pills laced with strychnine. He murdered Ellen Donworth, Matilda Clover and (on the same night) Emma Shrivell and Alice Marsh. Cream was an exhibitionist and this was a key factor in his capture. He wrote anonymous letters offering theories on the identity of the Lambeth poisoner and one letter, signed 'A. O'Brien. Detective', to a coroner offering to reveal the killer's name for a reward of £300,000.

He also tried to blackmail a doctor, Joseph Harper, by claiming that his son (a medical student who also lived at 103 Lambeth Palace Road) had committed the murders. Cream was arrested in June 1892 when a policeman recognised him from the description of a man seen with some of the victims. He was tried in October 1892. Seven bottles of strychnine had been found in his lodgings and a prostitute named Louise Harvey also told how she had spent a night with Cream in 1891. He offered her some pills but, being suspicious, she had only pretended to take them. The jury took 12 minutes to convict him. Cream was hanged in Newgate on 15 November 1892 and buried in Dead Man's Walk.

George Chapman

➤ **George Chapman and Bessie Taylor**
George Chapman was hanged in 1903. His real name was Severin Klosowski, and he was born and married in Poland where he worked as a surgeon and barber. He came to London in 1888 and worked as a barber in the East End. He married Lucy Baderski but his Polish wife then came to London, where all three lived in the same building until the Polish wife disappeared. Klosowski and Lucy went to America in 1890 but they separated and Lucy returned to London. Klosowski followed her in 1893 and again lived with her but she left him (taking their two children with her) because of his affairs with other women. Klosowski changed his name to George and adopted the surname Chapman after living for a short time with Annie Chapman (who also left him). He then lived with Mrs Mary Spink

and they went to Hastings where Chapman ran a barber's shop. He then used her money to set himself up as the landlord of the *Prince of Wales* public house on Bartholomew Square, near City Road in London. Mrs Spink fell ill, with abdominal pains and vomiting, and died on Christmas Day 1897. Chapman then employed Bessie Taylor as a barmaid and they pretended to friends that they had married in Southwark. They ran a public house in Bishops Stortford and then the *Monument Tavern* on Union Street in Borough. Bessie also fell ill, with vomiting and diarrhoea, and died in February 1901.

➤ **George Chapman and Maud Marsh**
Chapman employed Maud Marsh as a barmaid and then proposed to her. They did not actually marry but told her parents and their friends that they had done so. The couple moved to the *Crown* public house in Borough but Maud became ill with vomiting and diarrhoea and died in October 1902. The doctors were baffled but Maud's mother suspected poisoning. A post-mortem revealed that Maud had died of antimony poisoning. The bodies of Mrs Spink and Bessie Taylor were exhumed and they also revealed evidence of antimony poisoning. Chapman was convicted of Maud's murder at the Old Bailey and hanged on 7 April 1903 in Wandsworth Prison. Some writers have suggested that Chapman was Jack the Ripper because he was a murderer (albeit a poisoner) who had worked as a surgeon and was working as a barber in the East End in 1888. It is a weak case.

◄ **The Judge: Sir Henry Hawkins**
Henry Hawkins (1817-1907) was called to the Bar in 1843. He was a master of cross-examination and achieved fame for his advocacy in the trials of the Tichborne claimant (see page 95). He was appointed as a judge of the Queen's Bench Division and later the Exchequer Division, and tried many murder cases. Mr Justice Hawkins was a thorough and patient judge who favoured leniency for first-time offenders. However, he also became known as a hanging judge and was often criticised for summing up the evidence in a prejudicial manner. He is recorded as saying: 'No human being has the right to take the life of another human being and my business is to make this abundantly clear in the cases that come before me in court.' Hawkins pronounced the death sentences on Dr Lamson in 1882 and Dr Cream in 1892 and sentenced Charles Peace to life imprisonment in 1878 for the attempted murder of PC Robinson.

Dr Crippen

➤ **Hawley Harvey Crippen**

Dr Hawley Harvey Crippen is one of the most famous British murderers, but he was really American. He was also not a qualified doctor but merely had some diplomas in medicine and pharmacology. Crippen was born in Michigan in 1862. His second wife was Kunigunde Mackamotzki, who changed her name to Cora Turner and, hoping to be a music-hall artiste (despite her limited talent), used a stage name, Belle Elmore. The Crippens came to England in 1900 and lived from 1905 at 39 Hilldrop Crescent, Islington. Crippen could not practise medicine here so took jobs selling patent medicines. He was a mild-mannered man, dominated by his wife, who quarrelled with him and insulted him in public. In about 1907, Crippen began an affair with his young secretary Ethel Le Neve, often meeting her in seedy hotels in King's Cross. Cora disappeared in early 1910. Crippen told people that she had returned to America and died. He even placed an obituary in a showbusiness newspaper.

▼ **Ethel Le Neve**

Ethel moved into Crippen's house. Cora's friends saw Ethel wearing Cora's jewellery and furs and informed the police. A police search of the house found nothing suspicious but Crippen changed his story, telling the police that his wife had left him for another man and that he had been too humiliated to admit it. Alarmed by the police investigations, Crippen fled on the ship *S.S. Montrose* to Canada accompanied by Le Neve (and disguised as a father and son). Their departure led to another police search of 39 Hilldrop Crescent.

▼ **Mrs Cora Crippen**

Some remains of Cora Crippen (flesh, skin, internal organs and hair) were found buried in the cellar. Her head and bones were never found. This was the first major case for Bernard Spilsbury, later one of the most famous British pathologists. He was able to prove from scar tissue that the body was that of Cora. It contained traces of the poison hyoscin. It was also discovered that Crippen had purchased some hyoscin in January 1910. A warrant was issued for the arrest of Crippen and Le Neve and a description of the fugitives was circulated. The captain of the *Montrose* had become suspicious of Le Neve's ill-fitting clothes and of the affectionate behaviour of this father and son. He sent a radiogram to Scotland Yard (the first use of wireless in a murder case) and Chief Inspector Walter Dew took a faster ship, overtook the *Montrose* and arrested the couple on 31 July 1910. Crippen and Le Neve were tried separately, at the Old Bailey, before the Lord Chief Justice. Crippen was convicted of murder. Le Neve was accused of helping Crippen to escape, knowing that he had murdered his wife. She was acquitted. Crippen was hanged at Pentonville Prison on 23 November 1910.

▲ **The Convict Office**
The Convict Office of the Metropolitan Police, shown here in 1883, was responsible for supervising convicts who had been freed from penal servitude, before the expiration of their sentence, on tickets of leave. These were licences to which certain conditions were attached, for example reporting to the Convict Office each month. The office also kept a register (with photographs) of habitual criminals. This office developed into the Criminal Records Office, the registers of which could be consulted by policemen throughout the country.

▲ **Lord Alverstone, Lord Chief Justice**
Richard Everard Webster (1842-1915) was educated at Charterhouse and Trinity College, Cambridge. He was called to the Bar at Lincoln's Inn in 1868. He was a Conservative MP and Attorney-General (1885-86, 1886-92 and 1895-1900). He was created a Baronet and Master of the Rolls in 1900 and then appointed as Lord Chief Justice. He was the judge at the trials of Crippen and Le Neve.

▲ **Oscar Wilde**
Oscar Fingal O'Flaherty Wills Wilde (1854-1900) was a famous Irish playwright. Two of his plays, *A Woman of No Importance* and *The Importance of Being Earnest*, are still regularly performed. He was also the principal figure in three trials at the Old Bailey in 1895. He was educated at Trinity College, Dublin and Magdalen College, Oxford. He married and then lived in London but had a lover, Lord Alfred Douglas, known as Bosie. Wilde unwisely brought an action for criminal libel against Bosie's father, the Marquess of Queensberry, who had called him a sodomite. Queensberry gathered evidence of Wilde's associations with homosexuals and Wilde was forced to withdraw his prosecution on 5 April 1895. Queensberry's solicitors then sent their evidence to the Director of Public Prosecutions. Later the same day, Wilde was arrested at his hotel in Sloane Street, taken to Bow Street Magistrates Court and charged with committing acts of gross indecency with another man (such conduct between males in private had only become an offence by a statute of 1885). Wilde was held in Holloway Gaol until his trial at the Old Bailey. The jury failed to agree but he was convicted at a second trial in May 1895 and sentenced to two years' imprisonment with hard labour. Wilde served six months in Wandsworth Prison and was then transferred to Reading Gaol. He was exposed to public gaze wearing convict clothes, on the platform of Clapham Junction, on his way to Reading. Wilde lived in France after his release in 1897 and died in 1900.

◄ **Adolf Beck 1904**

Beck was imprisoned as a result of witnesses incorrectly identifying him as the man who swindled them, and he was also wrongly identified as a man who had been convicted of similar offences. Beck was born in Norway in 1841 and lived in South America and England. He was arrested in London in 1895 when he was recognised by Ottilie Meissonnier. She said that he had pretended to be a lord, obtained a watch and ring from her and given her a cheque for £40 that turned out to be forged. Many other women made similar complaints and ten of them identified Beck as the swindler (who had pretended to be Lord Wilton or Lord Winton de Willoughby). These crimes were also similar to those committed by John Smith, who had been sentenced at the Old Bailey in 1877 to five years' penal servitude. An expert reviewed handwriting exhibits from that case and advised that the handwriting of Beck and Smith was the same. Beck was tried on 3 March 1896 at the Central Criminal Court. None of the ten charges referred to the 1877 convictions and so the defence was not permitted by the judge to raise the issue of whether or not Beck was the John Smith who had been convicted in 1877 of similar crimes. Some evidence was ruled inadmissible, such as that of a witness who had met Beck in Peru in 1880 (when Smith was in prison). The jury was therefore unaware that another man, who looked like Beck, had committed similar crimes. Beck was convicted, principally on the basis of the women's identification evidence. He was sentenced to seven years' penal servitude and sent to Wormwood Scrubs. Beck sent 15 petitions to the Home Secretary complaining of a miscarriage of justice.

◄ **William Augustus Wyatt,** *alias* **John Smith, 1881**

Beck's solicitor discovered that John Smith had also used the names Wilhelm Meyer and William Augustus Wyatt and that he was circumcised (which Beck was not). This proved that Beck and Smith were different men. However, the Home Secretary refused to interfere with Beck's sentence because he had been convicted on the women's identification of him as the swindler and not because of his identification as the John Smith who had been convicted in 1877. Beck was finally released on ticket-of-leave in 1901 having served five years of his sentence. However, in 1903 there was a resumption of the type of frauds for which Beck had been convicted. One of the new victims was taken by the police to see Beck and she identified him as the swindler. Beck was tried in May 1904 at the Old Bailey. He was convicted but the judge, Mr Justice Grantham, delayed sentencing for a short period.

◄ **William Augustus Wyatt,** *alias* **William Thomas, 1904**

A few days later, a man named William Thomas was arrested and charged with three offences similar to those of which Beck had been convicted. It transpired that Thomas was the John Smith, *alias* Meyer, *alias* Wyatt who had been convicted in 1877. He and Beck looked extremely similar. Beck was released and received a free pardon and compensation. A Committee of Inquiry found that a primary cause of the miscarriage of justice was the prison authorities' failure to include a note of Smith's circumcision on his record. The case also highlighted the need for a process by which those convicted could appeal. This resulted in the creation of the Court of Criminal Appeal in 1907.

Murder of a Police Officer

➤ Frederick Guy Browne

Frederick Browne was born Leo Brown in Catford in 1881. He met William Kennedy in Dartmoor Prison and both had many convictions for burglary and theft. They were executed for murdering a policeman. The body of PC Gutteridge was found in a country lane near Romford on 27 September 1927. He had been shot four times (two of the shots in his eyes), his notebook and pencil lay on the ground, near tyre marks of a car, and he had apparently been questioning a motorist. A stolen car had been seen in the vicinity that day and this was found abandoned in London, with blood on its bodywork and a spent cartridge case on the floor. Browne had a garage in Clapham and was arrested on suspicion of having stolen some cars. A revolver, loaded with obsolete ammunition of the type used to kill Gutteridge, was found in the garage.

➤ William Henry Kennedy

William Kennedy had worked at Browne's garage in Clapham. He was arrested and admitted being in the car with Browne on the day of the murder. He claimed that Browne had shot PC Gutteridge twice and then (as Gutteridge lay on the ground) said 'What are you looking at me like that for?' and shot him in the eyes. The ballistics evidence showed that Browne's revolver made distinctive marks on cartridge cases, exactly the same as marks on the case found in the stolen car. Browne and Kennedy were tried at the Old Bailey in April 1928 and sentenced to death by Mr Justice Avory (see page 57). Browne was hanged at Pentonville Prison and Kennedy at Wandsworth Prison on 31 May 1928.

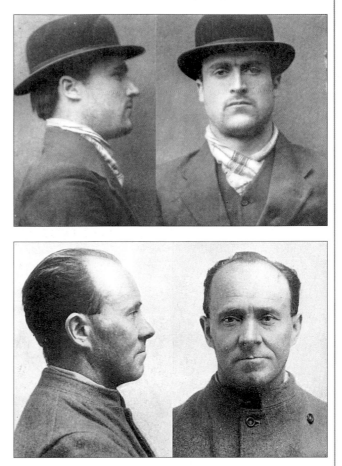

▼ Misleading photographs; unique fingerprints

These photographs show how similar men can be distinguished by fingerprints. Sir William Herschel used fingerprints to identify soldiers and illiterate prisoners in India. However, the significance of this for identification in criminal investigations was not realised until 1880 when a Scottish physician, Henry Faulds, working in Japan, showed that a suspect could not have been a thief (who had left prints of sooty fingers in a house).

Sir Francis Galton verified that everyone's fingerprints were unique (even identical twins' prints had differences) and were not inherited. He also established that prints do not change with age. He worked on a system of classifying fingerprints by sorting them between their arches, loops and whorls. The system was perfected by Sir Edward Henry, who became head of the CID and founded the Fingerprint Bureau in 1901. Those arrested often gave false names to hide their previous convictions and fingerprint checks overcame this problem. The value of fingerprints in detection work, especially in identifying fingerprints on weapons or at crime scenes, was shown in 1905. An elderly man and his wife were beaten and robbed in their shop in Deptford, and they both died. One of their assailants had left a thumbprint on a cash box that had been broken open. The police made inquiries about local criminals and suspected two brothers, Alfred and Albert Stratton, who had a record of committing violent burglaries. They were arrested and their fingerprints taken. The print on the cash box was Alfred Stratton's. He and Albert were convicted of murder and hanged.

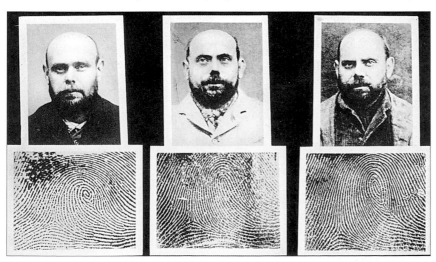

Ronald True

▼ Ronald True

True was born in Manchester in 1891. As a child, he lied, played truant from school and was cruel to animals. When he left school, he was sent abroad to work by his stepfather. True worked in Canada, New Zealand, Mexico and Argentina but was dismissed from his jobs or walked out of them. He became addicted to morphia. He joined the Royal Flying Corps in 1915 but crashed on his first solo flight, sustaining head injuries. His behaviour became very odd: he was tense, unstable and boastful. He was invalided out of the RFC but managed to obtain a job as a test pilot and then, in America, as a flying instructor. He married and returned to England but was now severely addicted to morphia and had a split personality; he might be courteous and charming but was often violent. He also believed that a man was impersonating him. True spent periods in hospital for his morphia addiction and mental problems, then left his wife in 1922 and moved to London. He spent his time womanising, drinking and dancing in clubs. He also stole money and obtained hotel rooms and a car without paying the bills.

◄ True's victim, Gertrude Yates

True met a prostitute named Gertrude Yates, also known as Olive Young. He saw her a few times and stayed in her flat in Fulham on the night of 5 March 1922. In the morning, he hit her with a rolling-pin, strangled her and stole £8 and her jewellery. However, he did not leave the flat until after Yates' maid arrived. She found the body and was able to identify True. He was convicted of murder at the Old Bailey in May 1922. The jury rejected medical evidence suggesting that True was insane and he was sentenced to death. He was again examined by doctors on the order of the Home Secretary and found to be insane. He was sent to Broadmoor Criminal Lunatic Asylum where he died in 1951.

The Murder of Percy Thompson

◄ Mr and Mrs Thompson

Percy Thompson was a shipping clerk in the City of London. His wife Edith also worked in the City, as a book-keeper, and they lived in Ilford. Edith had an affair with a family friend, Frederick Bywaters, a steward on P&O ocean-liners. He lodged with the Thompsons while he was on shore leave but left after quarrelling with Percy. Bywaters sailed to the Far East in September 1921 and he and Edith exchanged long letters during their separation. Bywaters returned to England on leave a few times in the next year and often met Edith. He returned again in September 1922 and secretly met Edith most days. On 3 October, they met in the City and that night, as Percy and Edith were returning home from a London theatre, Bywaters stabbed Percy to death in an alley.

► Frederick Bywaters

Bywaters was arrested and both he and Edith were tried for murder at the Old Bailey. Edith probably had no part in this killing. Bywaters gave evidence that he had gone to meet the couple that night on impulse and had asked Thompson to release his wife. An argument ensued and Bywaters pulled out

The Tichborne Claimant

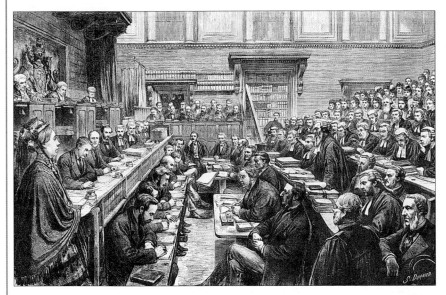

Lord Chief Justice ordered that Orton be charged with perjury and issued a warrant for his arrest. He was taken to Newgate Gaol. Orton's trial for perjury (pictured here) lasted 188 days during 1873 and 1874.

▼ **The Tichborne claimant arrives at Newgate Gaol**

Orton was convicted and sentenced to 14 years' penal servitude. He was released after 10 years and died in poverty. Edward Vaughan Hyde Kenealy QC (1819-80) was Counsel for Orton at his perjury trial. He was disbarred for his conduct of the case but became the MP for Stoke on Trent.

▲ **The trial of the Tichborne claimant**

The case of the Tichborne claimant was one of the most famous of the 19th century. His civil claim to a baronetcy and a family's estates (worth £40,000 a year) led to his prosecution and imprisonment for perjury. Arthur Orton was the son of a Wapping butcher. He had lived in Australia and was wanted there for horse theft. He claimed to be Roger Charles Doughty Tichborne (who had been lost at sea), the son and heir of Sir James Tichborne, 10th Baronet. The trial of Orton's unsuccessful action against Sir Henry Tichborne, 12th baronet, lasted 102 days in 1871 and 1872. At the end of the case, the

his knife. Edith had shouted 'Oh don't!' and, when questioned after the killing, she had named Bywaters as the killer. However, the prosecution case against Edith relied on her adultery and her love letters that appeared to include hints at how they could kill Percy. Both were convicted. Edith was executed at Holloway Prison and Bywaters was executed at Pentonville at the same hour on 9 January 1923.

chapter 6 Some Political Trials and Executions

MOST POLITICAL TRIALS in Britain have involved allegations of treason and most of those trials, as well as the punishment of the accused, have taken place in London. Treason has always been treated by the British criminal justice system as the most serious of crimes and therefore attracted the death penalty. British history is littered with the bodies of those who died as a result of this heinous crime. However, whether an act constituted treason usually depended on those in power afterwards. A few examples of treasonable acts and the trials of traitors have already been noted, such as those of the Gunpowder plot conspirators and James Sheppard. A few more are included here and in the following sections that deal with victims, executions, prisons and other punishments.

John Dudley and Lady Jane Grey

◄ **John Dudley, Duke of Northumberland**
Mary Tudor ordered the execution of the Duke of Northumberland on Tower Hill in 1553 for high treason in placing his daughter-in-law, Lady Jane Grey, on the throne after the death of Edward VI. Dudley was born in about 1502 and knighted in France in 1523. He held various offices during the reign of Henry VIII, for example serving as Warden of the Scottish Marches and as Great Admiral. When Henry died, Dudley was appointed joint regent for the young Edward VI but acquiesced in the other regent, the Duke of Somerset, becoming sole Protector in 1547. Dudley was created Earl of Warwick and High Chamberlain in 1547 and then Earl Marshal and Duke of Northumberland in 1551. He procured the execution of Somerset in 1552 and then, intending to alter the succession, married his son Lord Guildford Dudley to Lady Jane Grey in 1553. On the death of Edward VI later that year, Dudley placed Jane on the throne. However, Mary Tudor, the eldest daughter of Henry VIII, was proclaimed Queen by her supporters a few days later and took her throne as Dudley's supporters melted away. Dudley was sentenced to death. He tried to save himself by becoming a Roman Catholic but was nevertheless sent to the scaffold.

▶ **Lady Jane Grey**
When Edward VI died in 1553, Lady Jane Grey was aged 16. She was a descendant of King Henry VII, being the grand-daughter of Mary (the sister of Henry VIII) and Charles Brandon, Duke of Suffolk. Jane had been married to Lord Guildford Dudley the same year and was placed on the throne by her father-in-law, the Duke of Northumberland. She occupied it for only nine days and was imprisoned in the Tower of London when Mary Tudor was proclaimed Queen on 19 July 1553. Jane and Lord Guildford Dudley were tried for treason at Guildhall in the City of London. They were sentenced to death but their executions were delayed and they were held in different towers within the Tower of London. Sir Thomas Wyatt then led a rebellion against Mary Tudor. This sealed the fate of both Jane and Lord Guildford Dudley. Dudley was beheaded first, on 12 February 1554 on Tower Hill. Jane watched his headless body being brought back to the Tower in a cart. She was then taken out and executed on Tower Green.

The regicide Miles Corbet

Corbet was a barrister, MP for Great Yarmouth and an officer of the Court of Chancery. He was one of those responsible for the execution of Charles I (see pages 98-9). Corbet attended only one meeting of the Commission that tried Charles but also signed the death warrant. He fled to Holland in 1660. After his Restoration, King Charles II had to deal with Corbet and the other regicides, that is, those who signed his father's death warrant and others who were closely involved in his trial. The death warrant was signed by 59 men: John Bradshaw, Thomas Lord Grey of Groby, Oliver Cromwell, Edward Whaley, Michael Livesay, John Okey, John Danvers, John Bourchier, Henry Ireton, Thomas Mauleverer, Hardress Waller, John Blakiston, John Hutchinson,

MILES CORBET.
(Executed at Tyburn 1662)

Miles Corbet

William Goff, Thomas Pride, Peter Temple, Thomas Harrison, John Hewson, Henry Smith, Peregrine Pelham, Richard Dean, Robert Titchburn, Humphrey Edwards, Daniel Blagrave, Owen Roe, William Purefoy, Adrian Scroop, James Temple, Augustine Garland, Edmond Ludlow, Henry Martin, Vincent Potter, William Constable, Richard Ingoldsby, William Cawley, John Barkstead, Isaac Ewer, John Dixwell, Valentine Walton, Simon Mayne, Thomas Horton, John Jones, John Moore, Gilbert Millington, George Fleetwood, John Alured, Robert Lilburne, William Say, Anthony Stapeley, Gregory Norton, Thomas Challoner, Thomas Wogan, John Ven, Gregory Clement, John Downe, Thomas Waite, Thomas Scott, John Carew and Miles Corbet. Many others were incriminated. John Cooke, Solicitor-General, was Charles' prosecutor. Francis Hacker supervised the execution. Lord Monson, Sir Henry Mildmay, Robert Wallop and William Hevingham had sat at Charles' trial (although they withdrew before the death sentence and did not sign the death warrant). The Reverend Hugh Peters had often preached against the King. Daniel Axton (or Axtell) commanded the soldiers guarding the King at the trial and was disrespectful to him, often laughing during his speeches.

Twenty regicides escaped trial by their death before the Restoration including Oliver Cromwell, John Bradshaw, Henry Ireton, Thomas Grey, John Venn, William Constable and Thomas Horton. This did not stop the Royalists taking revenge. The corpses of Bradshaw, Cromwell and Ireton were exhumed and gibbeted at Tyburn in 1661. Their rotting heads were cut off and placed on spikes on the roof of Westminster Hall. Sir William Constable had been buried in Westminster Abbey but his body was dug up and thrown into a pit.

Lord Monson, Henry Mildmay and Robert Wallop escaped trial by an Act of Indemnity that had been passed as part of the settlement restoring Charles II. However, Charles had them thrown into the Tower of London. Each year, they were dragged on hurdles to Tyburn and back to the Tower. Wallop died in the Tower, Monson died in the Fleet Prison and Mildmay died while being transported to Tangier. Some regicides escaped abroad: Edward Whalley, John Dixwell and William Goff to New England; Valentine Walton and Daniel Blagrave to

Germany; Edmund Ludlow and William Cawley to Switzerland; and William Say and Thomas Challoner to Holland. Most of these men died in exile. Thomas Scott had also fled to Holland, but was persuaded to return and faced a trial. Colonel Okey and Sir John Barkstead escaped to Germany and Miles Corbet fled to Holland. They thought they were safe.

Twenty-nine regicides were tried for treason (some in absentia) before 34 commissioners, including peers and senior judges. The trial started on 9 October 1660 at Hicks' Hall then continued at the Old Bailey. Some of the accused, such as Colonel Thomas Harrison, Adrian Scroop, John Jones, Thomas Scott, Gregory Clement, Robert Tichborne, John Okey, John Barkstead, James Temple, Robert Lilburne, Gregory Clement and Vincent Potter had signed the death warrant. The Reverend Hugh Peters, John Cooke, Francis Hacker, Daniel Axton and Isaac Pennington were also tried for their role in the King's death. Ten regicides were executed between 13 and 18 October 1660. Thomas Harrison suffered first. He was dragged on a hurdle to Charing Cross, where a crowd waited. King Charles II and many ladies of the court were also watching. Harrison was hanged on a gibbet facing Banqueting House (where Charles I had been executed). He was cut down while still alive and therefore watched as his intestines were drawn out and thrown on a fire. His body was then cut into quarters. Harrison's head was taken back to Newgate and attached to the hurdle used to drag the next victim, John Cooke, to his death. Hugh Peters was taken to the place of execution with Cooke, tied to the rails of the scaffold and forced to watch as Cooke was hanged, drawn and quartered. Peters then suffered the same fate. John Jones, John Carew, Adrian Scroop, Thomas Scott, Gregory Clement, Daniel Axton and Francis Hacker were also executed.

Colonel Okey and Sir John Barkstead had been condemned in their absence. They went to meet Miles Corbet (who had also been condemned) in Holland in 1662. The three men were seized, handed over to the English and taken to London. As they had already been tried they were hanged, drawn and quartered at Tyburn a few days later. Okey's relatives were permitted to bury the parts of his body. The quarters of Corbet and Barkstead were displayed on the City gates. Corbet's head was placed on a spike on London Bridge and Barkstead's on Traitor's Gate at the Tower.

The other regicides suffered various punishments. George Fleetwood and Augustine Garland were transported to Tangier. Simon Mayne and Owen Rowe were spared the death penalty but died within a year in the Tower. Peter Temple also died in the Tower in 1663. William Hevingham was imprisoned at Windsor Castle until he died in 1678. Robert Lilburne was imprisoned for life on St Nicholas Island in Plymouth Sound. James Temple, Thomas Waite, Gilbert Millington and Hardress Waller were imprisoned for life on Jersey. Colonel John Hutchinson was, rather surprisingly, let off completely.

The Trial of Charles I

◄ The trial of Charles I

Charles' reign was marked by unsuccessful wars and arguments with Parliament, which refused to authorise taxes for his needs and criticised his ecclesiastical policies. Charles ruled for ten years without Parliament but was forced to recall it due to lack of money. The English Civil War followed in which Charles' forces were finally crushed by the Parliamentarian army. Parliament then had to decide what to do with the King. The leaders of the army demanded that he be put to death and Royalist risings in 1648 confirmed the dangers of keeping him alive. The Commons therefore passed an Ordinance creating a Commission, styled the High Court of Justice, to try the King. Three judges were to sit with a jury of 150 commissioners, but the judges refused to act so the Commons declared that the Commissioners would sit as both judge and jury. They would include Oliver Cromwell, Henry Ireton, General Fairfax, some lawyers, a few peers, baronets, knights and various others. John Bradshaw was appointed as the Lord President (the presiding judge) of the Commission. Charles' trial took place, before meetings of the Commissioners in Westminster Hall, from 20 January 1649 and lasted four days. Many Commissioners failed or refused to attend the meetings (only 65 attended the first meeting). Charles was charged with high treason in levying war against Parliament and the Kingdom of England in order to gain unlimited power. He refused to acknowledge the authority of the court or plead to the charges and was convicted and condemned to death.

► John Bradshaw

The regicide John Bradshaw (1602-59) was called to the Bar in 1627, then appointed a judge of the Sheriff's Court in London (in 1643) and Chief Justice of Chester (1647). Parliament found it difficult to find judges to try King Charles in 1649 and finally appointed Bradshaw as Lord President of the Parliamentary Commission. He therefore presided at the King's trial and pronounced the sentence of death. Bradshaw continued work in various judicial posts but opposed Cromwell's gradual assumption of power and retired from public life in 1653. He died in 1659 and therefore escaped being tried with the other regicides for their role in the King's death. However, Bradshaw's body did not escape the wrath of the returning Royalists. It was exhumed in 1660 and hanged at Tyburn and his head was placed on a spike on the roof of Westminster Hall.

▼ The execution of Charles I

The King was executed on 30 January 1649 on a scaffold that was erected outside the Banqueting House of Whitehall Palace. He was brought out of a window of the hall, made a brief speech declaring himself the 'Martyr of the People' and was then beheaded. The execution was watched by thousands of spectators who were packed into Whitehall and lined the rooftops nearby. The identity of the executioner remains uncertain. Richard Brandon was the official London executioner at the time but he said publicly that he would not execute the King. An attempt was made to bribe him to do the work and, when that failed, soldiers were sent to collect Brandon and bring him to the place of execution. Two executioners, dressed in black, were on the stage when Charles was beheaded. Both wore masks and false beards so that their identity is unknown, but they were probably Brandon and his assistant William Lowen. One of them, probably Brandon, cut off the King's head with a single blow of the axe. The other executioner held the head before the crowd, shouting 'Behold the head of a traitor!'.

◄ **Chief Justice Hale**
Sir Mathew Hale (1609-76) was called to the Bar at Lincoln's Inn and acted as counsel for Archbishop Laud during his impeachment in 1645. He is said to have offered his services to Charles I for his trial in 1649. Hale was created a Judge of the Common Pleas by Cromwell in 1654 and became an MP in the same year. He was the senior judge sitting as a commissioner at the trial of the regicides in 1660. Hale was also appointed as Lord Chief Baron of the Exchequer in 1660, then knighted and appointed Chief Justice of the King's Bench in 1671. He wrote many legal texts that were published after his death.

▲ **The regicide Colonel John Okey**
John Okey served with distinction in the Parliamentarian army, for example at the battle of Naseby in 1645. He signed the death warrant of Charles I in 1649. He served in the Scottish war in 1651 and became an MP in 1654. He opposed Cromwell becoming Protector, which led to his discharge from the army, and was arrested in 1658 for renewed opposition to Cromwell. Okey fled to Germany upon the Restoration in 1660 but was later arrested in Holland, brought back to England and executed.

➤ **A 'seditious Anabaptist and Quaker', Thomas Venner**
Thomas Venner was a cooper and the leader of a fanatical sect known as the Fifth Monarchy men. At first, the sect supported the government of Oliver Cromwell, who was installed as Lord Protector in 1653, believing that it would become the Fifth Monarchy (in succession to the monarchies of Assyria, Persia, Greece and Rome). The sect believed that, during this Fifth Monarchy, Christ would reign with a government of saints (that is themselves) for one thousand years. When it was proposed that Cromwell should assume the title of King, the Fifth Monarchy men planned a rising. Many were arrested and sent to the Tower. They attempted a second rising after the Restoration of Charles II, seeing him as a usurper in Christ's dominion. Many members of the sect met on 6 January 1661 in a house in Swan Alley, Coleman Street, where Venner preached that the time of the Fifth Monarchy had arrived and that the reign of Jesus was beginning that day. Sixty armed members of the sect marched around the City for the next two days. They killed a man who shouted support for the King and routed the City militia sent against them but they failed to capture the Lord Mayor. A group led by Venner fought with the Horse Guards in Wood Street and many sect members were killed or captured. Venner was beheaded and quartered on 19 January and ten other sect members were executed.

THOMAS VENNER,
Preacher at the Conventicles of the Fifth Monarchy Men, & Seducer of Libertines. Captain of the seditious Anabaptists & Quakers in the City of London. Beheaded & Quartered 19 Jan.ᵉ anno 1661.

chapter 7 Victims of Crime

IT IS A SAD FACT that many criminals are remembered long after their crimes but their victims are usually forgotten. We should remember both the direct victims of crime, such as John Hayes, Gertrude Yates, Thomas Briggs and Cora Crippen, but also those who are indirectly affected by crime, such as Sarah Whitehead (see page 105 below).

Sir Thomas Overbury

▲ Sir Thomas Overbury

Sir Thomas Overbury (1581-1613) was a barrister and poet. He was murdered, by poison, in the Tower of London and Robert Carr, Viscount Rochester (later Earl of Somerset) and his wife Frances were convicted of the murder. Overbury was an adviser and favourite of Rochester, who was the private secretary and favourite of King James I. It has been suggested that Overbury was part of a homosexual triangle that consisted of himself, Rochester and James. Indeed, it was a common joke at court that 'Rochester ruled the King and Overbury ruled Rochester'. Rochester fell in love with Frances Howard, the wife of Robert, Earl of Essex. Frances petitioned for divorce from Essex (they were later separated by a decree of nullity on the basis of his impotency) so that she could marry Rochester. Overbury and the Howard family were enemies and so he tried to dissuade Rochester from the marriage. They argued and became estranged. Frances was so angry at Overbury that she decided to ruin him and persuaded Rochester to help. She used her influence to arrange for King James to offer Overbury an appointment as Ambassador to Russia and Overbury was then persuaded by Rochester to refuse the post. Frances and Rochester used Overbury's refusal to get him arrested on a trumped-up charge of contempt for opposing the King's wishes. He was committed to the Tower of London.

➤ Sir Gervase Elwes

Frances persuaded Sir Gervase Elwes, Lieutenant of the Tower, to employ Richard Weston, one of her servants, as the personal gaoler to Overbury. She also arranged for Anne Turner, who dabbled in magic, and James Franklin, a City apothecary, to supply poison. Weston used it to poison Overbury's meals. Overbury became very ill and finally died in September 1613. In November, Rochester was created Earl of Somerset and, with Overbury out of the way, he married Frances.

▼ Mrs Anne Turner

Unfortunately for Rochester, he was supplanted as the King's favourite by George Villiers (later Duke of Buckingham). At the same time, rumours began to circulate about the death of Overbury. Villiers' supporters appear to have obtained information about the poisoning and used it to ensure Rochester's downfall. Turner, Weston, Franklin and Elwes were arrested and convicted of murder in November 1615. They were executed but only after confessing that Rochester and Frances had procured the murder. As the Earl and Countess of Somerset, they were entitled to trial by their peers in the House of Lords. Frances was tried on 24 May 1616. She pleaded guilty. Rochester's trial started the next day. He pleaded not guilty but was convicted. They were both sentenced to death. The King pardoned them but they were detained together in the Tower for six years by which time they were said to have hated each other. Frances died of a painful disease (possibly cancer) in 1632, aged 39. Rochester died in 1645.

▲ Miss Ann Porter

Women in London in 1789 and 1790 were in terror. A man was stabbing women in public and often in daylight. This mystery fiend, referred to as the Monster, was said to dress well and have charming manners. He asked some women to smell a nosegay he was carrying but the flowers hid a sharp instrument that he jabbed in their faces. He also slashed at women's thighs, breasts and buttocks. Ann Porter was walking up St James's

Street with her sister on the night of 18 January 1790 when she felt a blow. She turned round and saw a man crouching. The girls fled home. Ann had been wounded on the thigh with a sharp instrument. The wound was about nine inches long and very deep.

◄ The monster: Rhynwick Williams

A few months later, Ann saw a man in a park and identified him as her attacker. He was Rhynwick Williams. Seven other victims also identified him as the culprit. Because of certain legal arguments, Williams faced two trials, one at the Old Bailey and one at Hicks' Hall, but the evidence and verdict at each were the same. Williams worked for an artificial flower-maker who swore that Williams was working at the time of the attack on Ann Porter and other employees corroborated this evidence. However, Ann seemed so certain of her identification of Williams as her attacker that he was convicted. He was sentenced to two years' imprisonment in Newgate for assault and also had to find sureties for his future good behaviour. Although there were no more attacks by the Monster, many people doubted that the right man had been caught. Many of the Monster's victims said that he had been much better educated than Williams and some doubted the truth of the women's identification of Williams.

◄ Samuel Mathews, the Dulwich hermit, murdered in 1802

Samuel Mathews was so grief-stricken at the death of his wife that he lived for several years in a cave in Dulwich Woods which were plagued by highwaymen and footpads. He became known as the Dulwich hermit but was murdered in 1802. His killer was never found.

Mrs Rudd and the Perreaus

↟ Mrs Margaret Caroline Rudd at the bar in the Old Bailey

Robert and Daniel Perreau were twins and almost impossible to tell apart. They were executed at Tyburn in 1776 for forgery but were possibly victims of a fraudster named Mrs Margaret Caroline Rudd. Robert was an eminent London surgeon. Daniel lived the life of an affluent gentleman. Mrs Rudd was a fashionable courtesan who had lived with Daniel since 1770 and bore him three children. Daniel had been declared bankrupt in 1770 following the failure of his business. The brothers and Mrs Rudd speculated in insurance funds, stocks and shares but, by 1771, all Robert's savings had gone and Daniel was again bankrupt. His return to wealth by 1776 may have been due to fraud and forgery but was possibly financed by Mrs Rudd who continued to entertain wealthy lovers with Daniel's knowledge. Mrs Rudd told the brothers that she was a relation of William Adair, a rich government contractor. She said that Adair wished to benefit her (by providing money to Daniel to buy a larger house) and that Adair planned to open a bank in partnership with the brothers. However, she also said that Adair sometimes needed to raise money in secret. He therefore sent his bonds to her with a request that Daniel or Robert Perreau raise cash with them (and pass that cash to him via Mrs Rudd). This happened a number of times. On 10 March 1775, Mrs Rudd handed another bond to Robert, for £7,500, purportedly signed by Adair. Mrs Rudd said that Adair again needed to raise money in confidence and had requested that Robert use his contacts to raise £5,000. He asked the bankers, Messrs Robert and Henry Drummond, for £5,000 on the security of the bond. They had doubts about the authenticity of Adair's signature, and Robert Perreau and Henry Drummond visited Adair. He denied that it was his signature, so Robert reported the forgery of the bond to a magistrate. Sir Thomas Frankland and a Doctor Brooke then discovered that their loan bonds were also forged.

↟ Robert and Daniel Perreau

The brothers and Mrs Rudd were arrested. Mrs Rudd gave evidence against the brothers to the prosecution and so had to be tried separately. She claimed that Robert Perreau had asked her to imitate Adair's handwriting and that Daniel had forced her to sign the forged bond under threat of death. The brothers were tried at the Old Bailey Sessions in June 1775. There was evidence that, when arrested, Mrs Rudd had admitted forging the Adair bonds herself and stated that the Perreau brothers were innocent. Servants in Daniel Perreau's house swore that Mrs Rudd often wrote letters, purportedly from Adair, to herself or the Perreau brothers and many witnesses gave evidence of the brothers' good character. A scrivener named Watson stated that he had drawn up eight bonds at the request of one of the brothers. He was unsure which of the twins had employed him but thought it was Daniel. If true, this suggests that Daniel Perreau and Mrs Rudd had committed the forgeries together and that only Robert was the unwitting victim. The brothers were convicted and lay in prison for seven months, hoping that new evidence might arise at Mrs Rudd's trial.

Unfortunately for the Perreau brothers, Mrs Rudd was acquitted of forgery in December 1775. She left court on the arm of her new lover, a notorious rake, Lord Lyttelton, but her final fate is unknown. There was much sympathy for the brothers and many leading merchants and bankers of London signed a petition to the King, requesting that mercy be shown. Robert's wife petitioned the Queen, imploring her to save her husband. However, at that time, the crime of forgery was considered so heinous that mercy was rarely granted. The brothers were taken to Tyburn on 17 January 1776 and hanged in front of 30,000 spectators.

Martha Ray

▼ Miss Martha Ray

Martha Ray was murdered by the Reverend James Hackman outside Covent Garden Theatre. She was the daughter of a staymaker and apprenticed to a mantua-maker in St John's Lane, Clerkenwell. She was seen there by Lord Sandwich, First Lord of the Admiralty, who took her, when she was 14 or 15 years old, to be his mistress in his house near Huntingdon. James Hackman was born in Gosport, Hampshire. His character was too volatile for a career in business and so his father purchased him a commission in the army. Hackman was heading a recruiting party at Huntingdon in 1774 and was invited to dine with Lord Sandwich. He met and fell in love with Martha, despite the fact that she had lived for 19 years as Sandwich's mistress and had borne him nine children. Martha and Hackman exchanged love letters for four years. Failing to obtain promotion in the army, Hackman became a clergyman and was appointed to a parish in Norfolk in 1768. He accompanied Lord Sandwich and Martha (who was fond of music) to a number of concerts. Martha and Hackman were considering living together but, in March 1779, Martha decided to end the relationship, and continue living with her children and their ageing, yet wealthy, father rather than with an impecunious younger man (and probably be barred from contact with her children). Hackman wrote to a friend hinting that he was considering suicide. On 7 April 1779, he was lodging in London, saw Martha get into a coach and followed her to Covent Garden Theatre. He then went to his lodgings, loaded two pistols and returned to the theatre. When the play was over, Martha was about to step into her coach when Hackman came forward and killed her with one pistol. He discharged the other at himself, but it misfired. He then beat himself on the head with the pistol butt.

▼ The Reverend Hackman

Hackman was carried before Sir John Fielding, who committed him to Tothill Fields Bridewell. Hackman was tried at the Old Bailey Sessions, before Mr Justice Blackstone, and was sentenced to death. In the condemned cell of Newgate Gaol, Hackman received a letter from Lord Sandwich, offering to use his influence to save him. Hackman declined the offer, saying that he wished for death. He was hanged at Tyburn on 19 April 1779 and his body was taken to Surgeons' Hall for dissection. This is another example of swift justice. Only 12 days separated a murder and a dissection.

Isaac Blight

▼ **Mrs Blight, widow of the victim Isaac Blight**

Richard Patch was executed for murder in 1806. He was born near Exeter in 1770, the son of a farmer and smuggler who later became a turnkey at Exeter Gaol. Richard was a farmer, who fell into debt, and so left his farm and went to work for Isaac Blight in Rotherhithe (for whom his sister worked as a servant). They discussed the possibility of Patch buying a partnership in Blight's business as a ship-breaker and so, in 1804, Patch sold his farm. He received £350 and paid £250 of this to Mr Blight as a part of the purchase-money. Then, on 23 September 1805, Mr Blight was wounded, while sitting in his house, by shots from outside. He died the next day. Patch was tried for murder at the Surrey Assizes in the Sessions House in Horsemonger Lane, on Saturday 5 April 1806. The public took great interest in the case and a vast crowd surrounded the Sessions House. Many persons of rank attended the trial, including the Dukes of Sussex and Cumberland. Neighbours stated that no-one had run away from the house at the time of the shots and Patch was found in the house immediately after the shooting. Mrs Blight, the deceased's widow, told the court how her husband had been facing action by some of his creditors and, to fool them, had secretly agreed to sell most of his property to Patch for £1,250. Patch had only paid her husband the sum of £250 and it appeared that, having obtained a transfer of the property, Patch probably murdered Blight to save having to pay the other £1,000.

◄ **Richard Patch**

The jury convicted Patch and he was executed on Tuesday 8 April on top of Horsemonger Lane Gaol in Southwark. His body was then delivered to the surgeons for dissection.

▲ **The Bank Nun: Miss Sarah Whitehead**

Sarah Whitehead was 19 years old in 1811. Her brother Philip was a clerk at the Bank of England and forged a bill of exchange to clear debts that he had incurred in gambling on stocks and shares. He was executed at Newgate Gaol. Sarah's friends kept the truth of her brother's fate from her, saying that he had gone on a long business journey. Sarah believed this until she visited the Bank and another clerk told her the truth, the shock of which sent her out of her mind. Sarah then went to the bank every day for 25 years, dressed in a black gown and hood, asking whether her brother had returned from his journey.

The Brides in the Bath

► **The brides in the bath: George Smith and Bessie Mundy**

George Joseph Smith was a bigamist who was also known as the 'Brides in the bath' murderer. Smith was born in Bethnal Green in 1872. He was a petty criminal who was in and out of prison for offences such as theft and receiving stolen goods. His defence counsel, Marshall Hall, later said that Smith had an almost hypnotic power over women. He was also a callous killer, capable of passionate words and caresses whilst coldly planning murder. His first and only valid marriage was in 1898 (calling himself George Love) to Caroline Thornhill, a domestic servant. Smith bullied her into stealing from her employers and deserted her when she was arrested. He moved to London and bigamously married a woman there (he was never divorced from Caroline who moved to Canada on her release). Smith also went through marriage ceremonies with three other women in 1908 and 1909 and stole money from them. One of them was Edith Pegler, to whom he returned in between his later marriages (telling her that his absences were due to business trips). Smith then turned to murder. In 1910, he used the name Henry Williams when he married Bessie Mundy, who had a fortune of £2,500 in a trust controlled by her uncle. Smith discovered that the only way he could get this money was if Bessie died. In July 1912 he arranged for Bessie to make a will leaving everything she owned to him. On 13 July, Smith called the doctor to their house in Herne Bay because his wife had died in her bath. The verdict of an inquest was death by misadventure.

▲ **Alice Burnham**

Smith married Alice Burnham on 4 November 1913 and insured her life for £500. She made a will in favour of her husband and the couple moved to Blackpool. On 12 December, Alice was found dead in her bath. The inquest's verdict was misadventure and Smith collected the insurance. Smith used the name Charles James to marry Alice Reavil in September 1914. They lived on Battersea Rise. She was not worth killing but Smith made £90 by stealing her savings and selling her belongings.

◄ **Margaret Lofty**

Smith then met Margaret Elizabeth Lofty. An insurance policy for £700 was taken out on her life and, posing as John Lloyd, Smith married her in Bath on 17 December 1914. They took lodgings the next day in Highgate in London and Margaret made a will, leaving everything she owned to her husband. She died in her bath that night. An inquest again found death by misadventure. However, Alice Burnham's father saw a newspaper report of Margaret's death and contacted the police. Smith was arrested on 2 February 1915 on a holding charge of using a false name in a marriage register. He was held in Brixton Prison and then charged with murder. Smith was tried at the Old Bailey in June 1915 for the murder of Bessie Mundy. His defence counsel, Edward Marshall Hall, tried unsuccessfully to exclude evidence of the other two deaths, by which the prosecution showed Smith's system of murder. He was convicted and hanged at Maidstone Prison on 13 August 1915.

chapter 8 **Executions**

HANGINGS, beheadings and other methods of execution were public spectacles from medieval times until the 19th century and were staged in many places in London. The killing of criminals removed offenders from the population (a practical necessity for a country that had insufficient prisons to hold offenders as a punishment), displayed the power of the authorities and was thought to have a deterrent effect on other people.

England was a bloodthirsty country. It is estimated that 72,000 people were put to death in England and Wales during the 38 years of the reign of Henry VIII out of a population that was a fraction of that today. The number of offences that carried the death penalty was gradually increased to 220 by 1819. However, some of these offences were so trivial that in many cases juries became reluctant to convict offenders. Even those convicted of capital crimes often escaped the ultimate penalty. As the law became more savage, many judges and juries looked for ways to ameliorate the position. Many of the condemned received pardons or had the death sentence commuted to one of transportation from the realm. In the period 1749 to 1758, it is believed that 365 people were hanged in London and Middlesex, that is about 70 per cent of those condemned to death. Fifty years later, there were 804 convictions for capital offences in one year (reflecting the greater population and the increased number of offences carrying the death penalty) but only 126 of the condemned were actually hanged. The number of offences for which death was prescribed was then gradually reduced. By 1868, the death penalty was limited to the offences of treason, piracy, murder and arson in the Royal Dockyards.

Most condemned criminals were hanged. However, those of noble blood were usually beheaded and anyone convicted of treason should have been beheaded or subjected to the ritual of hanging, drawing and quartering. In these cases, the condemned was hanged but cut down while still alive, disembowelled and then decapitated. The body would be quartered and the head and quarters placed on display (for example on the gatehouse of London Bridge or on Temple Bar) for maximum effect on the populace. It was not until after 1800 that this punishment was reduced to hanging with decapitation after death (as in the case of the Cato Street conspirators in 1820).

The punishment for heresy and some other religious offences was burning, since it was symbolic of the destruction of the evil within a person. Burning was also considered a more decorous punishment for those women, such as the murderess Catherine Hayes, whose offence carried the penalty of hanging, drawing and quartering. Death by burning was finally abolished in 1790.

Henry VIII was responsible for an Act of 1530 that legalised boiling to death as a punishment for poisoners. A cook named Richard Rose suffered in this manner at Smithfield in 1532. The offender could be placed in cold oil and brought to the boil slowly or, perhaps more mercifully (everything is relative), plunged into oil that was already boiling. This dreadful punishment was repealed shortly after the accession of Edward VI.

Tower Hill, the Tower of London, Tyburn, Smithfield and Newgate were the main places of execution. However, many other places were used to kill criminals. Cheapside was the chief market place of medieval London and had a fountain known as the Standard, where Walter de Stapleton, Treasurer to Edward II, was beheaded in 1326 and two fishmongers were beheaded in 1351. St Paul's Churchyard was the venue for the execution of some of the Gunpowder plot conspirators in 1606. The other conspirators were executed in Old Palace Yard, Westminster, where Sir Walter Raleigh was also executed in 1618. Some of the regicides were executed at Charing Cross in 1660.

Executions also took place at the location of a crime. In 1586, Anthony Babington was involved in a conspiracy to kill Queen Elizabeth and place Mary Queen of Scots on the throne. He was hanged, drawn and quartered with 13 of his accomplices in Lincoln's Inn Fields, because they had met there to 'confer of their traiterous practices'. Vratz, Stern and Borosky were hanged in Pall Mall where they had committed the murder of Thomas Thynne in 1682. Thomas Savage was executed at Ratcliff Cross in 1668 for the murder of his fellow servant. The hangman John Price (see page 130) was himself hanged at Bunhill Fields in 1718 for murder. John Williamson was hanged on gallows opposite Chiswell Street in Moorfields for the torture and murder of his wife at his house there. Nathaniel Tomkins, brother-in-law of Edmund Waller (and implicated in Waller's plot of 1643 to seize London for Charles I), was hanged outside his house in Fetter Lane because it was the scene of some of the conspirators' meetings. John Plackett was hanged on the City Road near Islington in 1762 for a robbery there (and his body was then hung in chains on Finchley Common). The last criminal to be executed at the scene of the crime was John Cashman. He was hanged in Skinner Street in Clerkenwell in 1817 in front of a gunsmith's shop that he had burgled during a street disturbance.

The corpses of those hanged, particularly highwaymen and pirates, might also be hung in chains at various places around London. People travelling into London from the west, over Hounslow Heath, were usually greeted by the rotting corpses of highwaymen hanging from gibbets along the road. This practice continued until 1834.

Executions attracted large crowds. On 21 January 1664, Samuel Pepys stood on a cartwheel to watch the execution of Colonel Turner, who had robbed a merchant, Mr Tryan, in Lime Street, of £1,000 and jewels worth £4,000. Pepys went to Leadenhall Street, at the end of Lime Street, near where the robbery occurred, and then to St Mary Axe, where Tryan lived. Pepys paid a shilling to stand on the cartwheel. He had to wait an hour before the hanging took place because Turner delayed matters by long discourses and prayers in the hope of a reprieve. None came and at last he was flung off the ladder. Pepys estimated the crowd at between 12,000 and 14,000.

Most executions took place at Tyburn. The processions of the Sheriffs and condemned from Newgate Gaol to the place of execution were conducted with pomp and ceremony but also with an element of farce and degradation. The procession had to force its way through massive crowds that gathered to watch. The events became rowdy affairs, with traders trying to sell their wares to the spectators, and heavy drinking, fighting and theft continuing all day. It was little wonder that this spectacle came to be known as 'Tyburn Fair'.

Surgeons required bodies to learn their trade and examine the workings of the human body. In the 17th and 18th centuries, ten corpses of executed criminals would be passed each year to the Royal College of Physicians and the Worshipful Company of Barber-Surgeons. However, these were not sufficient for their needs and further corpses were provided to surgeons secretly by the hangmen (for a suitable fee). A statute of 1752 stated that, after execution, the bodies of murderers should be handed over to the surgeons for dissection and then exposed to public view. This Act was not repealed until 1832. Its purpose was to deter murderers but it also resulted in even worse scenes at the gallows. As the executioner cut down a body, the criminal's friends and relatives might try to seize the body so that they could bury it and keep it from the surgeon's knife.

The celebration surrounding executions was gradually erased. The processions from Newgate to Tyburn ceased in 1783, when public executions were moved to the open space outside Newgate Gaol in Old Bailey. Large crowds continued to gather for executions and some spectators were killed when panic broke out in the crowd watching the execution of Holloway and Haggerty in 1807. Public executions came to an end in 1868, partly because of complaints at such matters being a public spectacle but also because of the dangers caused by such large crowds.

The methods of execution were also restricted to hanging (except in the armed forces where shooting was permitted). Capital punishment was abolished in 1965 except for treason and certain types of piracy. The only surviving scaffold is in Wandsworth Prison.

➤ Colonel Despard on the gallows
Colonel Edward Marcus Despard (see page 162) was hanged and then decapitated in 1803 at Horsemonger Lane Gaol in Southwark. This engraving shows him on the gallows, with the hangman's noose around his neck, addressing the spectators a few minutes before the platform dropped.

▼ The beheading of the rebel Lords on Tower Hill

Class distinction has always been important in England; and this even applies to executions. Most people who were condemned to death were hanged at Smithfield, Tyburn or Newgate but nobles were usually beheaded before crowds of spectators on Tower Hill, near the Tower of London or in the relative privacy of the Green within the Tower. At least seventy-five people were executed on Tower Hill, including Edward, Duke of Buckingham (in 1521), Sir Thomas More (1535), Thomas Cromwell (1540), the Duke of Somerset (1552), the Duke of Northumberland (1553), the Earl of Strafford (1641), Archbishop Laud (1645), the Duke of Monmouth (1685) and Lord Lovat (1747). Most of the executions were for treason. However, Mervyn Touchet, Lord Audley and 2nd Earl of Castlehaven, was beheaded on Tower Hill in 1631 for arranging and assisting the rape of his wife by one of the household servants (he was acquitted of charges of sodomy with other servants). This class distinction for executions was again demonstrated in 1715. Seven nobles and about 300 other men, fighting for the Pretender James Stuart, were captured by the English army at the battle of Preston during the rebellion against George I, and brought to London. The soldiers were taken to Newgate or other prisons, tried before the Court of Exchequer and hanged at Tyburn. The nobles – the Earls of Derwentwater, Nithsdale, Winton and Carnwath, Viscount Kenmure and Lords Widdrington and Nairn – were imprisoned in the Tower of London and then impeached for high treason before the House of Lords in Westminster Hall on 19 January 1716. All of them except the Earl of Winton pleaded guilty and were sentenced to death. James, Earl of Derwentwater and William, Viscount Kenmure were beheaded on Tower Hill on 24 February 1716 by the executioner William Marvell. The Earl of Winton pleaded not guilty (claiming that he had surrendered on a promise that his life would be spared). He was also found guilty of treason but escaped from the Tower. The Earl of Nithsdale also escaped from the Tower, dressed as a woman, and reached Rome where he died in 1744. The other condemned lords were granted a reprieve. The rebellion of the Young Pretender in 1745 was also crushed. The Jacobite Lords Kilmarnock and Balmerino were executed on Tower Hill in 1746 and Lord Lovat was executed there in 1747. At his execution, one of the spectators' stands was so overladen (it is said with about 1,000 people) that it collapsed and crushed ten people to death instantly (and ten more died of their injuries). Lovat was the last man beheaded at Tower Hill (or anywhere in England) but not the last person to be executed there. Three of the Gordon rioters, two prostitutes (Charlotte Gardener and Mary Roberts) and a one-armed soldier (William McDonald) were hanged there in 1780.

Sir Thomas Wyatt

◄ **Sir Thomas Wyatt, executed on Tower Hill, 1554**
Wyatt was executed for leading a rebellion against Mary Tudor. Edward VI, the only son of Henry VIII, died in 1553. Lady Jane Grey occupied the throne for a few days but was sent to the Tower of London when Mary Tudor, the eldest daughter of Henry VIII, was proclaimed Queen on 19 July. Mary was a fervent Catholic and about to marry King Philip of Spain. Sir Thomas Wyatt led a rebellion, raising 10,000 men in Kent, and marched on Southwark. The drawbridge on London Bridge had been raised and the Tower of London was strongly held and so a river crossing there was impossible. Wyatt therefore marched west through Battersea to Kingston Bridge, crossed the river and marched on London from the west. The rebels reached Ludgate but found that gate barred against them. Mary's troops then attacked. By this time Wyatt's force was depleted. He was forced to surrender and taken to the Tower of London.

▼ **The beheading of Sir Thomas Wyatt**
Wyatt was tried in Westminster Hall for high treason on 15 March 1554 and beheaded on Tower Hill on 11 April. About 400 of his followers were executed in London, Maidstone and Rochester. Fifty-eight were hanged on gallows erected at each gate of the City of London and others were executed on gallows around London, for example at Cheapside, Leadenhall, Fleet Street, Smithfield and Charing Cross. The quarters of Wyatt's body were displayed and his head was exhibited on a gibbet at Hay Hill (near Piccadilly), from where it was stolen or secretly taken away by his friends for burial.

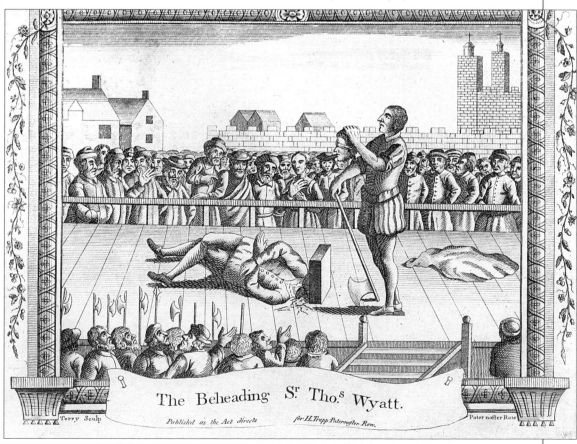

The Beheading S.r Tho.s Wyatt.

Terry Sculp. *Published as the Act directs* *for H. Trapp, Paternoster Row.* *Pater noster Row*

A. Doctor Vsher, Lord Prima-
   te of Ireland.
B the Sherifes of London.
C the Earle of Strafford.
D his Kindred and Friends.

▲ The execution of Thomas Wentworth, Earl of Strafford, 1641

During the reign of Charles I, the struggle between supporters of the King's Prerogative and those supporting Parliament's powers and privileges came to a head in the question of Charles' right to raise taxes without consulting the House of Commons. Strafford opposed the dissolution of Parliament and the imposition of ship money and other taxes but he was then taken into the King's favour in 1628 and became one of Charles' chief advisers in his attempt to rule without Parliament. Strafford used the Court of Star Chamber to suppress opposition, supported the dissolution of the Short Parliament and the collection of funds by force and urged that leading Parliamentarians be imprisoned in the Tower. In 1640, Strafford had to share some of the blame for the army's defeat by the Scots. Charles was desperate for money and had no choice but to summon Parliament to raise taxes. Parliamentarians spotted their opportunity and passed a motion to impeach Strafford and William Laud, the Archbishop of Canterbury (who was accused of tryng to restore Roman Catholicism in England). Strafford was tried before the House of Lords in Westminster Hall in March 1641, the prosecutors being members of the Commons. He faced 28 charges of treason, in particular that he had advised Charles to establish arbitrary government. The evidence was weak and Strafford defended himself well. The impeachment was therefore dropped and a Bill of Attainder proposed instead, simply declaring that Strafford was a traitor. The bill was passed by the Lords and Commons after it was revealed that Charles planned to seize the Tower of London and free Strafford. Fearing mob violence in London, Charles then felt compelled to assent to the bill. On hearing that his King had deserted him, Strafford declared, 'Put not your trust in Princes'. About 100,000 people watched his execution on 12 May 1641.

▼ James, Duke of Monmouth

James Scott was the illegitimate son of Charles II and Lucy Walters (James took the surname of his wife Anne Scott, Countess of Buccleuch). James was raised as a Protestant and created Duke of Monmouth. After his father's death in early 1685, he left Holland, where he had been living with his mistress, and landed in Dorset with a few followers. He called his uncle, the Catholic James II, a traitor and usurper and raised an army in the western counties. Monmouth marched on London but his army was defeated at the battle of Sedgemoor on 6 July 1685. Hundreds of prisoners were brought before Judge Jeffreys at the Bloody Assizes, and many were executed while others were transported. Monmouth had fled but was captured in the New Forest and taken to the Tower of London. He did not have a trial because Parliament had passed an Act of Attainder, based on his clear treason, that declared his life forfeit. Monmouth was executed on Tower Hill on 15 July. The executioner, Jack Ketch, failed to behead Monmouth with five blows of the axe and had to finish the job with a knife.

► **The place of execution on Tower Green, within the Tower of London**

Many important people were executed in the relative privacy of Tower Green rather than on Tower Hill. They included Queen Anne Boleyn in 1536, Margaret, Countess of Salibury (1541), Queen Katherine Howard (1542), Lady Jane Grey (1554) and Robert Devereux, Earl of Essex (1601). The last people to die on Tower Green were not royalty or nobles but three soldiers who were shot by a firing squad in 1743 for their part in a peaceful protest about their officers and conditions. This view shows the site of the scaffold, surrounded by a railing, and behind it the Chapel of St Peter ad Vincula, founded in the 12th century for the use of prisoners in the Tower. Many of those executed in the Tower or on Tower Hill were buried inside, including Anne Boleyn, Katherine Howard, Protector Somerset, Sir Thomas More, Lady Jane Grey and the Duke of Monmouth.

▼ **The execution of Margaret, Countess of Salisbury, 1541**

Margaret Plantagenet was the daughter of George, Duke of Clarence (and the niece of Edward IV and Richard III). She was 71 years old when Henry VIII ordered her execution. This was in part because of her Plantagenet blood but also because her son Reginald, Cardinal Pole, had severely criticised Henry's divorce from Catherine of Aragon, his assumption of Supremacy over the church in England and his break with Rome. The old lady refused to lay her head on the block. She was pursued around the block by the executioner until he hacked her to death with his axe.

▼ **The axe and the block at the Tower of London**

This axe is said to have been at the Tower since 1687 and the block was possibly that used for the beheading of Lord Lovat in 1747.

➤ Old London Bridge: heads displayed on the gatehouse

The first London Bridge was built by the Romans of wood. The first stone bridge was begun in 1176. Houses and a chapel were built on the bridge and there was a gatehouse at the Southwark end. The head of William Wallace, the Scottish patriot, was placed on a spike above this gatehouse in 1305. This gruesome custom continued until 1661. The heads were parboiled and dipped in tar to preserve them. They included those of Jack Cade (who led a rebellion in 1450), Thomas More, Bishop Fisher and Thomas Cromwell. A German visitor counted over 30 heads on display in 1598. This engraving of the bridge, by Alfred Ashley, is from G. Herbert Rodwell's romance *Old London Bridge*, published in 1831. The heads of traitors can be seen on the gatehouse on the left.

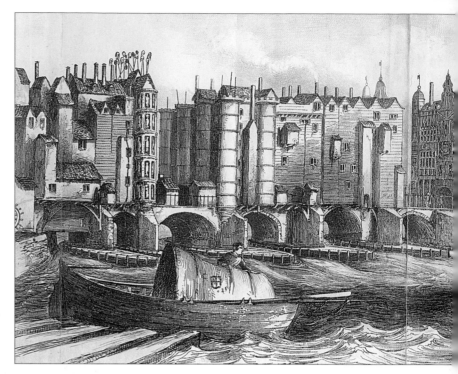

▲ The keeper of the Bridge Gate Tower
This engraving by Alfred Ashley, also from Rodwell's *Old London Bridge*, is a fictitious scene but so charming that I have to include it here.

➤ The heads of Townley and Fletcher exposed on Temple Bar, 1746

Temple Bar stood where Fleet Street became the Strand and marked the western boundary of the City of London. A timber gate on that site, built in the 14th or 15th century, escaped the Great Fire but was replaced by Wren's new gate, known as Temple Bar, in 1672. The heads of executed traitors (or other parts of their bodies) were displayed on spikes on the top of Temple Bar. The first occasion appears to have been in 1684, when parts of Sir Thomas Armstrong's body were displayed (having been boiled in salt so that birds would not eat them). The heads of some Jacobites were displayed following Bonnie Prince Charlie's failure to take the throne in 1745. Francis Townley, George Fletcher, James Dawson and a number of other Jacobite rebels were tried at the Court House at St Margaret's Hill in Southwark in June 1746. They were convicted of treason and sentenced to be hanged, drawn and quartered. Townley was a Catholic from Lancashire who had served in the French army. He joined the Pretender's army when it invaded England, raised a regiment at Manchester but was captured at Carlisle. Fletcher and Dawson, both from Manchester, had been commissioned as captains in the Pretender's army. The condemned rebels were held in Horsemonger Lane Gaol and dragged on hurdles to the place of execution on Kennington Common on 20 July 1746. Townley was cut down, still alive, after five minutes and his head cut off with an axe. His heart was cut out and burned. The others were dealt with in the same way and their bodies were quartered. The heads of Townley and Fletcher were placed on Temple Bar and could still be seen there until 1772, when they blew down in a gale, causing women to scream and faint. Temple Bar was moved in 1878 because it was so narrow that it caused traffic congestion. It was rebuilt in Theobald's Park in Hertfordshire, but it may soon return to London.

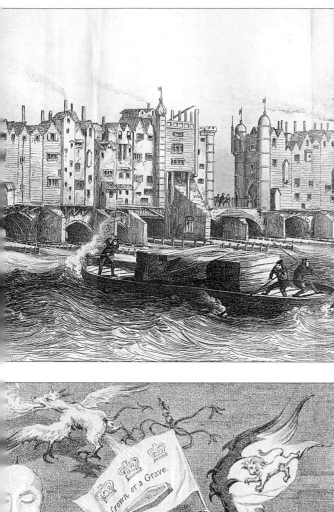

Executed at Kennington Common, July 30
Exposed on Temple Bar
Aug.st 2.nd 1746.

the Banner which would all enslave   While trembling Rebels at the Fabrick gaze
ned Traytors did so proudly wave   And dread their fate with horror and amaze
seems the project to despise   Let Britons Sons the Emblematick view
onfused from off the trophy flies,   And plainly see what is Rebellions due.

▲ **Execution of the Lollards**

The Lollards were inspired by the teachings of John Wycliffe.
Their beliefs were similar to Protestants of the 16th century.
They desired a bible in English, rather than in Latin, and they
criticised image-worship, pilgrimages and the holding of
secular offices by clergymen. Clearly, these dangerous heretics
had to be suppressed and both Henry IV and Henry V
supported the church in the suppression. An Act of 1401
permitted obstinate heretics to be burned to death. This
engraving shows the hanging and burning of Lollards at St
Giles' Fields on 12 January 1414 (39 suffered on that day) when
a large group of them had marched on London. Some thought
that it was a Lollard attempt to overthrow Henry V but the
crowd was merely going to a meeting to hear a preacher named
John Beverley. Sir John Oldcastle (upon whom Shakespeare
based his character Sir John Falstaff) had been arrested as a
Lollard sympathiser in 1413 but escaped. He was recaptured in
1417 and executed at St Giles' Fields by being suspended in
chains and roasted over a fire.

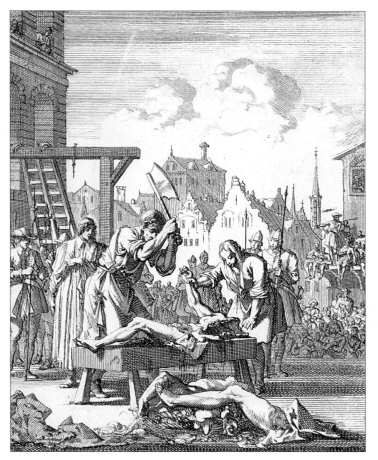

◄ The butchery of Thomas Armstrong

Sir Thomas Armstrong served under both Charles I and Charles II and became a friend of the Duke of Monmouth. He was one of the leaders of the Rye House Plot of 1683 in which the conspirators planned to kill Charles II and his brother James. After discovery of the plot, Algernon Sidney, Lord William Russell and Henry Cornish were tried and executed (see page 50). An order was made for Armstrong's arrest but he escaped to Holland. He was outlawed for high treason, captured in 1684 and taken back to England. Armstrong was denied a trial by Judge Jeffreys because he was an outlaw and was sentenced to death. He was hanged on the gallows on the left of this engraving, cut down, disembowelled and quartered. Parts of his body were displayed on spikes on Temple Bar.

▼ A mass burning at Stratford

Eleven Protestant men and two women were burned at the stake at Stratford for heresy on 27 June 1556, during the reign of Queen Mary. A crowd of 20,000 gathered to watch the burning of Henry Adlington, Thomas Bowyer, Lyon Cawch, John Derisall, Agnes George, William Hallywell, Edmund Hurst, Ralph Jackson, Lawrence Parnam, Elizabeth Pepper, John Routh, George Searles and Henry Wye. The men were bound to three stakes and the women stood with them inside a ring of firewood. A memorial to the martyrs was erected in 1879 at St John's Church, Stratford.

SMITHFIELD in the 12th century was a grassy, open space outside the City walls with a celebrated horse and livestock market. Bartholomew Fair was also held there from the 12th century until 1855, when its rowdiness and debauchery resulted in its suppression. Smithfield was also used for sports, tournaments and, because it was an open space conveniently close to Newgate Gaol (London's most important prison), it was also used for over 400 years to stage public executions. The Scottish patriot William Wallace was hanged at Smithfield in 1305. His head was the first to be exhibited on London Bridge and the quarters of his body were sent to Berwick, Newcastle, Perth and Stirling for display. Common criminals were also hanged at Smithfield, at first from trees and later from a gallows, until the 15th century, when the gallows at Tyburn became the preferred venue. Some offenders were still hanged at Smithfield, including a man named Perrott who was made bankrupt and later hanged for having hidden many of his assets from his creditors. Many offenders suffered at Smithfield by being boiled or burned alive. In 1532, a cook named Richard Rose was boiled to death for having poisoned gruel made for the household of Bishop Fisher of Rochester; 17 people were poisoned and two died. Rose was placed in an iron cauldron over a log fire and died two hours after the fire was lit. In 1542, Margaret Davy was also boiled to death at Smithfield for the offence of poisoning. In 1538, Prior John Forest was roasted alive in a cage for refusing to recognise Henry VIII as Supreme Head of the church. A statute of 1401 provided for heretics to be burned at the stake. This statute was repealed in 1533 but re-enacted a few years later and used, after the accession of Queen Mary, to punish Protestants and other heretics. At least 43 people (and perhaps as many as 200) were burned at Smithfield for heresy during Mary's reign. The first of these martyrs was John Rogers, a Protestant rector of St Sepulchre's Church, Holborn. He was imprisoned in Newgate and burned at Smithfield in 1554, for calling Queen Mary's religion 'pestilent popery, idolatry and superstition'. John Taylor, the vicar of St Bride, Fleet Street was also burned at Smithfield. He had denied the ancient faith and declared that the sacrament was merely bread and wine. He was imprisoned in the Fleet, Bread Street Compter and Newgate, and convicted by a commission that sat in the Lady Chapel of St Mary Overies Church in Southwark. Taylor was burned in Smithfield on 30 May 1555. Protestants had their revenge a few years later. An enormous number of Catholics were executed during the reigns of Elizabeth and James I, although the Protestants' preferred method of despatching Catholics was by hanging.

▲ **John Bradford and John Leaf: burned in Smithfield**
This engraving shows the burning of the Reverend John Bradford and John Leaf (a London apprentice) in 1555. Bradford was a barrister of Inner Temple who took up a career in the church. He was a chaplain to King Edward VI and became Prebendary of St Paul's Cathedral in 1551. Bradford was imprisoned (in the Tower of London then Poultry Compter, the King's Bench Prison and finally Newgate) on a charge of preaching heretical sermons. He was sentenced to burn with John Leaf who was imprisoned in Bread Street Compter, examined by Bishop Bonner, then condemned to death as a heretic.

Lord Ferrers at Tyburn

▲ Execution at Tyburn, 1760: Lord Ferrers

Tyburn was used for hangings from the late 12th century. The earliest recorded execution there is that of William Fitz Osbert who was drawn by horses to Tyburn from the City of London in 1196 and hanged for having killed a guard of the Archbishop of Canterbury. Tyburn was the preferred venue for hanging London's criminals from the 15th century until 1783. Executions then took place outside Newgate Gaol. It is estimated that over 60,000 people were hanged at Tyburn. The hangmen were appointed by the Sheriffs of the City of London and Middlesex. In the early days, offenders were hanged from trees or from gallows that were erected for each execution. A permanent gallows was built in 1571, a three-legged structure (illustrated on page 120) known as Tyburn Tree, from which up to 24 people (eight on each of three horizontal beams) could be hanged at the same time. It was demolished in 1759 and replaced by a moving gallows. One of the early victims of Tyburn was Perkin Warbeck, who was executed there in 1499. In 1535, John Houghton, Prior of Charterhouse, refused to take the oath recognising Henry VIII (rather than the Pope) as Supreme Head of the Church in England. Houghton and two other Carthusian priors were tried at Westminster Hall and condemned to death. They were dragged to Tyburn on hurdles, hanged and then (while still alive) cut down, quartered and disembowelled. Three monks of Charterhouse suffered the same fate a few weeks later. In 1534, Elizabeth Barton, the 'Holy Maid of Kent', was executed at Tyburn after making an unwise prophecy: that if Henry VIII married another woman, he would not be King a month later. Margaret Ward was hanged and quartered at Tyburn in 1588 for assisting the escape of William Watson, a priest, from Bridewell. Oliver Plunket, Roman Catholic Archbishop of Armagh, was executed at Tyburn in 1681 for treason, on the basis of the perjured evidence of Titus Oates. The highwayman Jack Sheppard was executed at Tyburn in 1724 and Jonathan Wild (the Thief-Taker General) in 1725. Thousands of other common criminals, murderers, forgers, highwaymen, thieves and rapists also

suffered there. The most bizarre hanging took place in 1660. The corpses of the regicides Oliver Cromwell, John Bradshaw and Henry Ireton were exhumed, dragged to Tyburn, hanged and beheaded (the heads were displayed on spikes at Westminster Hall). Laurence Shirley, Earl Ferrers, was tried by his peers and hanged at Tyburn in 1760 for the murder of his steward. Ferrers was normal when sober but acted like a madman when drunk. His wife left him and obtained a private Act of Parliament that awarded her an income out of Ferrers' property. Ferrers' steward, Mr Johnson, was appointed (with Ferrers' agreement) to collect the money for her.

➤ Lord Ferrers shooting his steward

Ferrers' seat was at Stanton, Leicestershire. In 1760, a Mrs Clifford was living with him, together with their four daughters and their servants. Mr Johnson lived on a farm near Stanton, that he rented from the Earl and visited Ferrers occasionally to settle the accounts. Ferrers developed a hatred for Johnson, because he collected the money for Lady Ferrers, and decided that Johnson was conspiring to damage his finances. Ferrers wanted revenge. He ordered Johnson to attend upon him at Stanton at 3pm on 18 January 1760. He told Mrs Clifford to take their daughters for a walk until 5.30pm. He also sent the male servants on errands, leaving only three maids in the house. Johnson arrived and was called in to Ferrers' room. Ferrers locked the door and, in a loud voice, heard by the maids outside, ordered Johnson to kneel. Ferrers cried, 'Declare that you have acted against Lord Ferrers! Your time has come – you must die!' He then shot Johnson. The maids came to the door, alarmed by the shot and Ferrers left the room and turned to drink. Johnson was put in bed and his family and a surgeon were called. Ferrers admitted that he had tried to kill Johnson but told his daughter that if her father died, he (Ferrers) would support her family on condition that they did not prosecute him. Ferrers then drank more, went to the room in which Johnson was dying and threatened to shoot him again. Johnson died the next morning. A group of Johnson's neighbours armed themselves and marched to Stanton. Ferrers gave himself up and was committed to Leicester Gaol. Ferrers was entitled, by reason of his rank, to be tried by the House of Lords. He was taken to London, committed to the Tower and tried on 16 April 1760 in Westminster Hall. Ferrers conducted his own defence, calling witnesses to say that he was not of sound mind, but was unable to prove that he was not responsible for his actions. He was convicted of murder and sentenced to be hanged and then anatomised. A scaffold was erected under the gallows at Tyburn with a platform raised by about 18 inches, that could be dropped when the signal for the execution was given. This was the first time that a drop (a falling trap-door) was used instead of the gibbet and cart. On 5 May 1760, Ferrers rode in his own coach from the Tower to Tyburn, dressed in the white suit in which he had been married. The procession included two Sheriffs in their carriages, troops of horse and foot soldiers, a coach for Ferrers' friends and a hearse and six horses (to carry his body to Surgeons' Hall after the execution). The mob was so dense that the journey to Tyburn took three hours. Ferrers mounted the scaffold and joined the Chaplain of the Tower in reciting the Lord's Prayer. He tipped the hangman and the chaplain five guineas each and then cried, 'Oh God, forgive me all my errors – pardon all my sins!'. He put on a white cap, his arms were bound and the hanging cord was placed around his neck. He climbed onto the platform on the scaffold and stood under the beam of the gallows. The cap was drawn over his face. Upon the Sheriff's signal, the platform fell from under his feet and he was hanged. After the customary one hour, his body

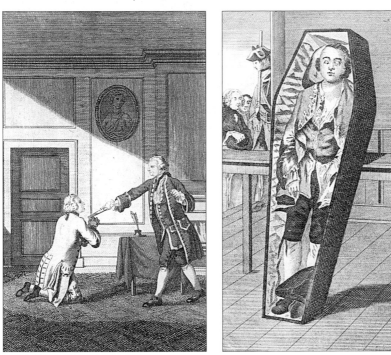

was taken in the hearse to Surgeons' Hall. A large incision was made from his neck to the bottom of the breast and another across his throat. The lower part of his belly was opened and his bowels removed. The body was exhibited in Surgeons' Hall and then delivered to Ferrers' friends for burial. While held in the Tower, Ferrers wrote this verse:

> In doubt I live, in doubt I die,
> Yet stand prepared the vast abyss to try,
> And undismayed, expect eternity.

◄ Ready for dissection: Lord Ferrers in his coffin

The bodies of executed criminals could be passed to surgeons for dissection and study. In this illustration, the body of Earl Ferrers is shown, in his wedding suit that he wore to his execution, on display in a coffin in Surgeons' Hall in Old Bailey.

➤ Extract from John Rocque's map of the cities of London and Westminster, 1746, showing the place of execution at Tyburn

John Rocque was of Huguenot ancestry and worked as a surveyor, principally of great estates. He also worked for nine years from 1737 on his map of the Cities of London and Westminster. This extract shows the place of execution at Tyburn, close to where Marble Arch now stands, near the north end of Tiburn Lane (now Park Lane). The map also shows Tiburn Road (now Oxford Street) heading back east towards Newgate. To the south of the gallows is the place 'where soldiers are shot'. Two soldiers, Hartley and South, were shot here in 1749 for desertion, after being held in the Savoy Prison.

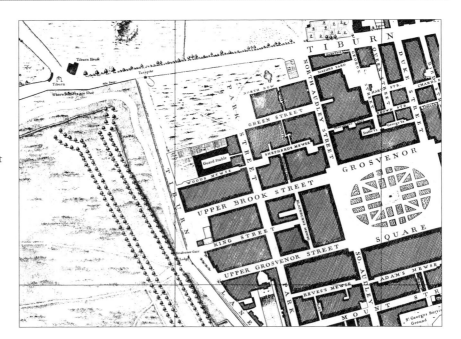

▲ The procession to Tyburn: the idle apprentice about to meet his end at Tyburn Fair

It is estimated that at least 60,000 people swung at the public hangings at Tyburn. Most hanging days were public holidays and they were loud, noisy events, attracting thousands of people, that became known as 'Tyburn Fair'. Some people gathered early at the execution site. Others followed the procession from Newgate. Hogarth published an engraving of an idle apprentice (Tom Idle) about to be hanged at Tyburn. Tom is in the cart to the left (although it was usual for three prisoners to be carried in a cart) with his coffin and a preacher exhorting him to repent. The chaplain of Newgate (known as the Ordinary) is in the coach in front of Tom, on top of which the hangman is lounging. The rope is being strung over the triple tree, on which sits the hangman's assistant, casually smoking his pipe. On the right of the picture is a grandstand known as 'Mother Proctor's Pews', whose seats were sold to those who desired a better view of the hanging. Prisoners originally climbed a ladder with the noose around their neck, then jumped (or were 'turned off', that is pushed). From the 18th century, a condemned person stood in the cart under the gallows while the noose was placed around his or her neck. The carthorses were then whipped and the cart pulled away. The condemned might give some money to the hangman hoping that he would, by his arrangement of the noose, grant a quicker end. Friends or relatives might pull on a condemned's legs to speed up death and shorten the suffering. There was also a curious belief that the touch of a hanged person was a cure for skin diseases, blemishes and other illnesses. For example, after six men were hanged before Newgate Gaol on 22 June 1786, 12 people climbed upon the scaffold and had the deceased's hands rubbed by the executioner upon their faces and necks. Hangings were attended by enormous crowds, perhaps as many as 200,000 at the execution of Jack Sheppard. They also attracted traders, ruffians, pickpockets, prostitutes and drunkards. In Hogarth's engraving, vendors are selling gin, oranges and gingerbread. A fight has broken out and a woman is prematurely selling a sheet entitled the 'last dying speech & confession of Tho. Idle'. The riotous behaviour and large crowds at Tyburn resulted in the authorities moving executions to the open area outside Newgate Gaol. The last execution at Tyburn was that of John Austin in 1783.

➤ The dying speech: Stephen Gardiner under the triple tree

Prisoners could choose the clothes they wore for their execution (if they had anything other than lice-infested rags). Some dressed well for their last day. Others chose to wear cheap and simple clothes such as a nightshirt or shroud in order to cheat the hangman who could claim the clothes of those he hanged. Stephen Gardiner was executed at Tyburn on 3 February 1724 for burglary. He was born in Moorfields and went to sea as a boy but was flogged on his first voyage for being idle and useless. He gave up the seafaring life after that one voyage and worked as a waterman. He lost all his money by gambling and so turned pickpocket. He was caught at his first attempt, during a drawing of the lottery at Guildhall, but managed to escape. One month later he was caught picking another pocket, beaten by a mob and dragged through a pond. Gardiner then worked with two thieves named

Garraway and Sly but all three were arrested. Gardiner was the youngest and so admitted an evidence against the others who were convicted and transported. He was then married in the Fleet to a woman who kept a public house. She had some money but this was soon spent and the couple turned to crime. They were arrested on suspicion of theft and held in St Sepulchre watch-house. They were released for lack of evidence but the bellman of St Sepulchre was in the watch-house at the time and a constable told Gardiner, 'Beware how you come here again, or this bellman will certainly say his verses over you'. Gardiner ignored the warning. He returned to crime, was arrested by Jonathan Wild's men for theft, convicted and sentenced to death. Before he left Newgate on execution day, Gardiner put on a shroud. He saw some friends in the Tyburn crowd and warned them to learn from his death, improve their lives and avoid following him to the gallows. He was then executed. This engraving from *The Newgate Calendar* shows Gardiner in a cart, about to be hanged from the triple tree. A Sheriff watches from the comfort of his carriage.

◄ Sarah Malcolm

Sarah was executed in 1733 for the murder of a wealthy old lady in the Inns of Court. She was born in County Durham in 1711 and compelled to work as a domestic servant because her extravagant father had spent all the family's money. Sarah worked at the *Black Horse*, a public house near Temple Bar, which was the resort of many criminals. She then worked as a laundress for some chambers in the Temple. One of her employers was Mrs Lydia Duncomb, a wealthy lady aged nearly 80 years, who had two servants Elizabeth Harrison aged 60 and Ann Price aged 17. Sarah decided to rob Mrs Duncomb's chambers on 3 February 1733. After the robbery, Mrs Duncomb and Elizabeth Harrison were found strangled. Ann Price's throat had been cut. The chambers had been stripped of all money, silver and other valuables. Sarah's lodgings were searched and a silver tankard was found. Its handle was covered

with blood. She was committed to Newgate and searched, one of the turnkeys finding her in possession of gold and silver coins. Sarah admitted that it was Mrs Duncomb's money but offered it to the turnkey if he kept quiet, but the turnkey told his superiors. At her trial, Sarah admitted robbery but denied the murders, saying that she had robbed the chambers with Martha Tracy and two brothers named Thomas and James Alexander but that she had merely kept watch. The court did not believe her and she alone was convicted and sentenced to death. Hogarth visited her in the condemned cell, drew her likeness and later issued a print of his drawing. This engraving is very similar to that by Hogarth but includes a chaplain looking over her shoulder and a picture of her execution. Sarah Malcolm was taken in a cart to the place of execution near Fetter Lane on 7 March 1733 and hanged there, aged 22.

↗ 'Half-hanged Smith'

John Smith was convicted of robbery in 1705 but reprieved while actually hanging on the scaffold. Smith was born in Yorkshire and worked as a packer in London. He then went to sea and later joined the army, in which he made 'bad connections', and turned to crime with some of his dissolute companions. Smith was convicted on 5 December 1705 of breaking into shops in Leadenhall Market and stealing 50 pairs of shoes, 148 pairs of gloves and 22 pairs of stockings. He was sentenced to death, carried to Tyburn on 12 December and 'turned off'. However, when he had hanged nearly 15 minutes, a reprieve arrived and he was cut down and recovered. He therefore became known as 'Half-hanged Smith'. He returned to a life of crime and was again tried at the Old Bailey in April 1715 for breaking into a warehouse and into the house of John Cooper. Fortune smiled on Smith again. He was acquitted on a point of law and an indictment against him, by the victim John Cooper as prosecutor, failed because Cooper died before the day of trial. Smith was again set at liberty.

◄◄ **Executions at Kennington Common**
Gallows were erected at the south end of
Kennington Common (now Kennington
Park). This was the main place of
execution for the county of Surrey. Most
of the hangings were of common
criminals but Jacobite rebels were
hanged, drawn and quartered here after
their trial in 1746. The last execution at
Kennington Common was of a forger in
the early 19th century. This print features
a triangular gallows (probably that
erected in 1746 for hanging the Jacobites)
and a gibbet from which hang the bodies
of highwaymen or murderers. The
Reverend Mr Whitfield is preaching a
sermon in the background.

◄ **John Hanna, executed 1739**
John Hanna was executed on Kennington
Common in 1739 for perjury. He had
been born in Lincolnshire and was 20
years old. He had been 'an evidence' in the prosecution of naval
captains named John Longdon and John Grant. Hanna had
charged them with running down a fishing boat with their ship
and then murdering the crew. Hanna later admitted that his
allegation was false and that he had been persuaded to swear it
by others. He was hanged.

◄ **A pirate hanged at Execution Dock, Wapping**
Pirates were hanged at a dock between Wapping New Stairs
and King Henry's Stairs until the early 19th century. They
included Captain John Massey and Philip Roche (both in 1723)
and Captain Kidd. Execution Dock was not only used for the
hanging of pirates. Captain William Codlin of the brig
Aventure was hanged here in 1802 for destroying that vessel (by
boring holes in her bottom) in an attempt to defraud the
insurers. John Smith and Robert Mayne were executed in 1762
for mutiny on the ship *King George*, and Captain James Lowry
was hanged here in 1752 for murder at sea. This engraving from
The Newgate Calendar shows a condemned man on the
scaffold with a chaplain. A mounted sheriff, on the left, is
supervising the execution and a constable stands on the right
holding a staff. The historian John Stow recorded that pirates'
corpses were left hanging until three tides had washed over
them. The bodies were then often placed in gibbets by the river.
Captain William Kidd was hanged at Execution Dock in 1701.
He was born at Greenock in Scotland. By 1695, he was an
experienced sailor based in New York and had often traded
with pirates in the Americas. He was commissioned by the
government to lead an expedition against pirates, particularly
in the Red Sea. French ships were fair game because England
and France were at war. Kidd also received a secret commission
from Lord Bellomont, the governor of New York, to act as a
privateer and share any prizes (the value of ships taken and
their cargoes) with a group of British politicians (including
many Cabinet ministers) and the King himself. Kidd lost many
of his crew during the voyage and had to replace them with
pirates whom he had to placate by attacking foreign ships. Two
of these were Armenian ships carrying French passes (letters of

protection). The powerful East India Company branded Kidd as a pirate for the attacks. Information about the secret syndicate also leaked out to opposition politicians in Britain. Bellomont and the British government therefore needed a scapegoat. Kidd was arrested by Bellomont when he returned to New York, sent to England and examined by the House of Commons. Kidd handed over the French passes to show that the Armenian ships were legitimate prizes but the passes then disappeared. Kidd was held in Newgate for two years and then tried for piracy by the Court of Admiralty at the Old Bailey Sessions House. The court decided that the passes had never existed (they have now been found in the Public Record Office at Kew) and Kidd was convicted of piracy. The execution procession made its way from Newgate to Execution Dock on 23 May 1701 and Kidd was hanged there with his companion Darby Mullins. After Kidd had been tied to the gallows, the rope broke and he fell to the ground. However, he was tied up again and hanged.

➤ **George Webb and Richard Russel at the place of execution on Shooter's Hill**
Webb and Russel were hanged on Shooter's Hill at Blackheath in 1805 for burglary. Webb was born near Bromsgrove, Worcestershire, the son of a clergyman. He came to London and worked in the docks at Woolwich and Deptford. He joined the West Kent Militia, deserted twice and then lived in Blackheath, near Richard Russel. He was born in Greenwich and had worked as a merchant seaman, butcher, dock-labourer and brickmaker. Webb, Russel and Russel's wife Sarah were arrested for theft from the houses of Thomas Taylor in New Cross and William Shadbolt in Deptford and examined by Magistrates at Bow Street. Officers searched the house of Webb's mother in Birmingham and found stolen goods there. Webb had given them to his family, claiming that he was now wealthy as a result of marrying a rich woman. Webb, the Russels and their accomplices John White and Edward Egerton were tried at Maidstone for burglary. Webb and George Russel were convicted (the others were acquitted) and then escorted by constables and cavalry to Shooter's Hill on 19 August 1805 to be hanged.

➤ **Cruickshank's Bank Restriction note**
Forgery was one of the most common offences for which people were hanged in the early 19th century. One morning, early in the 1820s, the caricaturist George Cruickshank saw two women hanged outside Newgate for passing forged £1 notes, a number of which were in circulation. He was appalled and designed a grim parody of a £1 note, adorned with a scaffold and signed 'J. Ketch', the nickname of the Newgate hangmen. It was published and sold by the radical pamphleteer and bookseller, William Hone, from his shop in Old Bailey, almost opposite Newgate Gaol. This infuriated the directors of the Bank of England, but the notes sold as quickly

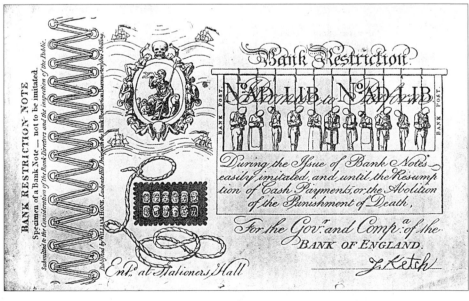

as they were be printed and they achieved their aim; never again was anyone hanged for passing forged bank-notes.

Newgate Gaol

known as Debtor's Door. The origin of the door's name is unclear but it may have been so-named because the condemned came out of it to pay their last debts. Every window overlooking the scaffold was filled with people, some of whom paid large sums of money for their view. The landlord of the *Magpie and Stump* tavern on Old Bailey, opposite the gaol, charged up to £50 (but also provided breakfast). About 100,000 people attended the execution of Henry Fauntleroy for forgery in 1824. About 50,000 gathered in 1864 for the execution of the railway murderer Franz Muller. Panic arose in a crowd of over 40,000 at the execution in 1807 of Haggerty and Holloway and at least 28 people were trampled to death or suffocated. The last example of a group of prisoners being executed outside Newgate was on 22 February 1864, when five men named Blanco, Leone, Duranno, Lopez and Watts were hanged for the murder of the captain of the ship *Flowery Land*. The last hanging outside Newgate was on 26 May 1868 when the Fenian Michael Barrett was executed for his part in the explosion at Clerkenwell House of Detention. Executions then took place inside prisons (Newgate, Wandsworth and later Pentonville). The tolling of a bell and a black flag flying over a prison indicated that an execution was taking place. The move of executions inside prisons, out of the public gaze, was not solely because the public or authorities believed that hangings were a revolting spectacle. The crowds that gathered for executions outside Newgate were a public danger (the authorities feared a repeat of the deaths that occurred at the hanging of Holloway and Haggerty). Large crowds also offered tempting opportunities for pickpockets. After the hanging of Muller in 1864, an article in *The Times* stated:

> Yesterday morning Muller was hanged in front of Newgate. He died before such a concourse as we hope may never be again assembled, either for the spectacle … or for the gratification of such lawless ruffianism as yesterday found its scope around the gallows.

The crowd had begun to gather the night before. Newgate was described as 'black in its blind massiveness except at one little point high over the walls, where one window in the new wing showed a little gleam of light'. By 3am, about 5,000 people had assembled and there was 'one long revelry of songs and laughter, shouting, and often quarrelling' and a 'half-drunken, ribald gaiety among the crowd'. The gallows was erected to cheers and hissing from the crowd. As the sun rose, all the space before Newgate was packed with people, some trying to get

▲▲ Ten on the gallows

Public hangings were moved from Tyburn to the open area outside Newgate Gaol in 1783. The first was on 9 December 1783, shown in this engraving, when 10 criminals were hanged by Edward Dennis. Instead of the old Tyburn gallows, the hangmen at Newgate used the 'new drop'. This was a portable gallows that was brought out of the gates of Newgate Gaol on execution days. It had a drop, that is a collapsible platform, on which the condemned stood and which fell when the signal for the execution was given. Twenty people could be hanged at the same time from the two parallel beams.

▲ A public execution at the door of Newgate Gaol, 1809

This engraving shows the second version of the 'new drop' in 1809. It only had one horizontal beam. The drop has already fallen and the three condemned have hanged. However, the drop was so short that the bodies remained in view and the criminals were probably strangled slowly by the rope. Large crowds gathered around Old Bailey to see executions. The condemned were brought out of a gate of Newgate Gaol

closer to the spot where Muller would die and some trying to avoid thieves. At eight o'clock, the bell of Newgate began to toll. Muller was brought out to the scaffold in a procession with a minister of a German church, the Sheriffs of London and the governor, surgeon and chaplain of Newgate. Muller is said to have admitted his crime as the crowd went quiet and the drop fell. By the time he was cut down, the laughing, filthy language, thefts and violence in the crowd had resumed.

▼ Anne Hurle and Mathusalah Spalding in the cart at their execution in Old Bailey, 1804

Anne Hurle, aged 22, was hanged outside Newgate on 8 February 1804 for forging a letter of attorney with intent to defraud the Bank of England. Spalding was hanged at the same time. He was convicted of what Jackson's *New and Complete Newgate Calendar* of 1818 described as 'an unnatural crime, a deed without a name … nature shudders at it'. The drop had been replaced temporarily by the old gallows (for which a cart was necessary). The prisoners were therefore brought out of Debtor's Door at Newgate, placed in the cart, then drawn a few yards to the gallows in Old Bailey. After prayers, caps

were drawn over the faces of the condemned. The cart drew away and left them suspended.

▼ The gallows in the execution shed at Newgate Gaol

This and the illustration below are postcards from a cheerful series entitled *Glimpses of Old Newgate*, published in about 1900 for a public that has always had a morbid interest in executions. From 1868, executions inside Newgate were carried out in a shed in the prison yard. The gallows was at ground level but above a pit. A condemned prisoner stood on the closed trapdoor with the hangman's rope, formed into a noose, around his neck. The other end of the rope was attached to the chain on the beam above. The trapdoor dropped open and the prisoner hanged. Prison governors might allow journalists to be present but this was discouraged because hangings rarely went smoothly. Many of the condemned did not die instantaneously but were slowly strangled. The last hanging in Newgate took place in May 1902, shortly before it was closed. The scaffold was then moved to Pentonville Prison.

➤ The waiting box and the execution shed at Newgate Gaol

Hangings took place in the timber shed on the right of this postcard. Lively greetings, such as 'Wish you were here', were probably written on copies of this card and sent to friends, relatives or employers.

➤ **The execution of Cundell and Smith at Horsemonger Lane Gaol, Southwark**
Horsemonger Lane Gaol was built (1791-98) as the Surrey County Gaol to hold 400 petty criminals and debtors. An adjacent building was used as the Sessions House for Surrey. Executions took place outside the gaol or on the roof of the gatehouse. Colonel Despard was executed here in 1803 (see page 162) for plotting to assassinate the King and seize the Tower and the Bank of England. On 16 March 1812, William Cundell and John Smith were hanged and then decapitated at Horsemonger Lane for treason. Charles Dickens watched the execution here in 1849 of Mr and Mrs Manning and then wrote letters criticising public executions. Horsemonger Lane Gaol was closed in 1878 and Wandsworth Prison became the place of execution for South London.

▼ **The scaffold at Wandsworth**
The scaffold was housed in a shed known as the 'cold meat shed'. This photograph shows the executioner's lever and the drop.

➤ **The execution of Catherine Webster**
Catherine Webster, *alias* Catherine Lawler, was hanged at Wandsworth Prison in 1879. She was born in Ireland, married twice and was known for robbing lodging houses. She worked as a servant to Mrs Thomas who lived alone in a cottage in Richmond. On 5 March 1879, a box was found on the banks of the Thames at Hammersmith, containing bits of human flesh that had been boiled, the remains of Mrs Thomas. In the meantime, Webster (calling herself Mrs Thomas) was selling the contents of the Richmond property. Webster had been sacked by Mrs Thomas and so killed her with a meat cleaver, cut up the body and boiled parts of it. Mrs Thomas' head was never found but it was said that Webster carried it around in a bag until she disposed of it. Webster fled to Ireland but was arrested and convicted of murder at the Old Bailey in July 1879. She was hanged at Wandsworth on 29 July.

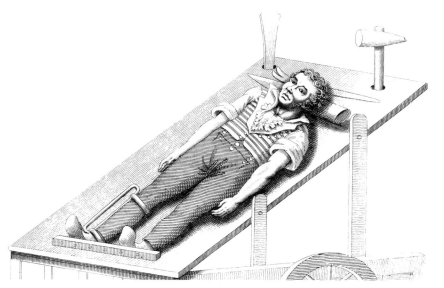

The exposure of the alleged murderer, John Williams

Seven people were murdered in two incidents known as the Ratcliffe Highway Murders in 1811. The first murders occurred on 7 December at 29 Ratcliffe Highway. Mr Marr (a draper) and his shopboy were found with their throats cut, in a blood-spattered downstairs room. Marr's wife and child had been killed upstairs. The murder weapon, a ripping chisel, lay on the shop floor. On 19 December, John Turner escaped, nearly naked, from a second-floor window of the *King's Arms* public house on New Gravel Lane. He had seen two men murdering the people in the house. The publican, Mr Williamson, his wife and maid were found with fractured skulls and cut throats. One of the murder weapons, a maul or crowbar, lay at Williamson's side. Terror spread and rewards were offered. After more than 40 false arrests, John Williams, a seaman lodging at the *Pear Tree* public house, was arrested on suspicion of being one of the murderers. There was little evidence against him but he hanged himself at Coldbath Fields Prison before the committal proceedings. The authorities decided to exhibit his corpse at the scenes of the crimes and so it was taken to St George's watch-house. A procession then moved around Wapping, halting at the buildings in which the murders had taken place. Williams' body lay on an inclined platform on a cart. The maul and chisel, with which the murders had been committed, were placed on either side of his head. The cart was escorted by the High Constable of Middlesex and hundreds of constables and parish officers. It was customary to bury suicides at crossroads and so the procession moved to the crossroads of Cannon Street and St George's Turnpike. Williams' body was placed in a pit, a stake was driven through it and the pit filled in. However, the case remains a mystery. There were probably two murderers and Williams may not have been one of them. It is also doubted whether Williams committed suicide. He may have been murdered, perhaps by someone who feared the truth coming out if Williams went to trial.

A murderer's body exposed in Surgeons' Hall, Old Bailey

The bodies of murderers might be dissected after execution. A number of criminals who suffered this fate, such as Elizabeth Brownrigg, Lord Ferrers and John Bellingham, have already been mentioned. Spectators often filled the galleries in the dissection room. This engraving from *The Malefactors Register* shows the body of a murderer on the dissection table with most of his internal organs already removed. Two skeletons of criminals can be seen in the alcoves behind the spectators.

He rose from the dead: William Duell

William Duell (or Dewell) was executed for murder, but came to life again while being prepared for dissection in Surgeons' Hall. Duell had robbed and killed Sarah Griffin. He was hanged for murder on 24 November 1740 at Tyburn and his body was taken to Surgeons' Hall to be anatomised. A servant was washing the body but noticed him breathing. Duell was soon able to sit in a chair. That evening, he was returned to Newgate. His sentence, which might have been repeated, was commuted to transportation.

chapter 9 The Hangmen

EXECUTIONERS WERE popular when they hanged or beheaded a criminal hated by the public. However, if they had to execute a popular figure, the executioner himself became a figure of hate to the crowd. As a result, executioners sometimes wore masks to hide their identity (for example at the execution of Charles I in 1649). The hangmen were primarily executioners but they were also responsible for inflicting whippings and other punishments such as branding and mutilation.

The illustrations in this section show four well-known hangmen who worked at Tyburn and Newgate Gaol; Price, Calcraft, Marwood and Berry. John Price was hanged for murder in 1718 but many of the other hangmen are also interesting characters.

The earliest recorded London hangman was named Cratwell or Gratnell. He was appointed in 1534 but was himself hanged in Clerkenwell in 1538, in front of about 20,000 people, for a robbery at Bartholomew Fair. Another hangman, named Derrick, was sentenced to death for a rape. He was reprieved at the request of the Earl of Essex. However, Derrick was the executioner who had to behead Essex at the Tower of London in February 1601.

Gregory Brandon was executioner for the City of London and Middlesex from 1611 until his death in 1640. He was succeeded in the post by his son Richard. Gregory Brandon had killed a man in 1611 and only escaped the gallows himself by pleading benefit of clergy. Richard Brandon was held in Newgate Gaol in 1641, charged with bigamy, but was released. He executed the Earl of Strafford later that year, Archbishop Laud in 1644 and was probably one of the executioners of Charles I in 1649.

Jack Ketch (or John Catch) was the London executioner from 1678 (and perhaps earlier) until 1686. Ketch executed Lord William Russell in 1683 but it took a few strokes of the axe to finish the job. He executed about 200 of Monmouth's rebels in 1685 but bungled the beheading of Monmouth himself at Tower Hill by using a blunt axe. After five attempts, Ketch had to use a knife to remove Monmouth's head. Ketch was removed from his office shortly afterwards but all the London hangmen were thenceforth popularly known as 'Jack Ketch'. Ketch was replaced as hangman by Pascha Rose (a butcher by trade). However, Rose was convicted of burglary a few months after his appointment and Ketch was reinstated to hang Rose.

John Price was the London hangman from 1714 to 1718 but was hanged for murder. His successor, William Marvell, was convicted of burglary in 1719 and transported. John Thrift was appointed as hangman in 1735 and beheaded Lord Lovat in 1747. In March 1750, he stabbed a man in a quarrel. A crowd gathered outside Thrift's house, shouting 'Jack Ketch, Jack Ketch' and he ran outside with a drawn cutlass and killed one of his tormentors. Thrift was convicted of murder and condemned. However, he was pardoned and returned to his work at Tyburn until his death in 1752. He hanged the highwayman James Maclane. The hangman Edward Dennis executed the Perreau brothers, Dr Dodd and the Reverend Hackman. Dennis was himself sentenced to death for his part in the Gordon riots of 1780, but was reprieved and then hanged some of the rioters. Also illustrated below are the three best-known Victorian hangmen: Calcraft, Marwood and Berry. Unlike most of their predecessors, these executioners were not criminals.

Executioners were paid for their work. Calcraft was paid a guinea a week plus a guinea for each execution that he carried out. He earned extra money for floggings. In earlier times, executioners received various perks. They were entitled to the clothes worn by the condemned and, if the criminal had been notorious, the rope used to hang him could be sold. Before 1752, surgeons were always short of corpses and might secretly pay the hangmen to supply a few extra bodies.

John Ellis was born in 1874 and hanged Dr Crippen, Sir Roger Casement, Edith Thompson and 200 other men and women over a period of 23 years. He also worked as a barber. He tried to commit suicide twice, being successful on the second occasion, in 1932, with a cut-throat razor. Three members of the same family were among the last of Britain's hangmen. They were Henry Pierrepoint, his brother Thomas and Henry's son Albert. This dynasty served for over 50 years between them. Albert worked from 1931 to 1956 and hanged the murderer John Reginald Halliday Christie as well as Ruth Ellis, the last woman to be executed in Britain. Pierrepoint prided himself on being humane to the condemned by his speed. Once a prisoner was brought to the scaffold, Pierrepoint placed the cap over his head, positioned him on the drop, placed the noose around his neck and operated the lever. The process might take as little as 15 seconds. Pierrepoint resigned in 1956 and wrote his autobiography. He stated:

> During my twenty-five years as executioner, I believed with all my heart that I was carrying out a public duty. I conducted each execution with great care and a clear conscience. I never allowed myself to get involved with the death penalty controversy.
>
> I now sincerely hope that no man is ever called upon to carry out another execution in my country. I have come to the conclusion that executions solve nothing, and are only an antiquated relic of a primitive desire for revenge which takes the easy way and hands over the responsibility for revenge to other people. It is said to be a deterrent. I cannot agree. There have been murders since the beginning of time, and we shall go on looking for deterrents until the end of time.

▲ **The arrest of John Price, hangman, on the way to Tyburn**
John Price was born in St Martin's in the Fields in 1678. His poor widowed mother apprenticed him to a rag dealer but John ran away after serving only two years. Some sources say that Price joined a group of pickpockets, was caught in Bristol, whipped and sent to serve on a merchant ship and then on naval vessels. It is also said that he stole from other sailors and was whipped, keel-hauled and discharged. Price returned to London. He was committed to Newgate for theft but then married a woman who was employed to run errands at the gaol. Through that connection, Price managed to obtain employment as hangman for the county of Middlesex. Price had a reputation for cruelty and spent most of his money on drink. He was arrested for debt on the way to Tyburn with a prisoner John Meff, a burglar and highwayman. That execution had to be delayed. Price paid the debt (in part with money he got for the clothes of men he had hanged) but he was arrested for another debt a few months later and held in the Marshalsea for a year and a new hangman was appointed. Price and another prisoner escaped by breaking a hole in the wall. A few days later, he was walking across Bunhill Fields. He was drunk and carried out a violent sexual assault on Elizabeth White. Two men heard the woman's cries and arrested Price, taking him to the watch house on Old Street. The woman died from her injuries and Price was sent to Newgate. He was convicted, then attended daily (but drunk) in Newgate Chapel. He was hanged at Bunhill Fields on 31 May 1718. His body was hung in chains at Holloway.

▲ **William Calcraft, hangman**
William Calcraft (1800-1879) was a cobbler who became the best known of the Victorian hangmen and was also one of the longest serving executioners. His career at Newgate started when he was paid to flog juvenile offenders. He was appointed hangman in 1829 and served for 45 years, hanging Daniel Good, the Mannings and Franz Muller. He also performed the last public hanging (of Michael Barrett) outside Newgate on 26 May 1868. Calcraft was a kind man who was fond of children, animals and gardening but was a very inefficient hangman. Some of his efforts were little better than strangulation because he favoured a short drop that was usually insufficient to break a man's neck. Over the years, Calcraft used longer drops (giving the condemned 'more rope') but criminals still had to be hanged for the customary hour to ensure that they were dead. After the hanging of Mr and Mrs Manning, Charles Dickens wrote that Calcraft's jokes, oaths and intake of brandy should be restrained. Dickens also criticised Calcraft's 'unseemly briskness'. However, Dickens had paid 10 guineas to use a roof from which to obtain a good view of the hanging and he had waited up all night (with a picnic hamper) to see the Mannings hang. Dickens' criticism may therefore have been caused by his disappointment that, after such waiting and cost, the actual hanging was so quick. The last hanging conducted by Calcraft (when he was aged 74) was that of James Godwin, a wife-killer, inside Newgate Gaol. Calcraft was then gently forced to retire on a pension of a guinea a week.

▲ William Marwood, executioner

Marwood was appointed executioner in 1874. He is famous for inventing the long drop. Like Calcraft, he was a cobbler by trade. He had heard that many of the condemned were actually strangled by the rope and that some of them survived, writhing in agony, for a long time after they were turned off. He began experimenting with a series of drops designed to break a man's neck. This required exact calculation, taking into account the prisoner's body weight. If the drop was too long, the condemned might be decapitated. If it was too short, the result was slow strangulation. In general, about eight feet was about right. Marwood wrote to the Governor of Lincoln Prison, explaining his methods. After an interview and demonstration, he was asked to carry out an execution in 1872. He then worked as one of the official executioners around the country until his death in 1883, hanging about 170 people, including Henry Wainwright in 1875, Charles Peace and Catherine Webster in 1879, Percy Lefroy in 1881 and George Lamson in 1882. Marwood also developed a modern form of noose (fixing a metal eye to one end of the rope and bringing the other end through it) to replace the slipknot that was customarily used. Marwood never allowed people to address him as hangman, preferring the term executioner. He would say, scornfully, that Calcraft had throttled prisoners, whereas he executed them.

▲ James Berry, hangman

Berry served with both the Yorkshire and Nottinghamshire police forces and was appointed as an executioner in 1884, aged 31. He carried out about 130 executions until his retirement in 1891. He is best remembered for his failure, three times, to hang John 'Babbacombe' Lee at Exeter in 1885. Berry had calling cards printed stating: 'James Berry, Executioner. Bilton Place, Bradford, Yorkshire'. He also published his memoirs *My experiences as an executioner*. He died in 1913.

chapter 10 The Prisons of London

LONDON had more prisons than any other British city, partly because of its greater population but also because of the location in London of the central courts. Many prisons are included in this section such as the Tower of London, Newgate Gaol, Bridewell, Ludgate, the Fleet, Millbank Penitentiary, Brixton Prison and the Houses of Correction and Detention in Clerkenwell and Westminster. Many prisons were located in Southwark such as the Clink, Marshalsea, King's Bench and Horsemonger Lane Gaol. Some more modern prisons such as Wandsworth and Holloway and some lesser known prisons, such as the City Compters, are also featured.

In general, prisons were not intended to hold people for long periods of time until the 19th century. Offenders were punished by the whip, stocks, pillory, hanging or transportation. Sheriffs were obliged to hold prisoners in custody until their trial and were therefore responsible for the upkeep of prisons. The conditions in prisons were so bad, most prisoners living in miserable filth, disease, cold and hunger, that a long-term sentence of imprisonment was to condemn a person to a lingering but fairly certain death. The hulks were no better and often worse. Transportation to the colonies was sometimes a merciful alternative to the horrors of gaols such as Newgate.

The Tower of London was used as a prison from the 11th century and all the City gates were used as prisons at some point, the most famous being Newgate. These were insufficient to hold the vast number of debtors, vagrants and prisoners awaiting trial.

A statute of 1576 required each county to construct and maintain a House of Correction. These were administered by Justices of the Peace and were known as Bridewells after the House of Correction built within Bridewell Palace in London. Their regime of forced labour was meant to be unpleasant. They were originally intended to hold vagrants and to put idle beggars to work. Within a few years, they were also used to hold petty offenders and those awaiting trial or transportation. A statute of 1720 confirmed that Houses of Correction should also be used as prisons for offenders and by the late 18th century there was little practical difference between the Sheriff's prisons and the Houses of Correction. In addition to Bridewell, there were Houses of Correction in London at Clerkenwell, Tothill Fields, Brixton and Wandsworth.

As more offenders had to be incarcerated, so the number of prisons increased. This led to the building of Horsemonger Lane Gaol, Coldbath Fields, Millbank Penitentiary, Holloway, Pentonville and Wormwood Scrubs.

Throughout London, there were also small places of detention known as cages and lock-ups. These were used to hold drunks or those breaching the peace, especially at night, until they could be taken before Magistrates the next morning. They were generally maintained by the parish authorities and the stocks or whipping post were often located nearby. The cage at London Bridge is featured on page 139 below and Willesden Cage is on page 144. Many lock-ups were small wooden structures but the larger, richer parishes constructed large brick round-houses (but not always round) or watch houses. London watch houses and round-houses were used as the headquarters of the ward or parish watchmen (the inside of St Marylebone Watch House is shown on pages 30-1). Offenders could be held there for short periods, usually overnight. St Martin's Round House was located opposite the church of St Martin's in the Fields and was the scene of an outrage in July 1742. One night, a group of drunken constables decided to enforce the law against disorderly persons and arrested as many women as they could. One room in the round-house was used to hold 25 women, with little air and no water. The next morning, four women were found to have suffocated and another two died later. The local inhabitants were so enraged by this cruelty that they tore the building down the next day. William Baird, the keeper, was convicted of murder and transported to America.

One of the principal reasons for the appalling conditions in prisons was that the keepers or gaolers were usually unpaid (or received only a pitiful salary). They therefore had to make money however they could, mainly by charging prisoners extortionate fees. Fees known as garnish were payable to the turnkeys (and sometimes to other prisoners) on a prisoner's admission to a gaol. Fees would also have to be paid to the gaolers for better accommodation, food, bedding and even for being released from chains or irons. It was not until the 19th century, particularly after the campaigns of John Howard and Elizabeth Fry, that prisoners' conditions substantially improved. Further improvement came after The Prison Act of 1877. This placed control of all British prisons in the hands of five Prison Commissioners who were responsible to the Home Secretary. They had power to establish a single code of prison discipline and standard conditions. Since that time, there has been a steady improvement in the conditions in prisons, both as regards diet, hygiene and labour for prisoners but also in the pay and conditions for prison staff.

Some prisons were intended primarily to hold debtors, for example the Fleet (one of the oldest prisons in London), the King's Bench and the Marshalsea. From the 14th to the 19th centuries, at least as many people were imprisoned for debt as for crime. The Crown started imprisoning those who owed it money in the 12th century, partly as punishment and partly to encourage other debtors to pay. The law gradually extended the power of imprisonment to civil debts. A creditor could obtain a warrant for the imprisonment of a debtor by swearing that the debt was due. The Sheriffs' officers who executed warrants could obtain fees from the creditor and, if they imprisoned him, from the debtor as well. The debtors' prisons therefore began to fill up very quickly. In the 18th century, there were also over 100 sponging (or spunging) houses. These were small prisons operated by Sheriffs' officers to hold debtors whom they had arrested. The sponging house operated by James Bolland was a typical example. Men who were truly insolvent might spend years in prison, unable to clear their debts. The process of bankruptcy (clearing the slate for a percentage of all the debts due) was only available to traders. It was not until 1844 that any man could go into bankruptcy and only in 1869 that imprisonment for debt was abolished (except where it was proved that a man had the means, but refused, to pay a valid debt).

Three other prisons deserve mention here. Belmarsh, in Woolwich, is the only prison that was built in London in the 20th century. It opened in 1991 and was recently in the news because of its inmates Jonathan Aitken and Jeffrey Archer.

The Liberties of the Tower of London were the area within the Tower walls, the land on Tower Hill and, from the 17th century, the small areas of the Minories, Old Artillery Ground and Wellclose. The Liberties were outside the jurisdiction of the City of London or Middlesex and had their own court and a small prison. These were located (with a tavern) in an old house on Wellclose Square (the prison was also known as Neptune Street Prison). Most of the prisoners were debtors. By 1792, the prison was little used and described as ruinous. In the 19th century it became a lodging-house.

In the 19th century more and more people thought about reforming criminals and preparing them for a return to society, rather than seeing prison simply as a punishment and deterrent. A reformatory for young females was built by the government in Fulham in 1856 and known as the Fulham Refuge. It was intended to teach women, close to the end of their sentence, the skills that would help them to find work as domestic servants when they were released. There were 180 places. The refuge gradually became more like a prison, it was surrounded by a high wall and its gateway was topped by spikes. A serious disturbance amongst the inmates led to changes in policy, for example requiring the prisoners to eat alone in their cells. By 1871, it was realised that the experiment had failed and that charities were providing some training. The institution was therefore expanded to accommodate 400 women and its name was changed to Fulham Prison. It was closed in 1888.

➤ **The Clink Prison**
We should start with the prison from which derives the slang 'in the clink'. In medieval times, it was common for bishops to have cells in their palaces to hold those who offended against ecclesiastical law (or priests and monks who were exempt by benefit of clergy from punishment by the lay courts). Cells existed in Lambeth Palace, the London home of the Arch-bishops of Canterbury (see page 138) and in the London house of the Bishops of Ely, built in the 13th century in Ely Place, Holborn. A group of cells in the Bishop of Winchester's palace in Southwark, just to the south of Bankside, became known as the Clink Prison. The dungeons had manacles, chains and fetters to hold prisoners securely (and in discomfort). The 'clinking and clanking' of these may have given the prison its name. As lord of the manor, the Bishop of Winchester also had power to punish people who offended against the laws of the manor or who breached the peace. This included those who breached the peace in or around the brothels on Bankside, known as the 'Stewes', which were licensed and supervised by the Bishop. Winchester Palace was rebuilt in the 14th century and a new prison was built in the cellars. Debtors were also

incarcerated there. The gaolers in the Clink extorted money from prisoners (on their admission or release, for a bed or for removing their manacles) and also tortured them. Prostitution was carried on inside the Clink, with a share of the proceeds being paid to the keeper of the prison. A pillory and ducking-stool were also located outside the prison for the punishment of offenders. During the reign of Henry VII, the Clink became a Royal Prison, although it remained under the supervision of the Bishops of Winchester. One of the 16th-century bishops was Stephen Gardiner. He had a reputation for spending too much time with his own whores (known as the 'Winchester Geese') and was said to have been 'bitten' by some of them (meaning that he caught venereal diseases). However, this did not prevent him being appointed Archbishop of Canterbury by Henry VIII and Lord Chancellor by Queen Mary. Gardiner rebuilt the prison in three buildings next to his palace. Conditions were awful. The 'Common' side of the prison had bare beds which were full of vermin. The only food was that which arrived as alms. Many prisoners were naked and suffered from disease.

The 'Hole' was a dark, rat-infested dungeon where many prisoners were left to die. Gardiner was in charge of Mary's campaign against the Protestant heretics and the Clink was consequently used to hold many of them, such as William Hooper, Bishop of London and John Bradford, before their execution in 1555. During the reign of Elizabeth, many Catholics were held in the Clink with dissenting Protestants, debtors and criminals. The prisoners' conditions remained appalling. Many died of gaol fever, a form of typhoid, or during the regular outbreaks of plague. Royalist prisoners were held in the Clink in the early days of the English Civil War and, in 1642, the whole of Winchester Palace was appropriated to this use by Parliament. After that, the Clink became very decayed and it was little used, except to hold a few debtors. In 1732, it was recorded that only two prisoners were being held there. From 1745, a house on Bankside was used in its stead. This was burned down in the Gordon riots of 1780 and never rebuilt. The Clink Prison Museum is now located near the site of the prison.

The Tower of London

▼ **The Tower of London**

The Tower is London's most famous fortification. It extends to
13 acres and has been used as a prison (particularly for political
or religious prisoners), a court and place of execution. The
Tower has also housed the Crown Jewels, the Crown's armoury,
State records, the Mint, as well as a garrison and menagerie.
Prisoners have included royalty or other important
people, particularly traitors, prisoners
of war and military

mutineers. The keep was commenced by William I and
completed in 1097. It became known as the White Tower in the
13th century when its walls were whitewashed. Cells were built
below the keep, but prisoners were also held on upper floors of
the keep and in towers on the surrounding walls. This illustration is a drawing based upon one of the earliest
paintings of London, dating from about
1500. It shows the White

Tower and many of the surrounding towers and walls as they were in that year but represents the captivity of Charles, Duc d'Orleans (a nephew of the King of France) who had been captured at the battle of Agincourt in 1415. He was held prisoner for 25 years. The first recorded prisoner in the Tower was Ranulf Flambard, Bishop of Durham, in 1101, who was permitted to keep his servants. This shows how the accommodation and treatment of prisoners in the Tower varied depending upon the status of the prisoner and the reason for his incarceration. In 1278, Edward I imprisoned about 600 Jews in the Tower on false charges of coin-clipping. About 260 were executed and most of the others died of ill-treatment in the putrid Tower dungeons. John Baliol, King of the Scots, was a prisoner in the Tower in 1296 and King John II of France (captured at the battle of Poitiers in 1356) was imprisoned in luxurious conditions in the Tower for three years until a ransom was paid. Henry VI and George, Duke of Clarence were both imprisoned and killed in the Tower. Anne Boleyn, the second wife of Henry VIII, was accused of adultery and imprisoned in the Tower in 1536. Princess Elizabeth was imprisoned in 1554, suspected of complicity in plots against her half-sister Mary Tudor but she was subsequently released. Philip Howard, son of the Duke of Norfolk, died in the Tower in 1595, having been a prisoner for ten years. Archbishop Laud was imprisoned in the Tower in 1641 and executed there in 1645. The notorious Judge Jeffreys was imprisoned in 1688 and died there in 1689. Many of the leaders of the Jacobite rebellion of 1745 were held in the Tower prior to their execution on Tower Hill. Sir Roger Casement was held there in 1916 until his trial for treason (he had sought German assistance for the nationalist cause in Ireland). He was later hanged at Pentonville Prison. William Joyce ('Lord Haw-Haw') was imprisoned in the Tower as recently as 1945, awaiting execution for treason.

▼ Inside the Wakefield Tower

Each of the towers in the Tower of London was used as a prison at some point, as were some of the houses within the walls. This photograph shows the basement of the Wakefield Tower where, it is said, many prisoners taken at the battle of Wakefield in 1460 were imprisoned. King Henry VI was held in the upper chambers of the Wakefield Tower in 1465 and murdered there in 1471. Sir Thomas More was held in the Bell Tower before his execution in 1534. Lady Jane Grey was held in the Lieutenant's House and her husband, Lord Guildford Dudley, in the Beauchamp Tower prior to their executions. Sir Walter Raleigh was imprisoned by Queen Elizabeth for seducing one of her maids. He lodged with his cousin, the Master of the Ordnance, in the Brick Tower. Raleigh was again imprisoned by James I, accused of plotting to place Arabella Stuart on the throne. He spent almost thirteen years in the Bloody (or Garden) Tower but made a home there with his wife, son and servants. After a temporary release, Raleigh was again imprisoned in the Tower but in less comfortable conditions, until his execution at Westminster. Arabella Stuart was a cousin of King James I. It was an offence for those of royal blood to marry without the monarch's permission but Arabella did so. Her husband William Seymour was imprisoned in St Thomas' Tower and Arabella in a private house in London. Both escaped but Arabella was recaptured and imprisoned in strict seclusion in an upper chamber of the Bell Tower. She went insane and died four years later.

◄ Traitors' Gate

This gate was originally known as the Watergate but became known as Traitors' Gate during the Tudor period. It was the entrance to the Tower from the River Thames and the convenient entrance for those prisoners arriving by water from their trials in the courts at Westminster. Many famous people passed through the gates, rarely to return to freedom.

York, who was proclaimed King Edward IV in 1461. Henry was captured in 1465 and imprisoned in the Tower of London until 1470. He was restored as King by the Earl of Warwick but recaptured by Edward IV. Henry was murdered in the Wakefield Tower on 21 May 1471 but it was announced that he had died 'of pure displeasure and melancholy'. George, Duke of Clarence was a younger brother of Edward IV. He was imprisoned in the Tower in 1478 for plotting against Edward. He was killed there, according to contemporary chroniclers and later Shakespeare, by being drowned in a 'butt of Malmsey'. After Edward's death in 1483, his sons Edward V and Richard, Duke of York were held in the Garden Tower (only much later called the Bloody Tower). Their uncle Richard became Protector and was then proclaimed King as Richard III. The princes then disappeared. They were probably murdered but controversy still rages as to whether the culprit was Richard III, the Duke of Buckingham or Henry VII.

▲ **Murders in the Tower: Henry VI and George Duke of Clarence**
Henry VI (1421-71) was the son of Henry V, who died when his son was aged only one. Henry was a pious man who founded Eton College and King's College, Cambridge. However, he was a weak ruler who finally lost his crown to Edward, Duke of

◄ **The Lollards' Prison**
Lambeth Palace has been the official residence of the Archbishop of Canterbury since the 12th century. Clerical offenders were imprisoned in the palace and, during Elizabethan times, many Catholics were also held there. Lambeth Palace was sequestered by Parliament at the outbreak of the Civil War and used as a prison for Royalists until the Restoration. In addition, one of the palace's towers, built in 1435, became known as the Lollards' Tower because of a legend that Lollards, treated as heretics by the church, were imprisoned there in the 15th century. This photograph shows a prison cell on one of the upper floors of the tower, with iron rings set in the walls. However, this room was probably adapted as a cell only in the 17th century, too late to have held Lollards.

The City of London

THE MEDIEVAL City of London was a great and bustling trading centre, full of people and livestock which were bought and sold in the great markets. Crime flourished in this crowded area of narrow streets and alleys. Criminals, suspects and vagrants were held in cells in the gates of the City such as Newgate and Ludgate but also in a building known as the Tun and in gaols, known as Compters, operated by the City Sheriffs. The Tun was a building in Cornhill which was in the shape of a tun (a large wine cask). It was used as a prison from 1282 until at least 1401, particularly for drunks, prostitutes or their clients and others who broke the curfew then in force in the City (a City ordinance prohibited armed persons or those of suspicious appearance wandering the streets after dark).

The word Compter derives from 'counter', the counting or keeping of official records. The Compters were controlled by the City Sheriffs. They were principally intended for debtors, drunks, vagrants and, on occasion, prisoners such as those engaged in fraudulent trading. They also held other prisoners when the City's principal gaol at Newgate was full. The Compters were notorious for the fees and charges extorted from prisoners. Poultry and Giltspur Street Compters and Whitecross Street Prison (the last of the City debtor prisons) are illustrated below. In addition, there were Compters in Bread Street and Wood Street.

Bread Street Compter was built in the early 15th century. Richard Husband, one of the keepers of the Compter, was so cruel to prisoners that he was gaoled briefly in Newgate in 1550. He returned to his post and previous practices. He also offered cells as cheap overnight accommodation for thieves and prostitutes. The City authorities closed the Compter in 1555 and transferred the prisoners to a new Compter on Wood Street.

Wood Street Compter was built in 1555 (to replace that in Bread Street) to hold 70 debtors or those offenders who were arrested in the City prior to their removal to Newgate. Wood Street Compter was rebuilt after the Great Fire of 1666 but was notorious for ruthless exploitation and the neglect and diseased state of its inmates. It had five wards or 'sides' of varying conditions. A prisoner was placed in the side that he could afford. The Masters' Side was for the wealthy, the Knights' Ward for the comfortably off and then, in descending order of comfort and hygiene, there were the Twopenny Ward, the Common Ward and lastly the Hole for the destitute. So many prisoners (men, women and children) were sick in the Hole that it was compared with being in a churchyard because the prisoners lay together like so many corpses in their graves. Those prisoners who had money would pay the Keeper and gaolers for better quarters, food and drink. The office of Keeper of the Compter was therefore very profitable and was bought and sold until the 18th century. Some inmates, such as attorneys, physicians and shoemakers, continued to trade from inside the Compter so as to maintain themselves. Jonathan Wild was held in this Compter from 1710 to 1712 because of his debts and became an assistant to the gaolers. As a result of this experience, Wild turned to crime on his release. Conditions in Wood Street Compter remained poor throughout the 18th century. It was described by a visitor in 1776 as dark and full of filth and vermin. It was closed in 1791 and replaced by Giltspur Street Compter.

▲ **The Cage on London Bridge**
In 1553, Queen Mary ordered cages and stocks to be erected in every parish in London. This engraving shows a woman in the cage at the Southwark end of London Bridge.

Ludgate

➤ Ludgate

All the City gates were used as gaols at some point. Newgate is the most famous but a room at the top of Cripplegate was used as a prison in the 14th century and Ludgate held debtors and criminals for 400 years. The Romans built the first gate on the site. It was known as Lud Gate ('lud' probably derived from the word 'lode', meaning a drain of water into a larger stream). Ludgate was rebuilt in 1215 and images of the mythical King Lud and his sons were added in 1260. A prison was built inside the gate in about 1377 and enlarged in 1464. It was used for petty criminals, debtors, freemen of the City and clergymen. It was said to be the most comfortable of the City's prisons, at least for the wealthy. As in all debtors' prisons, the gaolers extorted money from the inmates as fees for lodging, food and turning the key (on entry or discharge). One room had a window from which inmates could beg from passers-by. Ludgate was rebuilt in 1586 and again after its destruction in the Great Fire. The main part of the prison was in the south side of the gate with wards on each floor and a chapel. The Master's Side of the prison, on the two floors directly above the gate, contained 10 rooms for wealthy prisoners, but prisoners in

the other wards lived in rags, filth and vermin. Ludgate held up to 100 prisoners in the early 18th century. This drawing shows Ludgate a few years before its demolition in 1760.

◄ Ludgate Prison

The prisoners from Ludgate were moved to a new Ludgate Prison that was built in a workhouse on Bishopsgate Street. The Master's Side had 11 rooms for debtors. There were two rooms for Common Side (or poor) prisoners. The number of prisoners was usually around twenty and food was provided by the City authorities. The prison was closed in 1794 and inmates were moved to Giltspur Street Compter.

◄ The gate of Poultry Compter

Poultry Compter was the oldest of the City Compters. It was built in the 14th century, rebuilt in 1615, destroyed in the Great Fire but again rebuilt. In the late 17th century, the smell in Poultry Compter was said to be worse than a Southwark ditch and the inmates were described as 'ill-looking vermin, with long rusty beards, swaddled up in rags'. The Compter held felons and debtors

(and debtors' families). In 1776 there were 52 debtors but also many of their wives and a staggering 163 children. The Compter was so decayed by 1801 that only part of it could be used. It was then holding 36 debtors and their families. This engraving shows a gaoler standing in the doorway, holding the key to the Compter door. Poultry Compter was demolished in 1817 and the last prisoners were moved to Whitecross Street Prison.

➤ Giltspur Street Compter

The City authorities built this Compter in 1791, opposite St Sepulchre's Church, to replace Wood Street Compter. It held debtors, minor offenders and night-charges (those arrested at night and held until they could be taken before a court in the morning). This engraving dates from 1813. Giltspur Street Compter was a small prison, intended to hold about 200 prisoners, but it was very busy. About 6,000 people were committed to it each year. Debtors were transferred to Whitecross Street Prison in 1815 and Giltspur Street was then used as a House of Correction for beggars and vagrants. It remained overcrowded. A visitor in 1850 found so many prisoners in some wards that they barely had room to lie down. Giltspur Street Compter was replaced by the City's new House of Correction at Holloway and closed in 1854.

Whitecross Street Prison

▼ Whitecross Street Prison

The last of the City's debtor prisons was on Whitecross Street which runs from Old Street to Chiswell Street. It was built by the Corporation of London and opened in 1815, to accommodate 490 debtors, because of the vile conditions at Poultry Compter and concerns about allowing debtors to mix with felons in Newgate. This watercolour of 1840 by Frederick Napoleon Shepherd shows the front of the prison. Changes in the law gradually reduced the number of debtors in prisons and the last 27 prisoners were transferred to Holloway. The prison was demolished in 1870.

◀ Release from Whitecross Street Prison

This illustration from *The Graphic* of 15 January 1870 shows the last prisoners being discharged (in fact, a few prisoners stayed until the next morning and a few others remained in the prison infirmary). One man had been in the prison for 27 years. He had nowhere to go and returned to the prison the next day asking for shelter in the only place he knew as home. Another man had been held for seven years for a debt of £40 (even though £40 was also the approximate annual cost of imprisoning a debtor).

Newgate

NEWGATE is perhaps the most famous of London's prisons. It was a prison for over 700 years and had a terrible reputation, being described as a 'tomb for the living'. In his *Complete history of the lives and robberies of the most notorious highwaymen*, Captain Alexander Smith described Newgate as:

> a dismal prison [that] is enough to deter all men from acting an ill thing …
> it is a place of calamity … an habitation of misery, and a tower of Babel, where all are speakers and no hearers …
> It is the grave of gentility … the poison of honour, the centre of infamy …
> There, he that yesterday was great, today is mean;
> He that was well-fed, there starves;
> He that was richly clad, is stark naked;
> He that lay in a good bed is forced to rest himself on the hard boards or cold stones.

Newgate was built later than the other City gates (probably in the ninth century). There are records of a prison in the gate from 1188. Newgate was a prison for the City of London and Middlesex, controlled by the Sheriffs who appointed the Keeper of the Prison (often selling this office to the highest bidder). Conditions were very poor. Some prisoners were held in dungeons and tortured. Disease flourished so much that, in 1414, the Keeper of Newgate and 64 inmates died of plague.

▶ Newgate in 1650

Newgate was rebuilt in 1423 with money left by the Lord Mayor. The new prison had five storeys and included a dining-hall for prisoners. It was also gradually expanded to include some adjacent buildings. However, the keepers of Newgate continued to torture and steal money from prisoners. New inmates were robbed of any money or possessions by the gaolers or other prisoners. Inmates also had to pay fees to the turnkeys, for example for being released from irons. The Keeper in 1449, William Arnold, was imprisoned for raping a female prisoner. During the reign of Henry VIII, 11 monks of Charter-house refused to sign the Oath of Supremacy and were imprisoned in Newgate. They were chained upright in a dungeon and 10 died from disease. The survivor, William Horn, was transferred to the Tower until his execution at Tyburn three years later. In the 16th century, many other Catholic and Protestant martyrs were held here. Newgate was badly damaged in the Great Fire of 1666 and so rebuilt in 1672. Prisoners in this gaol included William Penn, Titus Oates, Daniel Defoe (in 1702/3) and Jonathan Wild (in 1725). Newgate was overcrowded, unhealthy and miserable. It could hold 150 prisoners comfortably but it usually held between 250 and 300, most of whom were awaiting trial at the Old Bailey and so were only held for a few weeks. However, debtors might be held for years. On the south side of Newgate was the Press Yard, an exercise yard that measured only nine feet by fifty feet. Over-looking it was the Keeper's house and a two-storey building, known as the Master's Side, with the best and most expensive 'lodgings' for inmates. A wealthy prisoner could rent these rooms and even entertain his family and guests here, albeit at enormous cost. However, the prisoners in the Common Side lay on the floor or had to pay for a hammock or wooden boards on which to sleep. The water supply was inadequate, ventilation was almost non-existent and there was an appalling stench. The dungeons of Newgate were used for the punishment of prisoners or for those who could not afford the less unpleasant cells. There were frequent outbreaks of gaol fever, a form of typhoid, which probably killed more prisoners than the gallows. In 1726, 21 men and women were hanged at Tyburn but 83 died in Newgate. Ninety-two prisoners died there in 1729 and 62 in 1750. A windmill was built on top of the gate in 1752, connected to a ventilation system that withdrew some foul air from the cells

below and replaced it with fresh air, but otherwise conditions were little better. Prisoners were permitted to keep animals in the cells; dogs were not excluded until 1792 and pigs and poultry until 1814. Cheap alcohol was available and gambling and prostitution thrived. Between 1700 and 1707, the deputy-keeper of Newgate, William Robinson, virtually transformed the gaol into a brothel, permitting 'lewd women and common strumpets' to lie there all night. Sex was also offered by many women awaiting trial, hoping to become pregnant and thus escape hanging. City Aldermen visited Newgate in 1707 and found that Robinson permitted male and female prisoners to spend a night together for one shilling or visit one another for sixpence. A clergyman entered a condemned cell in 1766 and found the condemned man engaged in what he described as 'wanton intercourse' with a female prisoner. By the late 18th century Newgate was an obstruction to the increasing amount of traffic. The building of a new prison started in 1770 and the old gate was demolished in 1777.

➤ Escape from Newgate: Daniel Malden

Jack Sheppard is the most famous person to have escaped from Newgate but he was not the only one. There were so many visitors to the gaol that some inmates tried walking out of the gates in the hope of getting past the turnkeys without being recognised. In 1663, a prisoner was visited by his wife and swapped clothes with her in a dark corner of his ward. He left the gaol unnoticed but hid near Newgate and was captured the next day. In 1679, seven prisoners made a hole in a wall under cover of darkness and climbed out. Their absence was not discovered until the next day. The sewers under Newgate were another promising, if disgusting, escape route. In 1731, six prisoners broke through a dungeon floor into the sewer below. Two drowned and their skeletons were discovered years later, but four managed to climb out of the sewer into a shop on Fleet Lane. Daniel Malden was convicted of robbery in 1737 and broke out of the condemned hold into a sewer even though he was shackled with heavy irons. He escaped from the sewer after 48 hours, had his irons removed and fled to Europe. Rather

Drawn by I. Clarke Painter.

stupidly, he then returned to England and was arrested and hanged at Tyburn.

▼ The new Gaol at Newgate, 1770

A new gaol building, designed by George Dance the Younger, was commenced in 1770 at the top of the street named Old Bailey. Prisoners were transferred from the gateway and surrounding buildings into the new prison that was finally completed in 1780. Old Newgate was demolished in 1777. This new gaol was badly damaged by fire during the Gordon riots of 1780.

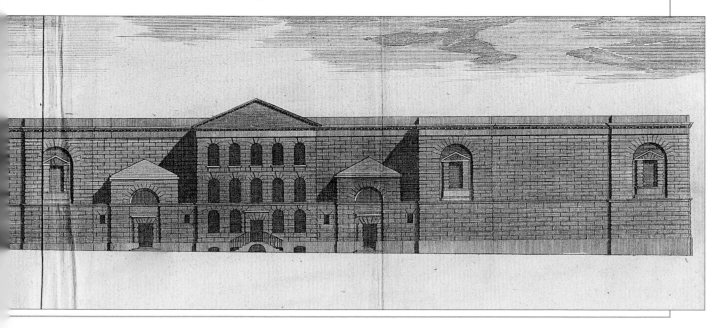

Jack Sheppard

▲ Jack Sheppard escaping from Newgate 15 October 1724
This engraving shows Newgate as rebuilt in 1672. As well as the gate spanning Newgate Street, the gaol included two annexes, each four floors high, adjoining the gate on either side of the street. It also had an exercise yard (the Press Yard) to the south west of the gate. The gaol was a rabbit warren of cells and dungeons. Its main entrance was a door on the south side of Newgate Street, close to the archway, which led into a large room known as the Lodge. This had a bar (where prisoners could buy beer, brandy, wine and tobacco) and the door to the condemned hold. The one small window of this cell looked onto Newgate Street but was under the arch so that the cell was always dark. A chapel was on the top floor.

Jack Sheppard was a burglar who became famous for escaping from Newgate but was executed at Tyburn in 1724. Although only 23 years old when he died, Sheppard was so notorious that his exploits were the talk of all ranks of society. His portrait was painted when he was in Newgate and books, pamphlets, songs and a pantomime were written about his exploits. John

Sheppard was born in Spitalfields in 1702. He and his brother Thomas were sons of a carpenter who died when the boys were young. Their mother went into service but placed Jack in a workhouse school in Bishopsgate Street and then apprenticed him to a cane-chair maker. Sheppard ran away from him because of his cruelty but a family friend, Mr Kneebone, arranged for him to be apprenticed to a carpenter in Wych Street near Drury Lane. After about four years, Sheppard began visiting the *Black Lion* tavern in Drury Lane and met a group of prostitutes, including Poll Maggot and Elizabeth Lyon (called Edgworth Bess as she had been born in Edgworth, now Edgware, in Middlesex). Sheppard was only five feet four inches high but strong and agile. He continued working as a carpenter but, under the women's tutelage, began stealing from houses in which he worked and burgling other premises. He also began quarrelling with his master and, in the last year of his apprenticeship, attacked his master and absconded. Sheppard continued to work as a carpenter since this made it easier to commit burglaries but he also joined one of Jonathan Wild's gangs. At this time, Edgworth Bess was arrested for stealing a gold ring from one of her clients and was locked up in St Giles Round House. Sheppard went to visit her but the beadle refused to admit him. Sheppard knocked him down, broke open the door and carried Bess away. He then carried out robberies with Bess and his brother Thomas until Thomas was arrested while trying to sell some stolen goods. He was held in Newgate and, hoping to be admitted an evidence, informed on Jack and Bess. Jack was caught and held in St Giles' Round House but escaped through the roof.

▼ A myth: Jack Sheppard escaping from Willesden Cage
This illustration is of one of the mythical exploits of Jack Sheppard. He did, however, make a similar escape from St Giles' Round House.

➤ Edgworth Bess and Jack Sheppard escaping from Clerkenwell New Prison in 1724
Soon afterwards, Sheppard and a thief named Benson were crossing Leicester Fields and attempted to steal a man's watch. Benson escaped but Sheppard was taken to St Ann's Round

House in Soho. Edgworth Bess visited him but was detained on suspicion of being one of his accomplices. The next day, they were committed to Clerkenwell New Prison and, passing as man and wife, were held together in a room known as Newgate Ward. Sheppard was visited by some friends, one of whom provided him with tools to make an escape. On 25 May, Sheppard filed off his fetters, broke a hole in the wall and tied a sheet and blanket together. He and Bess descended 25 feet to the yard in the Clerkenwell Bridewell next door. They then climbed the Bridewell's wall of 22 feet and escaped.

➤ **Jack Sheppard escaping from the condemned hold in Newgate**
Sheppard then committed some robberies with Charles Grace and Anthony Lamb. Lamb was caught, convicted and transported. At the same time, Jack's brother Thomas was also convicted of burglary and transported. Sheppard then worked with another notorious thief, Joseph Blake (*alias* Blueskin). They burgled the house of William Kneebone (Sheppard's old benefactor) and committed some daring robberies (including a highway robbery on a lady's coach near Hampstead) sometimes disposing of the goods to a receiver William Field. Field wanted to keep all the stolen property for himself and betrayed Sheppard and Blueskin to Jonathan Wild, who arrested Edgworth Bess, discovered Sheppard's whereabouts from her and then arranged his capture. Sheppard was tried at the Old Bailey Sessions in August 1724 for burglary. Field and Wild gave evidence against him and he was sentenced to death. Sheppard was held in the condemned cell at Newgate with nine other unhappy wretches but had been supplied with tools to escape. When he was visited on 30 August 1724 by Edgworth Bess and Poll Maggot, he broke through the door's hatch, even though some gaolers were drinking nearby. Sheppard hid in an ale-

house in Finchley but the Keepers of Newgate were informed of his hiding place, seized him and returned him to Newgate. To prevent any further escape, Sheppard was handcuffed, placed in heavy irons and chained to the floor of a strongroom known as the Castle, on the third floor above the gate. Excited by Sheppard's escapes, people of all ranks of society visited him. The gaolers ensured that no-one provided tools for an escape but Sheppard found a nail in the room with which, on 15 October, he unlocked the padlock that secured his chains to the floor and escaped from his handcuffs. Although he had iron fetters on his legs, Sheppard climbed up the chimney to the room above the Castle, then into the chapel and onto the roof. He descended to the ground using a blanket. Sheppard moved about London for the next few days, hearing people talk and sing about his escapes. He broke into a pawnbroker's shop in Drury Lane, stole a sword, clothes, rings and watches and then dressed as a gentleman. He dined with two women in Newgate Street and even passed under the arch of Newgate in a coach. However, he then dared too much. He was recognised in an ale-house (drinking with a girl named Moll Frisky), arrested, returned to Newgate and loaded with irons weighing 300 pounds to prevent any further escape. People flocked to see him, paying enormous fees to the gaolers for the privilege. Having already been convicted, Sheppard now faced execution. He still hoped to escape, during the execution procession, using a small knife that had been given to him, but it was found when he was searched on leaving Newgate. He was hanged at Tyburn on 16 November 1724 aged 23. There was rioting when he was cut down. His body was seized by the crowd to save it from the surgeons. It was then carried to the *Barley Mow* tavern in Long Acre and buried in the churchyard of St Martin's in the Fields. Edgworth Bess and four of Sheppard's other prostitutes or accomplices were captured and tried. Bess was sentenced to 14 years' transportation; the others were fined and imprisoned.

The Gordon Riots

➤ Lord George Gordon

Lord George Gordon was a son of the Duke of Gordon. He was educated at Eton, served as an officer in the Royal Navy and then became an MP (for one of the many rotten boroughs, the seats for which could then be purchased). In the late 1770s, Parliament was considering a number of bills to repeal some of the laws that discriminated against Catholics (for example, preventing them serving as officers in the army). Some people still opposed such changes and Gordon became President of the Protestant Association, campaigning against the bills. A crowd of 50,000 people assembled in St George's Fields, Southwark on 2 June 1780. They marched to Parliament, led by Gordon, with a petition against the bills and flags bearing the words 'No Popery'. Gordon lost control of the crowd and for five days there was the most serious rioting ever seen in London. Thousands of soldiers were called in to quell the riots. About 800 people were killed and an enormous amount of property was destroyed, including Newgate Gaol, other prisons and Catholics' chapels, shops and houses. About 135 people were tried for the rioting and 59 were convicted, including the hangman Edward Dennis (he was reprieved). At least 33 rioters were hanged at various places around London (many by Edward Dennis), including Richard Roberts and William Lawrence, who were convicted of destroying the house of Sir John Fielding. Gordon was arrested for inciting and assisting the insurrection, held in the Tower of London for eight months, then tried before the Court of King's Bench for treason. The jury was satisfied that Gordon was not responsible for his followers' violence and he was acquitted. Gordon converted to Judaism and was convicted of libel in 1787 and 1788. He was imprisoned in the rebuilt Newgate and died there from gaol fever in 1793.

▼ The Gordon riots in 1780: the burning of Newgate Gaol

Rioters broke the gates of Newgate Gaol with crowbars to release three fellow rioters who had been arrested. They also tore holes in the roof. About 300 prisoners escaped but some died in the fire that followed; Britain's newest and strongest prison was a smouldering shell. Rioters also destroyed the Fleet, King's Bench and Clink Prisons (releasing their inmates and those in Wood Street Compter and Clerkenwell Bridewell), and attacked Downing Street and the Bank of England, but were repelled.

▲ Newgate Gaol in the early nineteenth century

Newgate was rebuilt after the Gordon riots and subsequently modified but it continued to be crowded, poorly ventilated and dark. Despite the campaigns of Elizabeth Fry, conditions at Newgate remained harsh throughout the 19th century. Debtors were moved in 1815 from Newgate to Whitecross Street Prison or to the Fleet Prison, but Newgate was still overcrowded. It had been built to hold 500 prisoners but regularly had to accommodate over 800 (and over 1,000 at one point in 1817). The female felon's ward was built for 60, but 120 were there in 1873. A typical ward was about 15 feet by 30 feet and usually held up to 15 men but sometimes double that number. Members of the public could still pay to visit the gaol's cells and wards. Drink was sold in the gaol and many of the gaolers extorted money from prisoners or sold 'access' to the female wards.

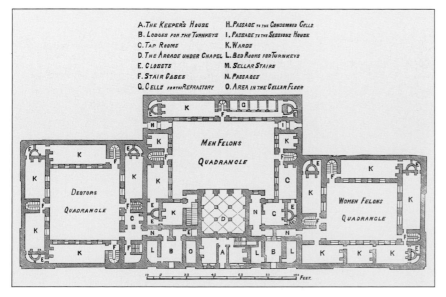

◄ A plan of Newgate, 1888

The opening of Holloway in 1852 resulted in Newgate only being used for the custody of prisoners awaiting either trial at the Old Bailey or execution. Further rebuilding was undertaken at Newgate in 1857 and 1858. Crowded wards were replaced by a block of five floors of cells built around galleries. The basement had reception cells and bathrooms. A similar block for women was built in 1862. Newgate was demolished in 1902 and many of the contents (such as leg-irons and doors) were sold off by auction. The Central Criminal Court was built on the site.

Life and Death in Newgate

▼ **Newgate Gaol in 1897**
This photograph was taken from a rooftop, looking east. It shows the grim exterior of Newgate Gaol in about 1897. The dome of St Paul's Cathedral is in the background. Newgate was designed to look like a fortress. It also resembled a tomb, which it was for those who were hanged and buried there.

▲ **Visitors arrive at a door of Newgate**
Prisoners at Newgate were allowed visitors, especially if the prisoner was wealthy and could afford the fees charged by the gaolers until the early 19th century. Some men, such as Jonathan Wild, even managed to continue their business whilst imprisoned. Security was improved after visitors were found to have been able to pass knives and tools for escape to prisoners such as Jack Sheppard.

◄ **The death sermon in the chapel of Newgate Gaol**
The Chaplain at Newgate was known as the Ordinary. He conducted services in the prison chapel but often had to shout to be heard over the noise made by prisoners. One chaplain complained of the evil smell in the chapel caused by prisoners relieving themselves in a corner. In the 18th and early 19th centuries there might be up to 50 prisoners at Newgate at any one time who had been condemned but who awaited the death warrant. They were given only bread and water and were obliged to attend the chapel on the Sunday before their execution, where they were confronted by a black coffin and had to sit through the notorious 'Death Sermon'. This aquatint by Pugin and Rowlandson of 1808 shows the interior of the chapel after Newgate was rebuilt following the Gordon riots. The condemned would sit in a railed enclosure in the centre of the chapel around a coffin and hear the chaplain preach at length as to their fate. The coffin was removed in 1817. Members of the public (seen in the balcony) could pay to attend these services until 1828. Some Ordinaries were no better than the gaolers or prisoners. They wrote and sold broadsheets about the lives and crimes of the condemned, often including the criminal's confession. If the condemned refused to confess or give an interesting story, the Ordinary could make one up. As late as 1814, the Newgate Chaplain Dr Forde did little for his annual fee of £300 except attend chapel and visit condemned prisoners. He never attended the gaol's infirmary, never saw prisoners in private and took no interest in the welfare of the children held in the gaol.

➤ Dead Man's Walk: the graveyard for murderers in Newgate, 1897

A narrow passage connected Newgate Gaol and the adjoining Sessions House, through which prisoners walked to and from their trial. It was named Birdcage Walk because it was open to the air but covered with an iron grating. It was also known as Dead Man's Walk because it was the last walking place of those awaiting execution and 97 executed prisoners are recorded to have been buried in quicklime under the paving slabs in the passage. The letters on the wall at the left are the initial letters of the surnames of those buried, recording their approximate burial places in the passage. The row of letters T, B, I, D and T indicate the burial place of the five executed Cato Street conspirators: Thistlewood, Brunt, Ings, Davidson and Tidd. Dr Neill Cream was also buried here after his execution in Newgate in 1892, and Franz Muller, who was hanged outside the gaol, was buried here in 1864.

➤ Interior of the chapel of Newgate Gaol, 1897

Male prisoners sat behind the railings in the centre of this photograph. Female prisoners sat in the gallery behind the tall slanting boards so that they could see the Chaplain but not the male prisoners.

◄ John Howard, prison reformer

Howard was the High Sheriff of Bedfordshire and so saw the terrible conditions in prisons. He toured many British prisons in 1774 and published *The State of the Prisons* in 1777. He argued for humane conditions and better design of prisons. Many penal reform groups around the world bear his name.

▲ Taking a prisoner's photograph

From the late 19th century, all prisoners in Newgate were photographed and their personal details and crimes were recorded in registers that are now held in the Public Record Office at Kew.

▼ Prisoners at exercise

The small exercise yard, or Press Yard, at Newgate was replaced by larger exercise yards as a result of the campaigns of John Howard and Mrs Fry. The prisoners in this drawing of 1873, wearing their own clothes, were probably in custody awaiting trial. Conversation in the exercise yard was prohibited.

◄ Mrs Elizabeth Fry, prison reformer

Mrs Fry was a Quaker who began visiting Newgate in 1813. She was shocked by the disgusting smell and the sight of starving, drunk women, with babies, lying on filthy stone floors for lack of bedding. She formed the 'Association for the improvement of the female prisoners in Newgate' and campaigned for change. She was successful in improving women's conditions (better food, clothing and bedding) and secured the replacement of the male gaolers in the women's side of Newgate with a matron and female officers. She also encouraged women prisoners to keep clean and reform themselves.

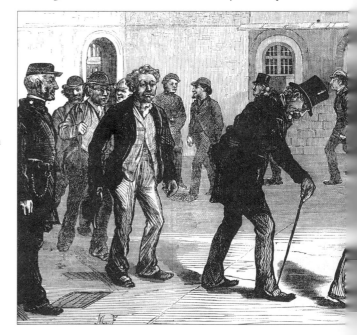

▲ A cell in Newgate, 1897
This is one of the cells in the new block, built in 1858. A prisoner's bedding is rolled up in the corner.

► The pinioning jacket
This was used to restrain prisoners who became violent or who had to be moved outside the prison and might try to escape. This drawing from *The Illustrated London News* of 1873 shows it being worn by a visitor to the prison.

▲ The exercise yard for female prisoners at Newgate
This was the central courtyard of Newgate after the rebuilding of 1858. The other exercise yards were on the other side of the wall tipped with iron spikes.

▼ The collection of plaster casts
Casts were taken from the heads of some of the murderers executed at Newgate, including Franz Muller. Following the demolition of the gaol, many of the casts were passed to Scotland Yard and they are now held in the Criminal Museum there.

▼ Visiting day
This drawing, from *The Illustrated London News* in 1873, shows how visitors were permitted to speak to prisoners through an iron grille.

The Fleet Prison

THE FLEET PRISON is the best known of the London debtor prisons. It was also the first building in London that was specifically designed to be a gaol. It was built in the 12th century, beyond the walls of the City of London, on an island formed between the east side of the Fleet River and some ditches filled with stagnant and foul water. The original prison had to be rebuilt in the reign of Edward III and again after it was razed by Wat Tyler's rebels in 1381. In the early years, the prison was used not only for debtors but also for those in contempt of the Royal Courts and those convicted in the Court of Star Chamber. Distinguished prisoners in the 16th and 17th centuries included the Earl of Surrey in 1543, the Earl of Pembroke in 1601 and the poet John Donne, later Dean of St Paul's Cathedral, also in 1601. The Fleet was later used principally to hold bankrupts and debtors, many of them famous such as William Penn. Debtors begged for money from passers-by through a heavily barred window. The Fleet was again burned in the Great Fire and in the Gordon riots of 1780 but rebuilt each time.

The Fleet was the scene of cruelty, extortion, drunkenness and depravity. The office of Keeper, or Warden, of the Fleet was hereditary (and could be sold). It included the right to receive fees from prisoners for their food, lodging or for short-term release into the lawless area surrounding the prison known as the Rules or Liberties of the Fleet. The Keeper of the Fleet made so much money out of the inmates that one Keeper named John Huggins purchased the office in the early 18th century for £5,000. Huggins later sold his office to his deputy warden, a solicitor named Thomas Bambridge, also for £5,000. Both Huggins and Bambridge extorted enormous fees from prisoners. None of the staff in the Fleet were paid and so they also lived on the fees that they levied from the prisoners. Some of the Fleet's inmates could afford the fees; they were wealthy men who had run up large debts and used the Fleet to hide temporarily from their creditors. The Fleet had some pleasures for the wealthy. It had spacious, comfortable rooms on the Master's Side, a taproom and a coffee-room. Racquets or rackets was played in the courtyard (a prisoner, Robert Mackay, became world rackets champion in 1820). However, the poorer inmates might lose their last possessions as garnish and have to hand over any proceeds of begging, or money received from family and friends, to the turnkeys. Many of the men, women and children lived in dirty conditions with no medical attention, particularly in a cellar named Bartholomew Fair, where the poorest prisoners lodged. Men and women drank heavily, mixed freely and often fought each other. The Fleet was also described as the largest brothel in England. Women in the Fleet sold themselves in order to be able to pay for better conditions. Prostitutes from outside the prison were able to visit inmates, especially the wealthier prisoners, without difficulty if they paid a fee to the gaolers.

The Fleet was also a popular venue for clandestine or irregular marriages (that is without licence or banns) from about 1680 until 1754. Marriages were performed in the prison chapel (for fees payable to the prison chaplain and warders) and then in marriage houses or taverns in the Rules of the Fleet. As many as 70 clergymen worked in the Fleet marriage trade over this period and the Fleet marriage registers record about 350,000 weddings.

Prisoners, their friends and relatives submitted petitions to Parliament in the period 1723-9 about the abuses at the Fleet. The petitions complained of the extortion and filthy conditions but also alleged that Huggins and Bambridge had murdered some prisoners. Parliament appointed a committee to investigate the abuses but Bambridge and Huggins were acquitted in a series of trials. Bambridge was finally removed as Keeper but conditions in the prison improved little and it remained overcrowded. In 1774, it held 243 prisoners (mostly debtors) and 475 others (mostly debtors' wives and children). Changes in the law gradually reduced the number of debtors in prison. The Fleet was closed in 1842 after serving as a prison for over 700 years. One prisoner had been there for 28 years.

▲ **The front of the Fleet Prison**
This engraving by Thomas Shepherd, published in 1827, shows the front of the Fleet Prison on Farringdon Street. A grate through which debtors begged is just behind the street lamp on the right.

The Fleet Prison

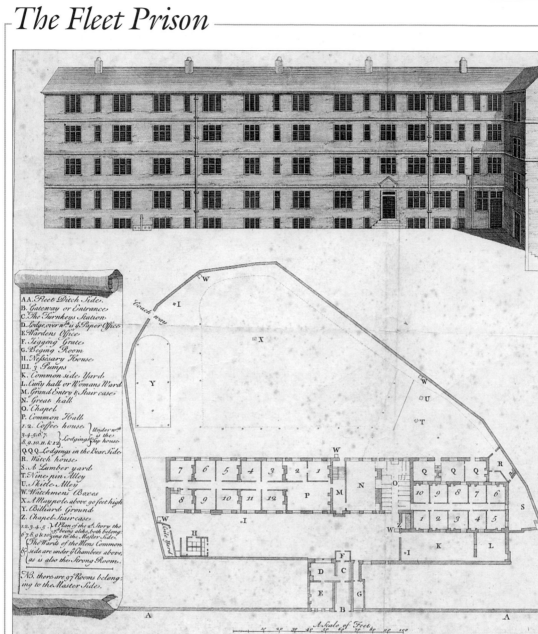

The plan legend reads:

A.A. Fleet Ditch Side.
B. Gateway or Entrance.
C. The Turnkeys Station.
D. Lodge, over w.ch is y Paper Office
E. Wardens Office.
F. Jigging Grate.
G. Beging Room.
H. Necessary House.
I.I.I. 3 Pumps.
K. Common side Yard.
L. Citty hall or Womans Ward.
M. Grand Entry & Stair cases.
N. Great hall.
O. Chapel.
P. Common Hall.
1.2. Coffee house.
3.4.5.6.7.
8.9.10.11.&12. } Under w.ch is the Tap house } Lodgings
Q.Q.Q. Lodgings in the Bear Side.
R. Watch house.
S. A Lumber yard.
T. Nine pin Alley.
U. Skitle Alley.
W. Watchmens Boxes.
X. A Maypole above 90 feet high.
Y. Billiard Ground.
Z. Chapel Stair cases.
1.2.3.4.5. } A Plan of the 2.d Story the
6.7.8.9.&10. } being alike, both belong
ing to the Master side.
The Wards of the Mens Common side are under y Chambers above as is also the Strong Room.
N.B. there are 97 Rooms belonging to the Master Side.

▲ Plan and elevation of the Fleet Prison, 1732
These drawings show the Fleet during the period of the trials of the Keepers Huggins and Bambridge.

➤ A courtyard in the Fleet Prison
This aquatint by Pugin and Rowlandson of 1808 shows the inner court of the prison, where the prisoners met and amused themselves with various games.

◄ 'Pray remember poor debtors'
The Fleet's inmates tried to support themselves by begging from passers-by through a grate in the wall.

➤ **The Keeper of the Fleet, Thomas Bambridge, before a Committee of the House of Commons at the Fleet**
A Parliamentary Committee was appointed to investigate the conditions in prisons in 1729. William Hogarth depicted the Committee's visit to the Fleet in February 1729 in a painting and this print. The Keeper Thomas Bambridge and his predecessor John Huggins were accused of extortion and murder. The Committee found that Bambridge had committed extortion, had taken bribes to permit escapes, put many prisoners in dungeons or irons and treated other prisoners in a 'cruel and barbarous manner'. Jacob Mendez Solas was placed in irons and thrown into a windowless dungeon, where he was held for two months. The dungeon was also used to hold the bodies (before their burial) of prisoners who died in the Fleet. Bambridge was also accused of murder. One prisoner, Robert Castell, had been deliberately exposed to smallpox when he was transferred from the Fleet to a sponging house in which smallpox was known to be raging. The Committee recommended the prosecution of both Bambridge and Huggins. They were committed to Newgate. Huggins was tried at the Old Bailey Sessions House in May 1729 for the murder of a prisoner, Edward Arne, who had been thrown in a dungeon by a prisoner who acted as a watchman at the Fleet. Huggins was said to have seen Arne twice in the dungeon, knowing that it was a death-trap but left him there despite Arne's pleas for mercy. Huggins blamed a deputy warden, named Gibbon, who had died by the date of the trial. The jury decided to give a special verdict. They stated that they were satisfied that Huggins knew the dangers of the dungeon, that Arne died as a result of being held there and that Huggins had seen Arne there 15 days before he died. Other courts then had to decide what this special verdict meant. Judges finally decided that Huggins must be acquitted because the verdict did not state that he was guilty of murder. Bambridge was tried in May for the murder of Robert Castell but was also acquitted for lack of evidence that he had been responsible for Castell catching smallpox. At this time, relatives of the deceased were entitled to insist on a second trial, by way of appeal. Bambridge was tried again, in January 1730, before Lord Chief Justice Raymond at Guildhall, but again acquitted by a jury. Bambridge also obtained an acquittal on a charge of stealing jewellery and other valuables from a prisoner, Elizabeth Berkeley. A special Act of Parliament was required to dismiss Bambridge from his position as Keeper. He committed suicide by cutting his throat about 20 years later.

Bridewell

▼ Bridewell Palace

Henry VIII's palace at Bridewell, where the Fleet River flowed into the Thames, was completed in 1520. However, its use soon changed. The poor and sick had relied for centuries on alms from the monasteries. Following the dissolution of the monasteries in the years after 1536, the poor had no means of support except charity. London was hardest hit since it attracted those hunting for work. It was soon said that beggars, drunkards and organised bands of thieves were 'swarming in the streets'. Petty theft and other crime also increased. Bridewell Palace was little used and therefore granted by Edward VI to the Corporation of the City of London for use as a hospital but for 'moral, not physical deformities'.

Bridewell became a House of Correction and House of Occupation, with two purposes, first as a training institute for destitute youths and second as a workhouse and house of punishment for vagrants, beggars, paupers, 'disorderly women' (that is, prostitutes) and petty offenders. Poverty and sickness were seen no differently from crime and were dealt with severely. Punishment and labour would, it was thought, reform the work-shy, drunkards and criminals. Bridewell was reopened on 16 December 1556. On that first day a woman was whipped at Bridewell and then pilloried in Cheapside for having abandoned her baby. In the next few years, many Roman Catholics, non-conformists and petty offenders were also imprisoned in Bridewell. It became notorious for chastising vagrants and prostitutes. They were whipped on arrival (12 lashes for adults and six for children) and disobedience led to further lashes. At first, whippings took place in a room next to the courtroom but, by 1638, a ducking-stool, stocks and whipping-post had been installed in one of the courtyards. Large crowds gathered twice a week for the public floggings of half-naked prisoners. The prisoners were given work; some with an element of skill, such as spinning, but most of it was little more than punishment, such as beating hemp, operating treadmills and cleaning sewers. The Bridewell regime (and its name) was copied elsewhere in London, for example at Westminster and in many other places in England.

▶ The Pass-Room at Bridewell

This aquatint by Pugin and Rowlandson of 1808 shows the women's Pass-Room at Bridewell. Paupers and vagrants who claimed a legal right of settlement in other parts of the country were confined for seven days before being sent off to those parishes. They were held in this room in Bridewell.

▼ Bridewell

Most of Bridewell was destroyed in the Great Fire but it was rebuilt as shown in this engraving. The stocks can be seen against the wall in the nearest courtyard. The flogging of women was abolished in 1791 and the prison was closed in 1855 (the last prisoners were transferred to Holloway). Most of the buildings were demolished in 1863. The Unilever Building now occupies part of the site.

Southwark

SOUTHWARK was the pleasure ground for London for centuries. In addition to its markets and taverns, there were gaming-houses, brothels on Bankside, theatres such as the Globe and bear-baiting and bull-baiting rings. Southwark was also a sanctuary for criminals. Even after the City of London gained jurisdiction over Southwark in 1556, there were areas, such as the Mint, where criminals felt secure from officers of the law. Despite this, Southwark's prisons were never short of clients. The area contained the Clink Prison, the Marshalsea, the White Lyon Prison, Borough Compter, Horsemonger Lane Gaol and the King's (Queen's) Bench Prison.

The Borough Compter was also known as the Southwark Compter. It was built in the 16th century inside the old parish church of St Margaret's (which also housed an Assize court). The Compter was used principally to hold debtors or petty offenders from Southwark. It was destroyed by fire in 1676 and a new Compter was built in part of the sprawling buildings of the Marshalsea Prison. Another new compter was built in 1787 on Mill Lane (running north from Tooley Street) in Bermondsey. This Compter was destroyed in the Gordon riots but an enlarged prison was built on the site. It was converted to a female prison in 1848, closed in 1852 and demolished in 1855.

▼ **Extract from John Rocque's map of the cities of London and Westminster, 1746, showing the south end of London Bridge and Southwark**

This map includes the southern end of London Bridge, the gateway to Southwark. The Marshalsea and the King's Bench Prison are marked, on the east side of Borough High Street. The map also includes Clink Street, the site of the Clink Prison, near the south bank of the Thames.

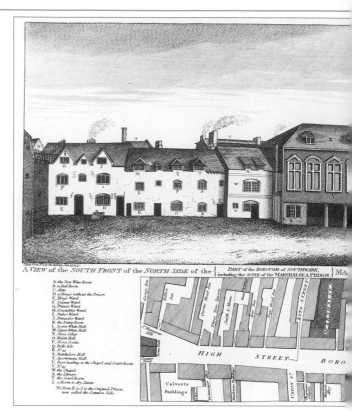

A VIEW of the SOUTH FRONT of the NORTH SIDE of the { PART of the BOROUGH of SOUTHWARK, including the SCITE of the MARSHALSEA PRISON.

A. the New Wine Room.
B. a Bed Room.
C. ditto.
D. a House without the Prison.
E. Kings Ward.
F. Queens Ward.
G. Princes Ward.
H. Constables Ward.
I. Dukes Ward.
J. Princes's Ward.
K. the Pump Room.
L. Lower White Hall.
M. Upper White Hall.
N. Stone Cellar.
O. Welsh Hall.
P. Nova Scotia.
Q. Belle Isle.
R. No 4.
S. Batchelor Hall.
T. Sportsmens Hall.
U. Door leading to the Chapel and Court Room.
V. No 1.
W. the Chapel.
X. the Library.
Y. the Court Room.
Z. a Room to dry Linen.

N.B. From E. to 3 is the Original Prison, now called the Common Side.

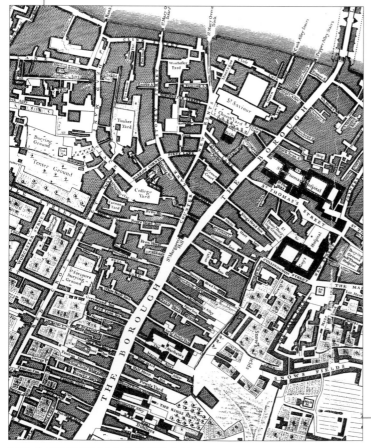

▲ **The Marshalsea Prison, Southwark**

The Marshalsea Prison in Southwark was probably built in the 14th century. Its name derives from the court once held by the Steward and Marshal of the Royal Household. This court moved with the King during his travels round the realm and had jurisdiction for 12 miles around his lodging (members of the King's Household were therefore subject to his court rather than a local one). The Marshalsea Prison was built in Southwark to house prisoners of this court. It acquired a reputation for vicious treatment of its inmates and was destroyed by Wat Tyler's rebels in 1381. The Marshalsea was rebuilt and then also held debtors. The prison grew and soon occupied a group of ramshackle buildings. Some comfort was available to wealthy prisoners but poor prisoners lived in squalor. During the Reformation, both Catholics and Protestants were held and brutally treated here, some in the lowest dungeon known as the Hole, or 'Bonner's Coal hole' after the last Catholic Bishop of London, who caused so many to be incarcerated here. A Protestant martyr, Gratwick, was held here in 1557 then burned in St George's Fields. When Elizabeth came to the throne, Bishop Bonner was brought here and died a prisoner in 1569. During Elizabeth's reign, the Marshalsea was used to hold many Catholics and became the most important of London's prisons after the Tower. In later years, most inmates at the Marshalsea were debtors

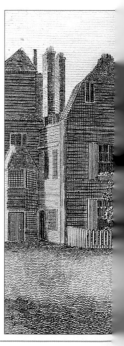

but other offenders were also incarcerated here. In the late 18th century, about 300 prisoners were held at any one time in very poor conditions. The Keeper, a butcher named William Acton (who paid £400 rent a year for the prison), recouped his money by extracting fees from inmates, sometimes by torture. Thirty or forty prisoners might be shut overnight in small wards. Prisoners who did not have friends outside to send them food might starve. Many sick women had to lie on the floor. Sick men lay on rows of boards, one row above another, with a line of hammocks above them. It was reported that a day did not pass without one death and there were often up to eight or nine deaths each day. Acton was tried at the Surrey Assizes at Kingston in 1729 for the murder of a prisoner named Thomas Bliss. He had been beaten and then held in irons in the 'Strong Room', a lean-to near the sewer, which was damp, dark and unventilated. Acton wanted to amuse some visitors one day and so sent for Bliss and put on him various instruments of torture: an iron skull cap, an iron collar and thumbscrews. Bliss had been a healthy man but was broken by this treatment and died soon after. Acton claimed that Bliss had been committed to the Strong Room because he had tried to escape and that his death had been caused by his catching a cold. Acton was also tried for the murders of John Bromfield, Robert Newton and James Thompson. They had also died in dungeons. Acton claimed that one of the deceased had stabbed another prisoner, another had tried to escape (and that all three had died of natural causes). Inquests had not been held on any

of the bodies. The judge made comments suggesting that Acton should be convicted but he was acquitted of all charges. It is unknown whether the jurors believed Acton's defences or were bribed or just had no interest in the fate of debtors and criminals. This engraving of the Marshalsea in 1773 was published in 1812. The different rooms or areas of the prison are listed; including the wards, chapel, library, lodging rooms, chandler's shop and drinking rooms. Some of the rooms had fanciful, inappropriate, names such as Nova Scotia, Belle Isle and Sportsman's Hall.

▲ **The interior of the White Lyon Prison, Southwark**
The White Lyon in Southwark was a small prison for the county of Surrey, situated on Borough High Street, near the Marshalsea and King's Bench Prisons. It was probably an inn that was converted into a gaol in the 16th century and it does not appear to have been used after about 1700. This watercolour by John Crowther dates from 1887, long after the prison closed.

◄ **A view of the interior of the Marshalsea**
By 1801, the Marshalsea was badly in need of repair and held only 34 prisoners (with eight of their wives and seven children). This engraving shows the buildings at that time. The prison was moved to a site north of St George's Church. In 1811, the government purchased the adjacent building (formerly the White Lyon Prison) and a new Marshalsea Prison was built on the combined site. This held debtors and petty offenders but also had two cells reserved for smugglers. Dickens' father was imprisoned for debt in the Marshalsea for three months in 1824. In his novel *Little Dorrit*, Dickens described the prison, in which the heroine was born, as 'partitioned into squalid houses standing back to back … hemmed in by high walls duly spiked at the top'. The prisoners in the Marshalsea were transferred to the Queen's Bench Prison in 1842. The Marshalsea was closed and the buildings demolished in 1897.

◄ **The Gordon riots, 1780: the mob setting fire to the King's Bench Prison and House of Correction in St George's Fields**
The first King's Bench Prison was built in the 14th century to the east of Borough High Street in Southwark, to hold prisoners for the Court of King's Bench. It was burned by Wat Tyler's rebels in 1381 but rebuilt. Many of the inmates were debtors but it was also used to hold Catholics and Protestants during the religious ferment of the 16th century. Conditions in the prison depended on the wealth of a prisoner (and his family and friends). Some lived in relative comfort but an inquiry of 1754 revealed many irregularities in the prison, including extortion and cruelty by the gaolers, overcrowding, filth, promiscuity and drunkenness amongst the prisoners. A new, larger King's Bench Prison, with 224 rooms and a courtyard surrounded by a high wall, was built in St George's Fields, on the corner of the present Borough Road and Borough High Street, in 1755-8. John Wilkes was imprisoned here from 1768 to 1770 for libel. The prison was burned in 1780 in the Gordon riots but quickly rebuilt.

◄ **A courtyard of the King's Bench Prison**
This aquatint of 1808 by Pugin and Rowlandson shows the high walls and courtyard of the prison after it was rebuilt in 1780. Rich prisoners enjoyed the prison's taproom, wine room and market (including a chandler's shop, a butcher's shop and a surgery). There were also up to 30 gin shops. A historian described the prison, in 1828, as 'the most desirable place of incarceration in England'. For a small fee, prisoners could obtain leave of

absence for a few days. For a larger fee, prisoners were allowed to live in the Liberties or Rules of the King's Bench, an area surrounding the prison that included St George's Fields and many taverns. Poor prisoners survived by holding a begging-box at the prison gate. They lived in filthy and overcrowded wards in conditions of 'vice, debauchery and drunkenness'. There was a sickening stench and the constant threat of gaol fever.

▲ **Sketches in the King's Bench Prison**
After the accession of Queen Victoria, the King's Bench was renamed the Queen's Bench Prison and received the remaining inmates from the Marshalsea and Fleet Prisons. Following the abolition of imprisonment for debt in 1869, the Queen's Bench was used as a military prison, then demolished in 1880. These drawings from *The Illustrated London News* in 1880 show the buildings just before their demolition, including the poor debtors' side at the lower right.

◄ **Gentlemen debtors**
The King's Bench Prison held many wealthy men and members of the upper classes. Some were debtors and some were convicted criminals. Lord Cochrane was found guilty of Stock Exchange frauds and imprisoned here in 1815. He made a dramatic escape over the prison walls using a rope that broke when he was 20 feet from the ground. However, he survived and went to the House of Commons to take up his seat, as MP for Westminster.

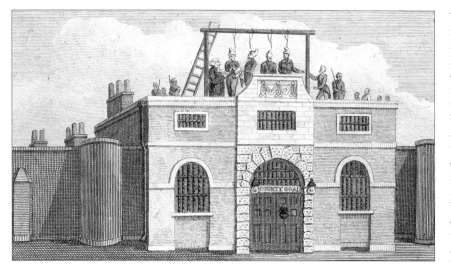

▲ The Surrey County Gaol in Horsemonger Lane

Horsemonger Lane Gaol was originally known as the New Gaol and built (1791-98) as the Surrey County Gaol for 400 prisoners. Behind a gatehouse was a three-storey quadrangle with three wings for petty criminals and a fourth for debtors. It was closed in 1878 and demolished in 1880. Executions took place outside the gaol or on the roof of the gatehouse. Mr and Mrs Manning were executed here in 1849 for murdering their lodger. This illustration shows the execution in 1803 of Colonel Edward Marcus Despard for treason. He was alleged to have plotted to assassinate the King and seize the Tower. Despard was born in Ireland, served in the army and was promoted to Colonel. Whilst serving in Honduras, some inhabitants accused him of various misdemeanours. He returned to England and was finally told, after two years, that there was no case against him worthy of investigation. He now had no official post but he did have a grievance against the authorities for their delay. He came into contact with some radical groups and reports on his activities were passed to the government. As a result, on the outbreak of the Irish rebellion in 1798, Despard was arrested as a 'suspected character' and imprisoned in Coldbath Fields. He claimed to have been treated cruelly and was released but he was then re-arrested and remained in custody until 1800. Despard was then drawn even more closely to radical associates at a time when the government was alarmed at the possibility of revolution in Britain following events in France since 1789 and the Irish rebellion. Government spies reported a conspiracy, involving Despard, to murder George III and overthrow the government. Despard and nearly 40 other soldiers and labourers were arrested at the *Oakley Arms* in Lambeth in November 1802 and examined by Magistrates at Union Hall in the Borough. Despard remained silent. He was committed to Newgate under a statute 'against seducing soldiers from their duty' and 32 other men were sent to Tothill Fields Bridewell or Clerkenwell New Prison. Despard was tried for treason on 7 February 1803 but again remained silent. The government relied on evidence from a defector from the alleged conspiracy who claimed that he had heard Despard and others discussing the kidnapping of the King. The jury found Despard guilty but recommended him to the King's mercy on account of his previous service to his country. He was sentenced to death. Twelve other prisoners were tried and nine were condemned.

Three were recommended for mercy and respited but the other six, John Francis and John Wood (both soldiers), Thomas Broughton and John Macnamara (both carpenters), James Wratton (a shoe-maker) and Arthur Graham (a slater), were to be executed with Despard. Traitors should have been hanged, drawn and quartered but this had been modified to hanging (until death) followed by decapitation. The executions took place at the New Gaol (later called Horse-monger Lane Gaol) on 21 February 1803. The drop, scaffold and gallows were erected on top of the gaol and soldiers were stationed on nearby roads. A block on which the condemned were to be beheaded was placed near the scaffold with bags of sawdust to soak up blood. The executioner, William Brunskill, then hanged the men. Despard's body was cut down first. His head was placed on the block and severed by a masked man. He took the head by the hair, showed it to the crowd and shouted 'This is the head of a traitor, Edward Marcus Despard'. The other bodies were then cut down, their heads severed and exhibited to the crowd with the announce-ment 'This is the head of another traitor'. The bodies were then taken away for burial.

▼ The Gatehouse, Westminster

The Gatehouse Prison was built in about 1370 in rooms over two gates, at right angles to each other, near Westminster Abbey (there were also some cells in the basement of the gates). One gate looked to the north and included the Bishop of London's prison for convicted clerics. The other gate looked to the west (across what is now Victoria Street) and included a gaol for lay offenders. Sir Walter Raleigh spent his last night here in 1618 before his execution in Old Palace Yard, Westminster. Samuel Pepys was held here for three weeks in 1690 on suspicion of supporting King James II (then in exile). In 1672, a female keeper of the prison was tried for cruelty and extorting fees from prisoners. The highwayman Maclane was also held here in 1750 awaiting his trial. Most of the Gatehouse was demolished in 1776.

▲ The Savoy

The Savoy Palace was built between the Thames and the Strand in the 13th century. It passed to the Earls and Dukes of Lancaster (and became the headquarters of the great Duchy of Lancaster) but was almost completely destroyed by Tyler's rebels in 1381. The palace was restored in the 16th century and became a hospital. However, the hospital declined within a few years and criminals stayed there, or in its grounds (part of the lawless area of Alsatia), claiming sanctuary from the law. The buildings were gradually converted to other uses, including an army barracks. A military prison was built on part of the site in 1695 and used to hold deserters or the army's offenders. Two deserters incarcerated here in 1749 were named Hartley and South, who were sentenced to death, marched to a spot near Tyburn that was used for military executions and shot. The Savoy also held men who had been pressed into the army (until they were sent to regiments) and convicts who were granted the option of military service over hanging. Daniel Defoe stated that the Savoy also included a civil prison, called 'The Dutchy', possibly named after the Duchy of Lancaster. The barracks burned down in 1776 but the military prison survived about another 20 years (this print was published in 1793, shortly before it closed). The site is now occupied by the *Savoy Hotel*, the Savoy Theatre and Embankment Gardens.

▼ David Dignan and George Barrington – prisoners on the hulks

David Dignan was committed to Tothill Fields Bridewell in 1777 and convicted at Westminster Guildhall for defrauding John Clark. He was sentenced to five years' hard labour in the hulks on the Thames. Dignan had defrauded Clark by pretending to procure, for a fee of £100, his appointment as a Customs officer in Dublin. Dignan had handed over a warrant to that effect signed by Lord Weymouth but it had been forged by Dignan. He was wealthy (probably as a result of other frauds that he had committed) and took a servant with him to the hulks at Woolwich. Dignan hoped that the servant could remain with him on the hulks but this was not permitted. Dignan attempted a further fraud, involving a promissory note for £500, while imprisoned on the hulk. His fraudulent scheme was exposed before any victim loaned money on the note.

George Barrington was known as the gentleman-pickpocket. He was well educated, well dressed and haunted those places that were frequented by the wealthier classes. Barrington's real surname was Waldron. He was born in Ireland in about 1755. He gained a good education but stabbed a fellow pupil with a penknife during a quarrel and was flogged. He then stole 10 guineas and a watch from his schoolmaster and ran away. He joined a company of travelling players, changed his name to Barrington and then began a career as a pickpocket. He moved to London in 1773 and was caught stealing a watch from a woman at Drury Lane Theatre in 1777. He was convicted at the Old Bailey Sessions in 1777 and sentenced to three years' hard labour on the hulk *Justitia*. After about a year he arranged for a petition to be presented to the court, praying that the remaining part of his sentence be remitted because of his good behaviour. The officers of the *Justitia* made a favourable report and Barrington was released. However, he was arrested a few days later for picking a pocket at St Sepulchre's Church. He was searched and various stolen goods were found on him. He was convicted in April 1778 and sentenced to another five years' hard labour on the hulks. Barrington obtained an early release on condition of his leaving England but, after short periods in Dublin and Edinburgh, he rather stupidly returned to London and again worked as a pickpocket. He was arrested for having returned to England in breach of the condition for his remission and held in Newgate for the remainder of the period that he should have served on the hulks. On his release, Barrington returned to picking pockets and was again arrested for the theft of a watch and 20 guineas at Enfield races on 1 September 1790. He was transported to New South Wales.

Tothill Fields Prison

▲ Tothill Fields Prison

Westminster Bridewell was built in 1618, at the north end of present-day Rochester Row, to hold petty offenders and vagrants. This Bridewell was the setting for Hogarth's engraving of the Harlot beating hemp (see page 191). It was closed in 1834. A new Tothill Fields Prison was erected on the north side of Francis Street. This large prison, with 549 cells holding up to 900 prisoners, is shown in this bird's-eye view which dates from about 1860.

◤ Boys exercising at Tothill Fields Prison

In 1862, Mayhew and Binney calculated that 12,000 juveniles passed through British gaols each year. Children were imprisoned for the most trivial of offences. One of the boys that they interviewed was aged 13. He had been imprisoned seven times in Tothill Fields and three times in Coldbath Fields. Mayhew watched boys such as those in this drawing trudging around the yard in Tothill Fields. He thought it ridiculous that such great efforts (visiting justices, warders, keys and cutlasses) were deemed necessary to hold the 'little desperate malefactors'. Many of them were so young that 'they seem better fitted to be conveyed to the place in a perambulator than in a lumbering and formidable prison van'. Tothill Fields was closed in 1884 and Westminster Cathedral stands on part of the site.

➤ Mothers and children exercising at Tothill Fields Prison

For centuries it was common for mothers to be imprisoned with their babies or small children and for debtors to be imprisoned with their families. However, many children were imprisoned because of their own crimes. Most of them never had any education apart from a schooling in crime from other criminals in the prison. Action was taken in 1845 to prevent children mixing with adult offenders. It was decided that

Coldbath Fields would hold only adult male convicts and Tothill Fields Prison would hold only males under the age of 17 and women. This drawing of 1860 shows women prisoners exercising in the prison yard with their children.

Hulks

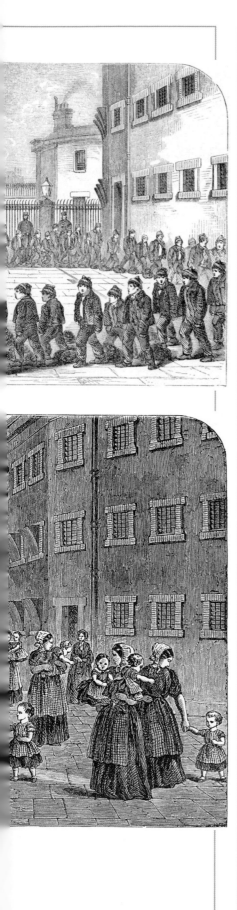

▲ **The *Warrior* convict hulk, Woolwich**
Thousands of criminals were transported to the British colonies in North America and the West Indies. The American Revolution prevented further transportation to North America and English prisons faced a severe problem of overcrowding. As a temporary solution, obsolete warships known as hulks were used as floating prisons and the convicts were put to hard labour ashore, including breaking rocks. The first hulk, *Justitia*, was anchored near Woolwich in 1776. When transportation recommenced, this time to Australia, the hulks were used to hold convicts until they boarded one of the transport ships that sailed in the convict fleets. By 1841, there were 11 hulks (holding 3,625 convicts) moored in the Thames or at Plymouth, Portsmouth, Sheerness, Chatham, Bermuda and Gibraltar. This drawing of 1846 shows the hulk *Warrior* at Woolwich. Hulks remained in use in England until 1859.

▼ **Inside the hulk**
Conditions on the hulks were dreadful, the food practically inedible and sanitary provision almost non-existent. Many convicts had to wear leg-irons and their clothes and bedding were infested with vermin. Deaths or illness from scurvy, typhus or dysentery were commonplace. The convicts on hulks also suffered badly during outbreaks of cholera. Within the first 18 months of use of the *Justitia*, 176 of the 632 convicts taken on board had died. Conditions did not improve much. The hulk *Warrior* held 638 convicts in 1841. Four hundred of these were admitted to hospital and 38 died.

Clerkenwell

CLERKENWELL was a hamlet to the north of the walls of the City of London. Its population increased rapidly from the 16th century, mainly by overspill from the crowded City streets. Sessions of the Justices of the Peace were held from 1612, in Hicks' Hall on St John Street and later at the Sessions House on Clerkenwell Green. Three prisons were built in Clerkenwell: a Bridewell, the New Prison (later called the House of Detention) and the House of Correction at Coldbath Fields.

◄ Samuel Bonner in Clerkenwell Bridewell, 1778

An Act of 1609 required each county to build a Bridewell to set 'rogues' and 'idle persons' to work. The Middlesex Bridewell opened in 1615 at Clerkenwell for the punishment and employment of the rogues and vagabonds of Middlesex. From the early 18th century, Bridewells were also used to hold offenders and suspects awaiting trial. In 1778, Samuel Bonner wrote a threatening letter to Mrs Sarah Teshmaker with intent to extort money from her. He was arrested and held in Clerkenwell Bridewell to await his trial. He is seen here begging Mr Day, an officer of the justices, to intercede for him as it was his first offence. Bonner was sentenced to death at his trial at the Old Bailey in December 1778 but was subsequently pardoned. The Bridewell was demolished in 1804.

▶ New Prison, Clerkenwell

The New Prison was built to the south of the Bridewell. It was burned down by prisoners in 1679 but rebuilt. Jack Sheppard and Edgworth Bess escaped from this prison in 1724. The New Prison was enlarged in 1774, to relieve the overcrowding in Newgate Gaol. Conditions at the New Prison were poor. Prisoners were crowded into cells and the Keeper and turnkeys extorted fees from the inmates (as payment for better cells, food or for sex with other inmates). This engraving of the New Prison dates from 1809. It was rebuilt and enlarged to hold 240 prisoners in 1818, utilising the site of the Bridewell.

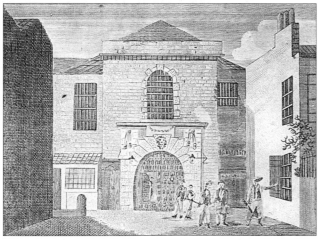

▲ Gate of the House of Detention, Clerkenwell
This engraving of 1860 shows the enormous gate of the prison that was built in 1846.

▼ Bird's-eye view of the House of Detention, Clerkenwell, 1860
The New Prison was rebuilt again in 1846, as shown in this engraving of 1860. It was renamed as the Clerkenwell House of Detention and designed to hold prisoners on remand. The two wings in the foreground of this illustration were for women, the two behind were for men. The prison's exercise yards can be seen in the background. It had 216 cells designed for single occupation but two or three prisoners were often held in the same cell. The House of Detention was the busiest prison in London between 1846 and 1878 because prisoners were held for only a short period, awaiting trial. In 1859 alone 5,422 men and 2,292 women passed through the gates. An attempt was made to rescue two Fenian prisoners, Richard Burke and Joseph Casey, from the House of Detention in 1867 (see page 42). The prison wall and a row of houses opposite were blown down, 12 people were killed and many injured.

The rescue failed and one of the bombers, Michael Barrett, was hanged outside Newgate in May 1868.

▲ Prisoners removed to Newgate
This drawing shows prisoners being marched (in a rather disorderly manner) from the New Prison to Newgate Gaol in the 18th century to await their trials at the Old Bailey Sessions House.

The House of Detention

▲ The collection of prisoners at the House of Detention

Black Marias were used to take prisoners from the House of Detention to their trials at Clerkenwell Sessions House or the Central Criminal Court. Some prisoners removed themselves from the House of Detention. William Hawkins was charged with theft and held in the prison in 1866. He was working in the prison's carpentry shop and used the tools to cut a hole in the wall. He fled, but only as far as a local pub, where he was found the same evening and taken back to prison.

► Interior of the House of Detention

After 1846 the House of Detention had galleries of cells in each block. Since most of the prisoners had not yet been tried, conditions were less unpleasant than in many other prisons and regular visits were permitted, as shown in this engraving of 1860. The House of Detention was closed in 1877 and much of it was demolished in 1890. The remaining parts of the prison, almost entirely underground, have been restored but are not open to the public at present.

Coldbath Fields Prison

▼ **Coldbath Fields Prison**
A House of Correction was built in 1794 on Coldbath Fields just to the north of the Bridewell and New Prison to house convicted criminals. Coldbath Fields was notorious for its severe regime and brutality. Punishments for the inmates included carrying cannonballs, sessions on the six treadmills or picking oakum (picking apart old ship ropes so that the fibre could be used again). Over 340 prisoners could work on the treadmills at a time and each prisoner might have to work on a treadmill for three or four hours a day. Prisoners were allowed to receive only one letter and one visit every three months. The management and staff of the prison were very corrupt. The first governor, Thomas Aris, was vicious and incompetent and the inmates in his care suffered from brutality, dietary cuts and overcrowding. Aris was not replaced until 1828. Conditions were so dreadful that the House of Correction was known as the Steel (after the Bastille) and, in 1799, Coleridge and Southey wrote in *The Devil's Thoughts*:

> As he went through Cold-Bath Fields he saw a solitary cell,
> And the devil was pleased, for it gave him a hint,
> For improving his prisons in Hell.

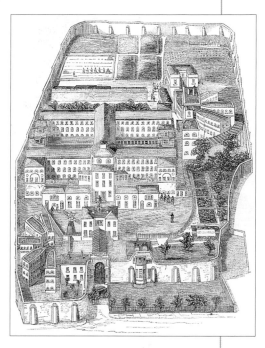

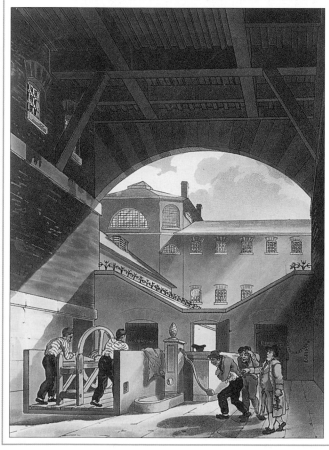

↗ **Bird's-eye view of Coldbath Fields Prison, 1860**
Coldbath Fields Prison was gradually expanded under the second governor, George Chesterton, to hold 1,150 prisoners. It became the largest prison in England. This view from 1860 shows the prison after its expansion. Ten thousand vagrants, drunks and petty thieves passed through Coldbath Fields each year. Chesterton rooted out corruption among the prison officers but he also had to control the inmates. In 1834, he introduced a regime of total silence and protesters were punished with leg-irons, solitary confinement and a diet of bread and water. Female prisoners were transferred to Tothill Fields Prison in 1850 but the prison remained overcrowded. About 1,450 prisoners were held at any one time at Coldbath Fields and this increased to about 1,700 in the 1870s. Up to half of them were imprisoned because they had failed to pay small fines and many others were petty offenders. Coldbath Fields was closed in 1885 and demolished in 1889. Mount Pleasant Post Office now occupies the site.

◄ **The water engine, Coldbath Fields**
This aquatint of 1808 by Pugin and Rowlandson shows two inmates at hard labour on the water pump. A turnkey is bringing two more inmates to relieve those on the pump.

Millbank Penitentiary

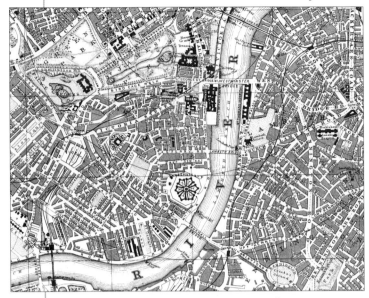

▲ **Plan of Millbank Penitentiary, Westminster and the surrounding area**
Millbank was built on marshy ground on the north bank of the Thames to hold convicts. It opened in 1816. This map from the late 19th century illustrates how Millbank was built in the shape of a six-pointed star within an outer octagonal wall (around which was a moat). Each point of the star was in the shape of a pentagon. In the centre of each pentagon was a tower from which warders could keep prisoners' blocks under perpetual surveillance. Millbank's corridors were three miles long and it had 1,000 cells. At the time, it was probably the largest prison in England.

◀ **Millbank Penitentiary in 1817**
The entrance to Millbank faced the river. This drawing of 1817 is a view of the prison from the opposite bank of the Thames.

▼ **The burial ground at Millbank**
The design of Millbank was based on Jeremy Bentham's ideas for prison management. The regime incorporated the separate system, designed to isolate convicts from each other and prevent them conspiring or corrupting each other. Prisoners were held in separate cells and forbidden to talk to each other

for the first half of their sentence so that they could contemplate their wicked lives. They were also given work (making shoes and mail-bags) and education to return them to the paths of righteousness. However, there was little concern for the prisoners' physical welfare. Epidemics of scurvy and cholera swept through the prison in 1822 and 1823. This illustration shows the prison's burial ground, alarmingly close to the vegetable patch! The burial registers of Millbank Penitentiary are held in the Public Record Office at Kew.

➤ **The reception ward at Millbank**
This drawing from *The Graphic* shows new inmates about to be examined by a medical officer. Convicts had to strip and bathe. They were searched for concealed weapons or other belongings, then examined by a doctor, principally for infectious disease, then measured, weighed and given a number.

➤ **Convicts at exercise**
Millbank was a costly failure. It did not reform criminals and the location, design and construction of the buildings made it damp and depressing. Pentonville Prison was opened to hold convicts in 1842 and this permitted the authorities to relegate Millbank to an ordinary prison and use it principally as a clearing depot for convicts prior to their transportation or transfer to other prisons. Its capacity was increased to about 1,500 prisoners (by the sharing of cells) and, since inmates were only held for a few months before transfer, over 4,000 passed through Millbank each year. It became a military prison in 1870, was closed in 1890 and demolished in 1903. The Tate Gallery now stands on the site.

▲ The central tower of one of the pentagons at Millbank Penitentiary
This photograph shows the block for female inmates and the central tower of one of the pentagons that gave a good view of the yards and blocks of cells.

➤ A cell in Millbank
This drawing from *The Graphic* shows a typical cell in Millbank. At first, prisoners were held in separate cells but this solitary system was found to send some prisoners insane. Furthermore, the severe mental problems of some offenders were discovered only after they had been convicted. Special cells were therefore built to hold them. The mad cell at Millbank had cushioned walls to prevent prisoners hurting themselves and an observation hole in the ceiling so that warders could see a prisoner in any part of the cell.

Brixton

▲ The House of Correction, Brixton

Brixton Prison was built in 1820 as a House of Correction for Surrey and is therefore the oldest of London's prisons that still receives prisoners. It was built for 175 but often held about 400 inmates. In addition, the cells were extremely small and so it became one of the unhealthiest of London's prisons. In 1821, Brixton became the first English prison to install a treadmill (see page 192) for prisoners who had been sentenced to hard-

labour. The treadmill was connected to corn-grinding equipment. The Surrey Magistrates closed Brixton in 1851 and built a new House of Correction at Wandsworth.

▼ Female convicts exercising at Brixton Prison

Brixton House of Correction was purchased by the government in 1853 to use as a prison for female convicts, who were now to face penal servitude at home rather than transportation to

Australia. Brixton was the first prison exclusively to hold female prisoners. The treadmill was replaced by a laundry so that the women had suitable work (taking washing from other prisons). The prison was in the charge of a woman superintendent instead of a male governor and was expanded to hold 700 convicts by the addition of further wings, a new chapel and houses for the superintendent and chaplain. However, many female convicts preferred transportation, followed by comparative liberty in Australia, to a long prison sentence in an overcrowded London prison. There were many disturbances and attacks on prison officers and Brixton's prisoners were transferred to Holloway. After serving as a military prison from 1882 to 1898, Brixton became the trial and remand prison for London and the Home Counties.

➤ The convict nursery at Brixton
Children over 12 months are now not allowed to stay with their mothers in prison. In earlier years, children were left in prison with their mothers until they were three or four years old.

▼ Plan of Brixton Prison, 1853
This plan is from a report of 1853 to Parliament by the Surveyor-General of Prisons concerning the discipline and management of the convict prisons. He reported the purchase of Brixton House of Correction and described the work being undertaken to rebuild it so as to hold female convicts.

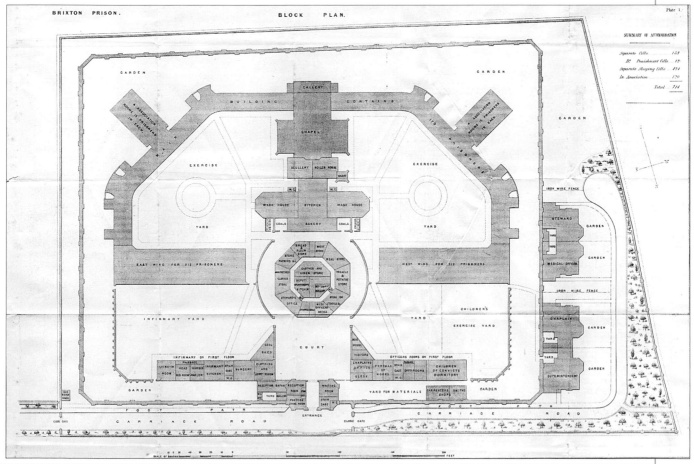

Wandsworth

▲ The Surrey House of Correction, Wandsworth

Wandsworth was built in 1851, as a House of Correction for Surrey, to hold 1,000 prisoners on the separate and silent system. The male section had five wings radiating from a central building. The female section was similar but had only three wings. Wandsworth had 100 cranks (see page 193) for those prisoners sentenced to hard labour. Most female prisoners worked in the laundry.

▶ A veiled female prisoner at Wandsworth

As part of the separate system, male prisoners wore masks and women wore veils. A prisoner's number was painted on his or her uniform and the cell number appeared on a brass disk on a man's arm or woman's belt. Warders addressed prisoners by their cell number rather than their name.

◀ An adult school in the chapel, on the separate system, in Wandsworth

Partitions between seats in the chapel ensured that prisoners could see only the chaplain (or a teacher during educational classes) and not the other prisoners.

▶ Letter-writing

Prisoners were permitted to write letters to family and friends. Times were fixed for the prisoners to write letters and the warders would then be kept busy reading them before they were sent.

▲ A Black Maria in Wandsworth
Wandsworth was used to hold short-term prisoners from 1877 and so Black Marias made regular visits to the prison. Oscar Wilde was held here for the first six months of his sentence in 1895. On the closure of Horsemonger Lane Gaol in 1878, executions for South London crimes were also carried out at Wandsworth. The prison gradually expanded and is now the largest in Britain.

Holloway

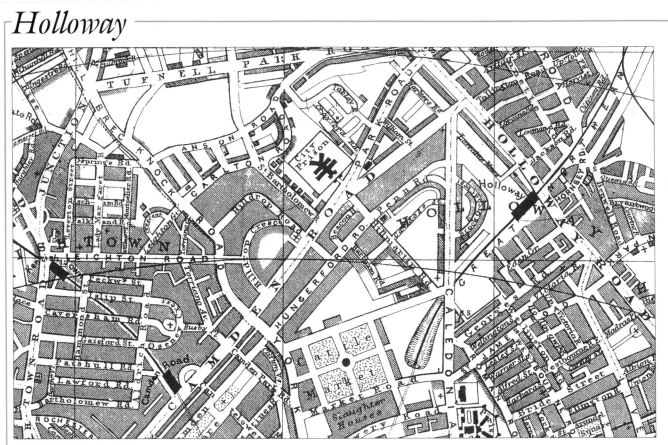

▲ **North Islington: Pentonville Prison and Holloway Gaol**
This map shows the relative proximity of Pentonville (opened in 1842) and Holloway (opened in 1852). Both prisons remain open although Holloway was completely rebuilt in 1979.

➤ **Holloway Gaol in 1897**
Holloway was taken into the state system of prisons in 1877 and then held some prisoners who had been convicted of serious offences. All female prisoners in the London area were transferred to Woking Prison in 1892 and, for a brief period, Holloway held only male prisoners (Oscar Wilde was held here in 1895, awaiting his trial). However, this policy was reversed in 1902 and only female prisoners were then held in Holloway. The prison was also enlarged to hold 975 inmates. Mrs Pankhurst and some other suffragettes were imprisoned here from 1906. A few days after the outbreak of the Second World War in 1939, Holloway's prisoners were transferred to Aylesbury Prison. Holloway was then used to hold people whose actions were thought to be prejudicial to the conduct of the war (including Sir Oswald Mosley and his wife) and also many people who were arrested simply because they were aliens. By 1942, Holloway had reverted to its role of holding convicted criminals. The first execution at Holloway took place in 1923. Edith Thompson was executed for allegedly murdering her husband in league with her lover Bywaters. She had to be heavily sedated when she was carried to the scaffold. Ruth Ellis was executed at Holloway in 1955, the last woman to be executed in Britain. The public outcry at the time should be contrasted with the lack of public interest when a Mrs Christofi, originally from Cyprus (an older, less attractive woman), was executed the year before.

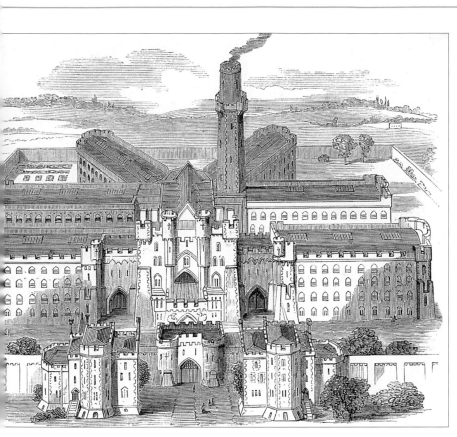

◄ **The House of Correction for the City of London, Holloway**
The Corporation of the City of London built this House of Correction to replace Giltspur Street Compter and relieve pressure on Newgate. It opened in 1852, held 350 prisoners and was known as Holloway Castle because of its tower (copied from Warwick Castle) and battlements. The words, 'May God preserve the City of London and make this place a terror to evil doers' were inscribed on its foundation stone. At first, communication between prisoners was forbidden but they received education, work (gardening and basketmaking) and there was a treadmill (which raised water for use in the prison). Daily attendance at chapel was compulsory.

Pentonville

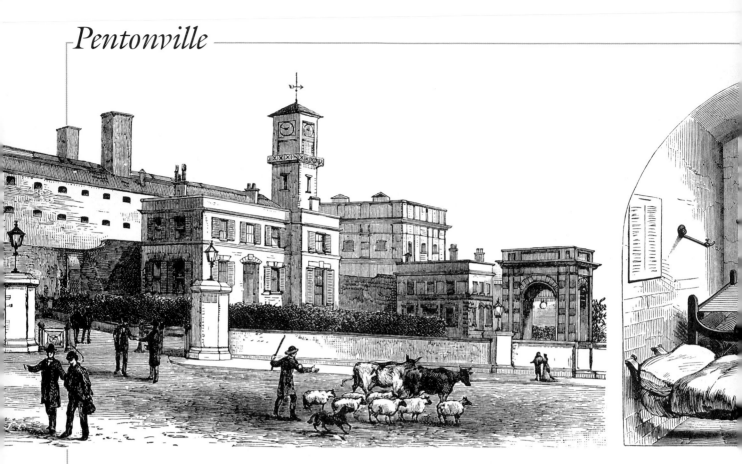

▲ **Pentonville Prison**
Pentonville Prison, on Caledonian Road, Islington, opened in 1842. It was built on the separate and silent system, with a 'frowning' entrance gate. It originally held convicts prior to their transportation.

◤ **A cell in Pentonville**
Prisoners had to wear masks to prevent them communicating or recognising each other. They worked, ate and slept alone in their cells.

➤ **Convicts exercising in Pentonville**
During the first part of their sentence, prisoners exercised alone in a small yard. They were later allowed to walk around a yard with other prisoners but they were not permitted to communicate with each other. This prolonged solitary confinement did not reform men to a life of honesty and virtue but drove some prisoners mad or to suicide. Masks were abolished and the exercise yards enlarged.

➤➤ **A corridor in Pentonville**
Transportation was replaced by long sentences of imprisonment with hard labour. Pentonville was one of the prisons used to hold these convicts. They had to work on hand cranks that did nothing but exhaust the inmates (they were said to 'grind the wind'). When Newgate was closed in 1902, its gallows was moved to Pentonville which became the hanging prison for North London (Wandsworth served the south). Those hanged at Pentonville included the murderers Crippen and Seddon but also Sir Roger Casement in 1916 (for treason in seeking German support for Irish nationalists). Pentonville Prison now holds about 800 prisoners serving short-term sentences.

Wormwood Scrubs

◄ **Wormwood Scrubs**
Wormwood Scrubs was built because of the failure of Millbank Penitentiary. It was constructed in the shape of four parallel blocks with an imposing gatehouse that incorporated the portraits of the prison reformers John Howard and Elizabeth Fry. The prison was built using convict labour (and completed in 1890) to hold 1,000 inmates, at that time the largest prison in Britain. Wormwood Scrubs cost only about £100,000 to build (mainly because of the use of convict labour) compared with the £450,000 that Millbank cost. It originally held both men and women serving short-term sentences but has held only men since 1902, including many imprisoned for serious offences. The cells (arranged in galleries) were large compared with other Victorian prisons, about ten by thirteen feet, with individual ventilation.

◄ **The search of a cell in Wormwood Scrubs**
This drawing, from *The Graphic* in 1889, shows a warder searching the cell of a convict before he is locked up for the night.

► **'Keeping the handcuffs bright': convict life in Wormwood Scrubs**
An attempt was made to provide prisoners with a more pleasant atmosphere than in earlier prisons but life in Wormwood Scrubs was hard. The prisoners' food was served to them in their cells and convicts worked on cranks and treadmills or had to pick oakum and make shoes, sacks and Post-office bags. This convict is engaged in the essential and fulfilling task of polishing the prison's store of handcuffs.

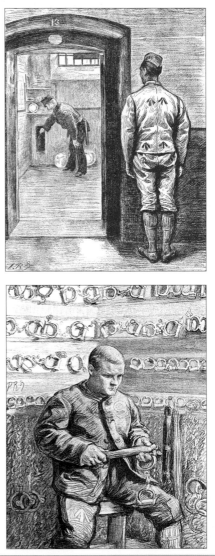

▲ **Dinner parade**

This drawing from *The Illustrated London News* shows convicts who worked as cooks at Wormwood Scrubs standing to attention and waiting for the governor. The arrows on the convicts' clothes are instantly recognisable to us as a symbol of a prisoner but were only used for about 50 years until 1922. The mark was originally used around 1700 to identify government stores, being copied from an arrow in the coat of arms of the Earl of Romney who was Master General of the Royal Ordnance from 1693 to 1702. The use of the mark on convict's clothes was intended to deter escapes because prisoners would find it difficult to move through the area around a prison in such distinctive clothes. Regulation clothes for today's prisoners are simple blue trousers and shirts.

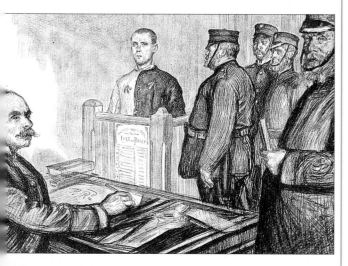

▲ **Breach of discipline; a convict brought before the Governor**
This drawing from *The Graphic* in 1889 shows a convict facing disciplinary charges at Wormwood Scrubs. His offence and the outcome of the hearing are not recorded.

◄ **The baby's parade, Wormwood Scrubs**
In late Victorian times, many of the women incarcerated in Wormwood Scrubs were held with their young children (and some women gave birth whilst serving their sentence). Babies were kept in a nursery but mothers were allowed to see them for a fixed period each day and walk with them around the exercise yard, as shown in this photograph from about 1897.

WHERE YOUNG CONVICTS are TURNED into HONEST CITIZENS
THE GATE OF BORSTAL PRISON AND A PEEP AT ITS INTERIOR

▲ **The Gate of Borstal Prison**
A committee of 1895 noted its concern at the treatment of young offenders, particularly those held with adult offenders. A new type of institution was suggested. The Borstal system was named after the village, near Chatham in Kent, where the first such institution was established. The Borstal system aimed to separate young offenders from older criminals who might corrupt them but also to provide them with training in useful skills. In those places where no separate institution was available, young prisoners could be placed in local prisons that had a section operating a Borstal system. Wormwood Scrubs operated such a system from 1904. One block of the prison was used only for young offenders and acted as an allocation centre in which young criminals were assessed before being sent to Borstal. After the First World War, a small block at Wandsworth Prison was taken over as a Boys Prison for London under a separate governor and regime from the rest of the prison. The youths were assessed, reports were made to court and, if they were sentenced to Borstal training, they were then allocated to suitable institutions. This role was transferred to Wormwood Scrubs in 1929 but the block at Wandsworth continued to be used for absconders from Borstal and those youths who were thought to need a more 'corrective' regime. The high hopes attached to the Borstal system can be seen from the caption that appeared with this photograph in *The Graphic* in 1911: 'Where young convicts are turned into honest citizens'.

chapter 11 Punishment

THE PUNISHMENTS of execution and imprisonment have already been considered. Imprisonment only recently became the most obvious form of punishment for criminals. Before this, there were many other ways of dealing with them. Fines have been imposed since Anglo-Saxon times. In the medieval period, a great part of a monarch's income arose from fines levied on offenders or those who were outlawed. The most common reason for someone to be declared an outlaw was because he had failed to appear before a court to answer charges brought against him. Such a man was treated as outside the law and he could be killed where he was found. His lands were forfeit to the Crown. A sentence of outlawry could be reversed but this involved the payment of a fine. Outlawry was only abolished in criminal proceedings in 1939.

The secular and ecclesiastical courts commonly imposed sentences that involved the public humiliation of offenders. The stocks and pillory were often used. The simple exhibition of offenders in public was a common punishment in medieval times. Many offenders, particularly women found guilty of adultery, might be sentenced to carry a lighted candle, in church or in a public procession. Public whippings of bare-backed offenders were commonplace. The public whippings at Bridewell were a popular spectacle. Offenders might also be whipped at the 'cart's tail', that is being roped to the back of a wagon and lashed along a street or at a whipping-post (usually located near to the parish stocks and pillory). Flogging was a whipping in which a 'cat-o'-nine-tails' was used, and birching (usually used for young offenders) involved the use of a thin cane on an offender's bare buttocks. Whipping, flogging and birching were not abolished as court sentences until 1948 or as a penalty for breach of prison discipline until 1967.

Mutilation is still a common punishment in many countries and was common in England until the 17th century. Those who uttered slanders might have their tongues cut out, prostitutes might have their noses slit and an offender's ears might be nailed to the pillory. William Prynne, a puritan barrister and pamphleteer, had parts of his ears cut off in the 17th century. Branding of criminals, usually with a letter or initials to indicate their crime, continued until the 19th century.

Torture was forbidden by English Common Law but this did not prevent its use by the Crown or by those courts, such as the Court of Star Chamber, that were controlled by the Crown and not bound by Common Law. As a matter of practice, if the King ordered someone to be tortured in medieval times or during the Reformation, no-one was going to oppose this. However, torture was rarely used in Britain compared with the rest of Europe. The exception was in the 16th and early 17th centuries. The religious conflict of the time led to a great increase in the use of torture. Priests, heretics and suspected plotters were subjected to agonising torture, especially in the Tower of London. Men and women were tortured into confessions and revealing the names, actions and intentions of their friends and associates. It did not really matter if, in their agony, the victims made things up. The authorities would then have other suspects to torture and the victim would have a break from the horrors of the torture chamber (at least until they were executed). The tortures used in England were not quite so imaginative as those used by the Spanish Inquisition but they were effective. The rack, press, chains, clamps, whips, hot irons and tools to pull teeth or nails were sufficient to obtain a confession or information from all but the hardiest of victims. Torture was abolished during the reign of Charles I.

Punishments were inflicted in many places in London. A fountain named the Standard on Cheapside was the scene of many public punishments. For example, three men had their right hands cut off here in 1293 for rescuing a prisoner. There was also a pillory in Cheapside, used especially for tradesmen selling short measures or rotten food. There was another pillory at Charing Cross. The open space on the north side of Westminster Hall was for centuries a place of punishment. Perkin Warbeck was placed in the stocks here in 1498 and Titus Oates was pilloried here in 1685. Stocks and a pillory were also located at the Stocks Market, a market on the site now occupied by Mansion House. In 1319, William Sperlynge of West Ham was pilloried there for selling rotten meat. A whipping post, stocks (and small prison) were located on St Martin's Lane, opposite the church of St Martin's in the Fields.

The poor conditions in prison were made worse by the punishments – some justified, some not – meted out upon the inmates. The most common offences were small transgressions such as talking (when silence was imposed), swearing and refusal to work. More serious matters were disobeying the orders of a warder, defacing the walls of a cell, damaging prison furniture, gambling, physical attacks on warders, fighting with other inmates, theft or sexual offences. Prisoners might be denied food and drink (or perhaps limited to bread and water), placed in solitary confinement, flogged or sentenced to extra work. The types of work given to the inmates of prisons were themselves forms of punishment and included hours on the treadmill, the crank or picking oakum.

The concept of punishment changed dramatically in the 20th century, with more emphasis being placed on the reform and rehabilitation of offenders. Fines and imprisonment became the normal sentence for most offences and all physical punishments, such as whipping, have been abolished. More thought has also been given to preventing young or first offenders becoming serious or habitual criminals. A statute of 1907 introduced the principle of supervision of offenders by probation officers. More recently, offenders may be subject to community service orders or perhaps curfew or tagging. It remains to be seen whether, in the long term, the crime rate will be affected by these changes.

➤ Death of a convict

The death of prisoners may not have been intended, but it was a common occurrence. This drawing of 1848 by George Cruickshank was from a series *The Drunkard's children*. An earlier series, *The Bottle*, showed how alcohol ruined a family. A man and his wife were reduced to debt, begging and violent quarrels. The husband then killed his wife in a state of drunkenness. The children also suffered: the daughter turned to vice and the son to robbery. He was sentenced to transportation but died on a hulk.

▼ In the stocks

Many offenders and vagrants were placed in the stocks and sometimes also whipped, so many parishes therefore had a combined stocks and whipping post. I included a photograph of the stocks and whipping post of the parish of St Leonard's Shoreditch in *Legal London*. William Brown of Westminster was to be a witness in a case in Westminster in 1610, but was drunk when he arrived at court. He was committed to the stocks for six hours. Cuthbert Foster was arrested in February 1612 for being drunk and disorderly in Tuttle Street. He was placed in the stocks for three hours and then whipped. This engraving shows four men in the stocks in Lollards' Tower at Lambeth Palace.

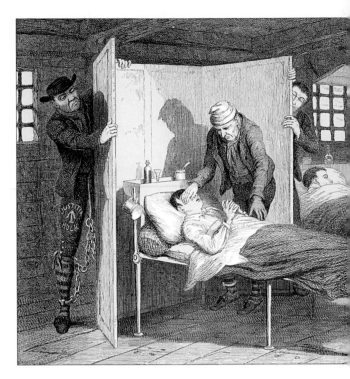

The BRANK or BRIDLE,
An ancient Instrument of Punishment for
Scolds and other "Unquiet Women".

► The ducking-chair

The ducking-chair or stool was a chair that was attached to a beam and used to duck women (and sometimes men) in rivers or ponds. This was a punishment for women who were gossips, slanderers and prostitutes or for tradesmen who sold goods that were underweight or of poor quality. This postcard shows a ducking-chair from Ipswich, which was hung by a chain from a horizontal beam. A ducking-stool was located near the Clink Prison on Bankside in Southwark in the 15th century. A woman who kept the *Queen's Head* ale-house in Kingston was ducked from Kingston Bridge, into the River Thames, in 1745 for being a scold. A crowd of almost 3,000 people gathered to watch.

◄ The scold's bridle

The brank, or scold's bridle, was a metal cage with a built-in gag that was clamped around a person's head. It was used to punish gossips or scolds (women who argued with neighbours and became a public nuisance). Alice Webb of Westminster was fitted with a brank in 1613 for abusing two constables. A brank from 1632 is preserved in Walton-on-Thames. This brank was used at Warrington in Lancashire.

► The racking of Cuthbert Symson

Torture was a popular pastime in previous centuries, particularly during the 16th century. John Holland, Duke of Exeter, introduced the rack into England in 1447. The rack set up in the Tower of London was therefore known as the 'Duke of Exeter's daughter' and those suffering on the rack were said to be 'wedded' to the Duke of Exeter's daughter. Cuthbert Symson was a Protestant from Islington who was committed to the Tower of London in December 1557. He refused to name the people who had attended a church service in English and was placed on the rack a number of times, then burned in Smithfield on 28 March 1558. Sir Thomas Wyatt was racked in the Tower after leading a rebellion against Queen Mary. Guy Fawkes was also racked in 1605 before signing his confession about the Gunpowder plot. It is thought that the rack was not used after 1640.

**➤ The burning of Thomas Tomkins'
hand by Bishop Bonner**

Edward Bonner became Bishop of
London in 1539. He was imprisoned in
the Fleet for two years and in the
Marshalsea for four years under Edward
VI for his refusal to accept the religious
reforms ordered by the King. He was
released on the accession of the Catholic
Queen Mary and soon became infamous
for his zealous persecution of Protestants.
Many people, accused of heresy, were
interviewed by Bonner in his palace at
Fulham or in Fulham Church, and many
of them were tortured and then burned.
This resulted in Bonner's imprisonment
in the Marshalsea after the accession of
Elizabeth in 1558. He died in that prison
in 1569. Thomas Tomkins was a
Protestant weaver from Shoreditch, who
was examined by Bonner in the hall of
Fulham Palace. During the examination,
Bonner took Tomkins by the fingers and
held his hand directly over a flame.
Tomkins was later burned in Smithfield.

**◄ Branding, or burning on the hand, at the Sessions House,
Old Bailey**

The punishment of branding with a hot iron dated from at least
Anglo-Saxon times. The branding caused great pain and was a
visible record of a conviction. From the 16th century, offenders
were branded with different letters, for example B for
blasphemer or T for a thief and vagrants might be branded
with the letter V. During the reign of Charles I, a Puritan
barrister and MP, William Prynne, was convicted of seditious
libel against the government. He was branded on the forehead
and had his nostrils slit and ears cropped. Three years later, he
was again branded with the letters SL (seditious libeller) on
each cheek and had the remainder of his ears cut off. Many
offenders were sentenced at the Old Bailey Sessions House to
be branded. The branding took place in court at the end of the
sessions and many members of the public remained to watch.
The last branding took place in 1799 and it was abolished as a
sentence in 1822. Some criminals escaped hanging by benefit of
clergy, an ecclesiastical privilege excusing clergy from punishment by the secular courts, but it was gradually extended to
persons who were eligible for ordination into the church; in
effect, most first offenders who could read. A simple test was
whether they could read from the bible and the same piece of
text was almost always used, a verse from the 51st Psalm that
became known as the 'neck-verse':

> Have mercy upon me, O God, according to thy loving
>   kindness;
> According unto the multitude of thy tender mercies, blot
>   out my transgressions.

The condemned person would have his sentence reduced,
usually to whipping, and be branded on the hand to prevent
him claiming the privilege after a second offence. There were
many abuses. Many illiterate criminals learned the verse by

TESTIS OVAT

◄ Titus Oates in the pillory

From as early as the 13th century, criminals might be placed in the pillory as a public humiliation and a method of allowing local people to make their feelings known about the offender, for example by pelting him with eggs, rotten food, rats and even dead cats. The Statute of the Pillory of 1226 provided for it to be used for perjurers, forgers and those who used deceitful weights and measures. A pillory was set up on Cornhill for the punishment of bakers, millers, bawds and scolds. From the 17th century, the pillory was also used for those who libelled the government or who published books or newspapers without a licence. Christopher Atkinson MP was placed in a pillory outside the Corn Exchange in Mark Lane in 1783 after being convicted of perjury (he was also imprisoned for 12 months, expelled from the House of Commons and fined £2,000). Titus Oates (1648-1705) was a clergyman, liar and perjurer. He gave false evidence about a Popish Plot in which Catholics intended to kill Charles II, take control of the government and massacre Protestants. His fabrications sent many innocent men (perhaps as many as 35) to the gallows including Oliver Plunket, Archbishop of Armagh in 1681. Oates gave evidence of Catholic plots to Sir Edmund Berry Godfrey. His murder soon afterwards seemed to confirm Oates' evidence. Oates received a pension of £1,200 a year and lived in comfort in Whitehall but suspicions grew as to the truth of his statements. Action was taken against Oates on the accession of the Catholic James II in 1685. He was tried for perjury before Judge Jeffreys in the Court of King's Bench at Westminster. Evidence was produced that Oates could not have been at meetings of Catholics that he claimed to have attended (and during which he claimed that people had discussed killing the King). Oates was convicted. He was sentenced to be whipped from Aldgate to Newgate and then from Newgate to Tyburn and then placed in the pillory on five days of each year for the rest of his life (at Westminster Hall, Charing Cross, the Temple, Royal Exchange and Tyburn). On his first day in the pillory outside Westminster Hall, Oates was almost killed by the mob. He was excused further time in the pillory but whipped and imprisoned for three years in the King's Bench Prison (and held in irons for the first year). He was released (and again paid a pension) in 1689 after the deposition of James II by William and Mary.

Egan and Salmon were two crooked thief-takers who worked with Stephen Macdaniel. They were convicted of conspiracy and pilloried in Smithfield in 1756. Egan was killed by a stone thrown by someone in the crowd. Popular men were treated very differently. Daniel Defoe was pilloried in 1703 at Charing Cross for his publication of a satirical pamphlet that attacked the government's suppression of non-conformity. The crowd drank to Defoe's health and adorned his pillory with flowers.

heart and it could sometimes be arranged, by a bribe, for the branding iron to be applied cold so that the criminal would be free to transgress in the future. Benefit of clergy was abolished for murderers in 1532 then gradually restricted and finally abolished in 1827.

This aquatint of 1808 by Pugin and
Rowlandson shows two men in the
pillory at Charing Cross, near the statue
of Charles I. Charing Cross was
frequently chosen as a suitable venue for
such punishment (for example for Daniel
Defoe in 1703) because there was an
extensive area for spectators. The use of
the pillory was abolished for all offences
except perjury in 1815 (and for perjury in
1837). It was last used in London in 1830
when James Bossy was pilloried for
perjury in Old Bailey.

▲ Dr Alexander Leighton

William the Conqueror abolished the death penalty for most
crimes but instituted the punishment of mutilation instead.
Many offenders had their hands or feet cut off or their eyes
gouged out during the Conqueror's reign. Mutilation
continued, although to a lesser extent, for many years. Dr
Alexander Leighton was a Scottish clergyman. He opposed the
attempt by William Laud, Archbishop of Canterbury, to force
various liturgical changes upon the Church in England and
Scotland. Leighton wrote a pamphlet in 1624 in which he
described bishops as men of blood (and ravens and magpies)
and criticised the abuse of their power by both church and
state. Leighton came to London in 1628 and was arrested under
warrant of the High Commission, signed by Laud. He was
convicted of sedition by the Court of Star Chamber in 1630 and
fined, pilloried, branded and whipped. One of his ears was cut
off and one of his nostrils was slit. Leighton was then sent to
the Fleet Prison. He was released 11 years later when his
sentence was reversed by the House of Commons. By this time,
Leighton was blind, deaf and hardly able to crawl. He no doubt
felt much better when he was told that his mutilation and
imprisonment had been declared illegal.

◀ **A man whipped in the Sessions House yard, 1779**

Floggings ordered at the Old Bailey Sessions were administered at Newgate Gaol, at Bridewell or in the yard of the Sessions House. A court might also order that an offender be whipped in public through the streets, often tied behind a horse-drawn cart. John Lumley was whipped through the streets of Southwark in 1810 for stealing pewter tankards from public houses. William Stroud was a notorious confidence trickster who was convicted of defrauding tradesmen of goods in 1752. He dressed as a gentleman, had a footman and obtained goods without paying for them (and then sold them). Stroud was imprisoned in Bridewell for six months and publicly whipped through the streets on six occasions.

Iames Nailor Quaker fet 2 howers on the Pillory at Weftminfter whiped by the Hangman to the old Exchainge London, Som dayes after, Stood too howers more on the Pillory at the Exchainge and there had his Tongue Bored throug with a hot Iron, & Stigmatized in the Forehead with the Letter:B: Decem: 17: anno Dom: 1656:

◀ **Thomas Hinshaw scourged by Bishop Bonner at Fulham**

Bishop Bonner was very keen on beating heretics himself. He is reported to have beaten John Miles with a willow rod so savagely that he wore it down to its stump and had to call for a birch rod to continue the scourging. Thomas Hinshaw was an apprentice, working in St Paul's Churchyard. Bishop Bonner ordered him to be placed in the stocks at Fulham. He was held there for eight days, with only bread and water. Hinshaw was then examined and taken to the palace orchard. There, he was scourged by Bishop Bonner, using two willow rods, and only released when he seemed near death. Hinshaw recovered and escaped further punishment by the death of Queen Mary soon after.

◥ **James Naylor: whipped, set in the pillory and his tongue bored through with a hot iron**

Whipping was the most common form of punishment in England until the 18th century. An Act of 1530 provided for vagrants to be tied to a cart and publicly whipped. Statutes also prescribed whipping for thieves (of goods worth less than 12 pence), blasphemers and unmarried mothers. Thus Eleanor Arnold of St Clement Danes was whipped in May 1612 for 'committing incontinency' with William Resworth and bearing his child. This print shows the punishment of James Naylor, a Quaker preacher, who claimed to be the Messiah. He was examined before Parliament in 1656 and found guilty of blasphemy. He was sentenced to be pilloried in New Palace Yard, Westminster then whipped through the streets to the City of London and pilloried. It was also ordered that his tongue should be bored through with a hot iron and his forehead branded with a B for blasphemer. He was then imprisoned in Bridewell. Naylor was released in 1659 and died the following year.

➤ The 'Boys' Pony' at the House of Correction, Coldbath Fields
This illustration is from *The Illustrated London News* in 1874. The pony was shaped so as to make a thrashing more effective and easy to administer.

▼ The whip and whipping-post, Wandsworth Prison
The public whipping of women was not abolished until 1791 and that of men not until 1817. Criminals might still be sentenced to be whipped, out of the public gaze, until 1850. Whippings also continued in prisons, as part of the disciplinary armoury available to warders, until the early 20th century.

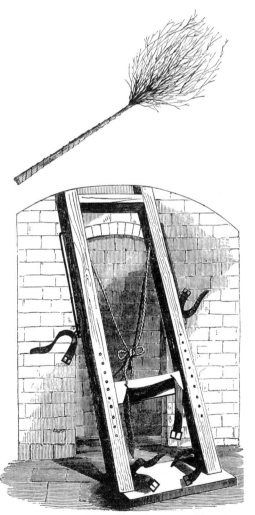

➤ William Spiggot under pressure in Newgate
An accused who refused to plead guilty or not guilty faced the punishment of 'Peine forte et dure' or pressing. This involved a man, almost naked, being laid on his back, with his arms and legs drawn by cords to sides of the room and being crushed with weights until he pleaded or died. A man might choose death in this manner to avoid a verdict of guilty (in which case his goods could be forfeited) and thus benefit his family. Major George

Strangeways was pressed to death at Newgate in 1658 for refusing to plead to the charge of murdering his brother-in-law. This avoided the forfeiture of the family estate. This form of punishment was abolished in 1772 and, from 1827, a defendant's silence was construed as a plea of not guilty. This engraving shows William Spiggot being pressed in Newgate. Spiggot was born in Hereford in 1692, apprenticed to a London cabinet-maker but then worked as a highwayman with Thomas Phillips and Joseph Lindsey, a clergyman of 'abandoned character'. They committed over one hundred robberies. On one occasion they were accompanied by a man named Burroughs, a lunatic who had escaped from Bedlam. They robbed Charles Sybbald on Finchley Common. Unfortunately, the lunatic Burroughs boasted about the robbery. The gang were captured and tried at the Old Bailey Sessions. Burroughs was sent back to Bedlam and Lindsey gave evidence for the prosecution to save his own neck. Spiggot and Phillips refused to plead. The court ordered that they be returned to Newgate and pressed. Phillips begged to be allowed to plead but Spiggot was put under the press. After 400 pounds was placed on his body he also asked to plead. Spiggot and Phillips were again indicted. They were convicted, principally on the evidence of Lindsey, sentenced to death and executed at Tyburn on 8 February 1721.

◀ The harlot beating hemp in Westminster Bridewell

The prisoners in Bridewells were put to work. In this engraving, Hogarth shows the harlot beating hemp but dressed in an expensive gown, probably a gift from one of her rich clients. One of the inmates has had her hands placed in the stocks (presumably for failing to work hard enough) which bear the declaration 'Better to work than to stand thus'.

▶ Convicts at Blackfriars Bridge, before being conveyed to Woolwich

A statute of 1579 authorised courts to banish vagabonds from the realm. This punishment was then extended to petty criminals and Quakers. From 1597, those convicted of capital crimes could also be transported. Transportation was seen as a convenient way of ridding England of wrongdoers. The period of transportation was often seven or 14 years, but it might be for life (particularly as an alternative to hanging). Many people were transported for trivial offences. For example, John Eyre was transported in 1771 for stealing a few sheets of printed paper. As late as 1827, a youth aged 18 was sentenced to transportation for life for theft of a handkerchief. Returning to Britain before the end of the sentence was an offence punishable by 14 years' transportation. If an offender returned a second time, the punishment until 1834 was hanging (and from then penal servitude for life). Perhaps 40,000 convicts were sent to the West Indies, Virginia, Maryland or the other American colonies and put to hard labour on the plantations. Convicts were marched in chains from Newgate down to Blackfriars Stairs, then taken in small boats to the transport ships moored in the Thames for the long passage across the Atlantic. Many convicts died on the way or shortly after arrival as a result of the poor conditions in which they were transported. The American Revolution brought an end to this traffic in 1776 and so the courts sent convicts to hulks moored in the Thames. It was then decided to found a penal colony at Botany Bay. The first fleet of convicts left England in May 1787. They landed in what is now Australia in January 1788. Forty convicts and five of their children died on the voyage. Conditions on the second fleet were even worse. More than 270 of the 980 convicts on the four ships died during the voyage. About 168,000 convicts were transported to Australia between 1787 and 1868.

▲ **The *Justitia* hulk with convicts at work on the bank of the Thames near Woolwich**
This engraving, from *The Malefactor's Register* of 1776, shows the hulk *Justitia* and convicts working near Woolwich. Convicts from the hulks were taken ashore to break stones, carry coal or clean sewers. Many convicts worked on the construction of new docks for London.

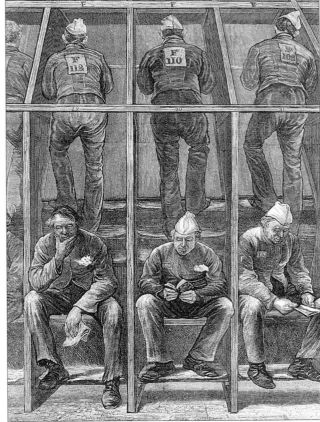

▲ **The treadwheel in the House of Correction, Coldbath Fields**
This drawing of prisoners on a treadwheel was published in *The Illustrated London News* in 1874. Coldbath Fields was notorious for its cruel regime and the poor health of prisoners held there. Riots took place at the prison in 1800 and 1830. The treadwheel and silent system were then introduced.

◄ **The treadmill at Brixton Prison**
Treadmills (or treadwheels) and cranks were installed in prisons for those prisoners sentenced to hard labour but also to punish prisoners for breaches of prison discipline. In 1824, Brixton was the first prison to be furnished with a treadmill. This was like a waterwheel, a large cylinder with steps on the outside. As prisoners stepped onto it, the wheel began to turn and the men had to climb onto the next step (to avoid falling backwards) and then continue climbing. A treadmill was an endless flight of stairs to nowhere. Treadmills sometimes had a useful function; perhaps grinding corn (as at Brixton) or bringing water up from a well, but sometimes they had no function at all except to punish prisoners. Treadmills were banned by Act of Parliament in 1898.

◀ Picking oakum in Wormwood Scrubs
Old tarred rope was separated into fibres and then used to
caulk the seams of wooden ships. The work made fingers raw
and painful. This photograph shows a woman picking oakum
in her cell in 1897.

**▼ A prisoner at crank-labour in the Surrey House of
Correction, Wandsworth**
A crank had to be turned by hand and was a punishment for
prisoners sentenced to hard labour. The crank was a box filled
with sand and a handle. The handle turned scoops inside the
box that scooped up the sand and then dropped it. Cranks were
intended to tire convicts and they had counters to record the
number of turns that a prisoner made. During his first month
of hard labour at Wormwood Scrubs, a prisoner had to turn the
crank 10,000 times a day. Cranks were banned in 1898.

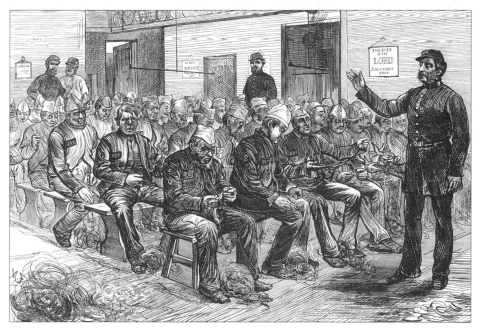

**➤ The oakum shed in the House of
Correction, Coldbath Fields**
Oakum-picking was performed in a shed
at Coldbath Fields that could accommodate up to 500 men. They worked in
silence or faced further punishment.
Notices on the wall encouraged inmates
to work hard and comply with prison
rules; one of the notices states that 'The
eyes of the Lord are in every place'.
Oakum-picking was also the chief work
for female prisoners and boys at Tothill
Fields. A shift of oakum-picking might
last as long as 12 hours.

◄ The needle-room in the House of Correction, Coldbath Fields
Prisoners at Coldbath Fields were also required to sew clothing and mailbags. The workroom was adorned with cheery signs such as that noting 'Be sure your sins will find you out'.

◄ A convict mat-making at Millbank
Another useful trade that a convict could learn was making mats. It is hardly surprising that few convicts were equipped to lead a hard-working life in an honest trade after their release.

◄ A dormitory at Coldbath Fields Prison
Lack of privacy was an everyday aspect of prison life. Even during the period when the separate system was operated, prisoners had no privacy from the warders. Having to sleep with this crowd as a punishment might have made even Ronnie Barker's character, Fletcher, decide to go straight.

A within the picture, note markings read:
A TURN 14,500 TIMES
PICK 180Z OAKUM
PER DAY
B TURN 12,500 TIMES
PICK 6OZ OAKUM
PER DAY.
C TURN 10,500 TIMES
PER DAY.

▲ The Convict Prison, Dartmoor

Many London criminals, or those who were sentenced by London courts, might serve their sentence in a prison outside London. In the 19th century, the authorities needed more prison accommodation for convicts because transportation to Australia was being brought to an end. Sentences of penal servitude (that is, imprisonment with the added punishment of hard work) were introduced and convict prisons were established at Portland, Chatham and Portsmouth but the most famous was at Princetown on Dartmoor. Most of the convicts were put to work on tasks outside the prison walls, quarrying granite, draining moorland or building roads. The prison officers who guarded them were armed with rifles and under orders to shoot a man who refused to halt if spotted trying to escape. There was also work inside the prison, as shown in this drawing from *The Illustrated London News* in 1884, including sewing, carpentry and a crank.

The LANCET Says:—
"COCOA ALONE IS AN
EXCELLENT FOOD AS WELL
AS A STIMULANT".
"CADBURY'S IS THE
STANDARD OF HIGHEST
PURITY."

CADBURY'S
COCOA

"Most Sustaining"

"The stimulating and strengthening properties of CADBURY'S Cocoa cannot be too highly appreciated."—*The Gentlewoman*.
"CADBURY'S Cocoa has in a remarkable degree those natural elements of sustenance which give the system endurance and hardihood, building up muscle and
bodily vigour with a steady action that renders it a most acceptable and reliable beverage."—*Health*.
"The favourite Cocoa of the day. For strength, purity, and nourishment there is nothing superior to be found."—*Medical Annual*.

CADBURY'S COCOA—ABSOLUTELY PURE, therefore BEST.

◄ Cadbury's Cocoa
I bring this volume to an end with a 19th-century advertisement. Police officers were often used as the subject in advertisements selling all sorts of goods. There is little doubt that a 'most sustaining' cup of cocoa would have helped these officers deal with any serious crime that night.

Bibliography

—, *The Bloody Register, a select and judicious collection of the most remarkable trials ...*, E. & M. Viney (1764) reprinted by Routledge/Thoemmes Press (1999)

—, *The Concise Dictionary of National Biography, from the earliest times to 1985*, OUP (1992)

—, *The handbook guide to Murder! Horror!*, London, Handbook Publishing (1998)

—, *Legal London*, catalogue to an exhibition in the Great Hall of the Royal Courts of Justice, London, 30 June to 30 July 1971 (1971)

—, *Lives of the most remarkable criminals who have been condemned and executed for murder, the highway, housebreaking, street robberies, coining or other offences collected from original papers and authentic memoirs*, J. Osborn (1735), reprint with an introduction by Arthur Hayward, Routledge (1927)

—, *Report on the discipline and management of the convict prisons and disposal of convicts, 1853, presented to both Houses of Parliament*, HMSO (1854)

—, *The Newgate Calendar, or Malefactors Bloody Register ...*, J. Cooke (n.d.)

—, *The Newgate Calendar or Malefactors Bloody Register ...*, Putnam (1932)

—, *The Newgate Calendar*, with an introduction by C. Emsley, Wordsworth (1997)

Abbott, Geoffrey, *The Who's Who of British Beheadings*, Andre Deutsch (2000)

Adam, H.L., *Notable British Trials, The trial of George Chapman*, William Hodge (1930)

Adcock, St John, *Wonderful London: the world's greatest city described by its best writers and pictured by its finest photographers* (no date or publisher, *circa* 1925-29)

Andrew, D.T. and McGowen, R., *The Perreaus and Mrs Rudd: forgery and betrayal in Eighteenth-Century London*, University of California Press (2001)

Andrews, William, *Old Time Punishments*, reprint, Dorset Press (1991)

Ashton, John, *The Fleet, its River, Prison and Marriages*, T. Fisher Unwin (1889)

Babington, Anthony, *A House in Bow Street, Crime and the Magistracy 1740-1881*, Macdonald (1969)

Babington, Anthony, *The English Bastille: A History of Newgate Gaol and Prison Conditions in Britain 1188-1902*, Macdonald (1971)

Barker, F. and Jackson, P., *London, 2,000 years of a city and its people*, Cassell (1974)

Barker, F. and Silvester-Carr, D., *The Black Plaque Guide to London*, Constable (1987)

Barlow, Derek, *Dick Turpin and the Gregory Gang*, Phillimore (1973)

Beattie, J.M., *Crime and the courts in England 1660-1800*, Oxford University Press (1986)

Begg, Paul and Skinner, Keith, *The Scotland Yard Files, 150 years of the C.I.D. 1842-1992*, Headline (1992)

Benson, Captain L., *The book of remarkable trials and notorious characters from 'Half-hanged Smith', 1700 to Oxford who shot at the Queen, 1840*, Chatto & Windus (n.d)

Besant, Sir Walter, *London in the Time of the Stuarts*, A & C Black (1903)

Besant, Sir Walter, *London in the Eighteenth Century*, A & C Black (1925)

Birkenhead, Earl of, *Famous Trials*, Hutchinson (n.d)

Birkenhead, Earl of, *More Famous Trials*, Hutchinson (1938)

Birkett, Sir Norman (ed), *The Newgate Calendar*, Folio Society (1951)

Birkett, Lord (ed), *The New Newgate Calendar*, Folio Society (1960)

Bland, James, *The Common Hangman*, Ian Henry (1984)

Bleackley, Horace, *Notable British Trials, Trial of Henry Fauntleroy and Other Famous Trials for Forgery*, William Hodge (1924)

Bleackley, Horace, *Notable British Trials, Jack Sheppard*, William Hodge (1933)

Bondeson, Jan, *The London Monster: A Sanguinary Tale*, Free Association Books (2000)

Borowitz, Albert, *The Bermondsey Horror*, Robson Books (1989)

Borrow, George, *Celebrated trials and remarkable cases of jurisprudence from the earliest records to the year 1825*, rev. ed. Jonathan Cape (1928)

Bridges, Yseult, *Poison and Adelaide Bartlett, the Pimlico poisoning case*, Macmillan (1962)

Bridges, Yseult, *How Charles Bravo died, the chronicle of a cause célèbre*, Reprint Society (1957)

Browne, D.G., *The Rise of Scotland Yard: A History of the Metropolitan Police*, Harrap (1956)

Budworth, G., *The River Beat: The Story of London's River Police since 1798*, Historical Publications (1997)

Burford, E.J., *A Short History of the Clink Prison* (n.d.)

Burford, E.J., *In the Clink*, New English Library (1977)

Byrne, R., *Prisons and Punishments of London*, Harrap (1989)

Byrne, R., *The London Dungeon Book of Crime and Punishment*, Little, Brown (1993)

Carswell, D., *Notable British Trials, trial of Ronald True*, William Hodge (1925)

Cheney, Malcolm, *Chronicles of the Damned*, Marston House (1992)

Cullen, Tom, *Crippen: The Mild Murderer*, Penguin (1988)

Engel, Howard, *Lord High Executioner, an unashamed look at hangmen, headsmen and their kind*, Robson Books (1996)

Farrington, K., *Hamlyn History of Punishment & Torture*, Hamlyn (1996)

Fido, Martin and Skinner, Keith, *The Official Encyclopedia of Scotland Yard*, Virgin (1999)

Fielding, Steve, *The Hangman's Record, volume I: 1868-1899*, Chancery House (1994)

Forbush, W.B. (ed), *Fox's Book of Martyrs: a history of the lives, sufferings and triumphant deaths of the early Christian and Protestant martyrs*, (1926)

Foss, E., *Biographia Juridica, a biographical dictionary of the Judges of England from the Conquest to the present time, 1066-1870*, John Murray (1870)

Gaute, J.H.H. and Odell, Robin, *The Murderers' Who's Who: outstanding international cases from the literature of murder in the last 150 years*, Harrap (1979)

Gaute, J.H.H. and Odell, Robin, *Murder 'Whatdunnit': an illustrated account of the methods of murder*, Harrap (1982)

Gillen, Mollie, *Assassination of the Prime Minister: the shocking death of Spencer Perceval*, Sidgwick & Jackson (1972)

Gordon, Charles, *The Old Bailey and Newgate*, Fisher Unwin (c.1903)

Green, Jonathon, *The Directory of Infamy: the best of the worst, an illustrated compendium of over 600 of the all-time great crooks*, Mills & Boon (1980)

Griffiths, Arthur, *The Chronicles of Newgate*, Dorset Press reprint (1987)

Heppenstall, Rayner, *Tales from the Newgate Calendar*, Constable (1981)

Heppenstall, Rayner, *Reflections on the Newgate Calendar*, W.H. Allen (1975)

Herber, Mark, *Legal London: A Pictorial History*, Phillimore (1999)

Honeycombe, Gordon, *The Complete Murders of the Black Museum*, Leopard Books (1995)

Hooper, W. Eden, *The history of Newgate and the Old Bailey and a survey of the Fleet Prison and Fleet marriages, the Marshalsea and other old London Jails. With extensive remarks on crime and punishment in England from mediaeval times to the present day*, Underwood Press Ltd (1935)

Howson, Gerald, *Thief-taker General: the rise and fall of Jonathan Wild*, Hutchinson (1970)

Howson, Gerald, *The Macaroni Parson: the life of the unfortunate Doctor Dodd*, Hutchinson (1973)

Irving, H.B., *Notable English Trials: Trial of Franz Muller*, William Hodge (1911)

Irving, H.B., *Notable English Trials: Trial of the Wainwrights*, William Hodge (1920)

Jackson, William, *The New and Complete Newgate Calendar or Malefactor's Universal Register* (1818)

James, P.D. and Critchley, T.A., *The Maul and the Pear Tree: the Ratcliffe Highway Murders 1811*, Sphere (1987)

Jones, Steve, *Capital Punishments, Crime and Prison Conditions in Victorian Times*, Wicked Publications (1992)

Jones, Steve, *London, the Sinister Side*, Wicked Publications (1998)

Kent, William, *An Encyclopedia of London*, revised by G. Thompson, J.M. Dent & Sons (1970)

Kenyon, John, *The Popish Plot*, Heinemann (1972)

Knott, George H., *Notable English Trials: Trial of William Palmer*, William Hodge (1912)

Lane, Brian, *The Murder Club Guide to London*, Harrap (1988)

Lane, Jane, *Titus Oates*, Andrew Dakers (1949)

Lewis, J.R., *The Victorian Bar*, Hale (1982)

Lock, Joan, *Tales from Bow Street*, Hale (1982)

Lock, Joan, *Scotland Yard Casebook: the making of the CID 1865-1935*, Hale (1993)

Lyons, Frederick, *Jonathan Wild, Prince of Robbers*, Michael Joseph (1936)

Manchee, W.H., *The Westminster City Fathers (the Burgess Court of Westminster) 1585-1901*, Bodley Head (1924)

Marjoribanks, E., *Famous Trials of Marshall Hall*, Penguin (1989)

Marks, Alfred, *Tyburn Tree: its history and annals*, Brown, Langham (n.d)

Marshall, Alan, *The Strange Death of Edmund Godfrey: plots and politics in Restoration London*, Sutton (1999)

Mayhew, Henry and Binney, John, *The Criminal Prisons of London and Scenes of Prison Life*, Griffin Bohn (1862)

Mayhew, Henry, *London Labour and the London Poor, those that will not work*, Griffin Bohn (1862)

Milne-Tyte, Robert, *Bloody Jeffreys, the hanging judge*, Deutsch (1989)

Mitchell, E.V., *The Newgate Calendar comprising interesting memoirs of the most notorious characters who have been convicted of outrages on the laws of England ...*, Bodley Head (1928)

Montgomery Hyde, H., *Notable British Trials: The Trials of Oscar Wilde*, William Hodge (1948)

Moore, Lucy, *The Thieves' Opera: the remarkable lives of Jonathan Wild, thief-taker, and Jack Sheppard, house-breaker*, Viking (1997)

Murphy, Theresa, *The Old Bailey: eight centuries of crime, cruelty and corruption*, Mainstream Publishing (1999)

O'Donnell, Bernard, *The Trials of Mr. Justice Avory*, Rich & Cowan (1935)

O'Donnell, Kevin, *The Jack the Ripper Whitechapel Murders*, Ten Bells Publishing (1997)

O'Donoghue, E.G., *Bridewell Hospital, Palace, Prison, Schools*, Bodley Head (1929)

Pelham, Camden, *The chronicles of crime, or the New Newgate Calendar being a series of memoirs and anecdotes of notorious characters who have outraged the laws of Great Britain from the earliest period to 1841*, T. Miles & Co (1891)

Pettifer, Ernest, *Punishments of Former Days*, Clegg, 2nd ed (1947)

Pierrepoint, Albert, *Executioner: Pierrepoint*, Coronet (1974)

Pringle, P., *The Thief Takers*, Museum Press (1958)

Rayner, J.L. and Crook, G.T. (eds), *The Complete Newgate Calendar*, The Navarre Society (1926)

Rowse, A.L., *The Regicides and the Puritan Revolution*, Duckworth (1994)

Rowse, A.L., *The Tower of London in the History of the Nation*, Weidenfeld & Nicolson (1972)

Ruddick, James, *Death at the Priory: love, sex and murder in Victorian England*, Atlantic (2001)

Rumbelow, Donald, *The Triple Tree: Newgate, Tyburn and Old Bailey*, Harrap (1982)

St Aubyn, Fiona, *Ackermann's Illustrated London*, Wordsworth (1985)

Scott, Sir Harold, *The Concise Encyclopedia of Crime and Criminals*, Deutsch (1965)

Sellwood, Arthur and Mary, *The Victorian Railway Murders*, David & Charles (1979)

Shepherd, T.H. and Elmes, J., *London and its environs in the nineteenth century, illustrated by a series of views from original drawings by Thomas H. Shepherd with historical, topographical and critical notices*, Jones & Co (1829)

Shore, W. Teignmouth, *Notable British Trials: The Trial of Frederick Guy Browne and William Henry Kennedy*, William Hodge (1930)

Shore, W. Teignmouth, *Notable British Trials: The Trial of Thomas Neill Cream*, William Hodge (1923)

Shore, W. Teignmouth, *Crime and its Detection*, Gresham (1931)

Smith, Capt. Alexander, *A complete history of the lives and robberies of the most notorious highwaymen, footpads, shoplifts, & cheats of both sexes*, 5th ed (1719), reprint by George Routledge & Sons (1926) with an introduction by A.L. Hayward

Symons, Julian, *Crime and Detection: an illustrated history from 1840*, Panther (1968)

Thornbury, W. and Walford, E., *Old and New London: a narrative of its history, its people and its places*, Cassell, Petter, Calpin & Co. (1873-78)

Todd, J. and Spearing, E., *Counterfeit Ladies: the life and death of Mary Frith, the case of Mary Carleton*, Pickering (1994)

Townsend, W., *Black Cap, murder will out*, Marriott (1930)

Treherne, John, *The Canning Enigma*, Jonathan Cape (1989)

Waddell, Bill, *The Black Museum, New Scotland Yard*, Little, Brown (1993)

Walker, Peter, *Punishment: an illustrated history*, David & Charles (1972)

Ward, David, *King of the Lags: The Story of Charles Peace*, Souvenir Press (1989)

Watson, E.R., *Notable British Trials: The Trial of George Joseph Smith*, William Hodge (1922)

Watson, E.R., *Notable British Trials: Adolf Beck (1877-1904)*, William Hodge (1924)

Weinreb, B. and Hibbert, C., *The London Encyclopaedia*, Macmillan, revised ed (1993)

White, Beatrice, *A Cast of Ravens, the strange case of Sir Thomas Overbury*, Murray (1965)

Wilkinson, George Theodore, *The Newgate Calendar improved, being interesting memoirs of notorious characters who have been convicted of offences against the laws of England ...*, R. Evans (1816) reprints by Panther (1962) and by Sphere (1991)

Wilkinson, George Theodore, *An Authentic History of the Cato Street Conspiracy*, 2nd ed (1820)

Whitmore, R., *Victorian and Edwardian Crime and Punishment*, Batsford (1978)

Young, F., *Notable English Trials: Trial of the Seddons*, William Hodge (1914)

Young, F., *Notable English Trials: Trial of H.H. Crippen*, William Hodge (1920)

Index

compiled by Auriol Griffith-Jones

Henry VIII, King, 107–8
heresy, 107, 116, 117
Herschel, Sir William, 93
Hevingham, William, 97
Hewson, Colonel, 7
Hewson, John, regicide, 97
Hicks' Hall Sessions House, 65
Hicks, Sir Baptist, 65
Hiden, Thomas, 20
highwaymen, 1–2, 7, 108
Highwaymen Act (1692), 24–5
Hill, Lawrence, 6
Hinshaw, Thomas, 189
Hitchen, Charles, 26
Hogarth, William, *The Harlot's Progress*, 16, 17
Holland, Anne, 10
Holloway, John, 14
Holloway prison, 132, 176–7
Homicide Act (1957), 18
Hooper, John, 20
Horn, William, 142
Horne, Captain, 7
Hornsey Lane, 7
Horsemonger Lane Gaol, Southwark, 126, 132, 158, 162
Horton, Thomas, regicide, 97
Hosey, John, 7
Houghton, John, 118
Hounslow Heath, 7, 14, 108
Housden, Jane, 11
House of Lords, court of, 59, 60
Houses of Correction, 132, 156, 172–3, 174, 193
Howard, John, prison reformer, 133, 150
Howard, Katherine, Queen, 113
Howard, Philip, 137
Huggins, John, Keeper of Fleet, 153, 155
Hunton, Joseph, 85
Hurle, Anne, 125
Hurst, Edmund, martyr, 116
Hutchinson, John, regicide, 97
Hyde Park, 37; riot (1866), 40

identification parades, 71
identity, mistaken, 92, 93
informers, common, 24
Ingoldsby, Richard, regicide, 97
Ings, James, Cato Street, 20–1, 149
insanity, 17, 18
Ireton, Henry, regicide, 97, 99, 118
Irish militants, 39, *see also* Fenians
Isaacs, Sir Henry, 63

Jack the Ripper, 17, 22–3
Jackson, Ralph, martyr, 116
Jacobite rebellion (1745), 110, 114, 122
James I, King, 101
James II, King, 50
Jardine, Mr., Magistrate, 68

Jeffreys, Judge George 'Bloody', 6, 49, 50, 112, 137
Jeffries, Elizabeth, 77
John II, King of France, 137
John, Percy, 53
Johnson, Mr., steward to Ferrers, 118–19
Johnson, Roger, 28
Johnson, William, 11
Jones, Jane, 85
Jones, John, regicide, 97
Jones, Mary, 10
Joscelyne, Ralph, 45
journalists, at executions, 125
Joyce, William ('Lord Haw-Haw'), 137
judges, 47–8, 50, 57
juries, 47–8
Justice, Ann, Fenian, 42
Justices of the Peace, 24, 48
Justitia prison hulk, 163, 165, 192

Kelly, Henry, 28
Kelly, Mary Jane, 22
Kelly, Peter, 30
Kenealy, Edward, QC, 95
Kenmure, William, Viscount, 110
Kennedy, William Henry, 57, 93
Kennington Common, 122
Ketch, Jack, executioner, 112, 128
Keyes, Robert, Gunpowder Plot, 4
Kidd, Captain William, 122–3
Kilmarnock, Lord, 110
King, Tom, highwayman, 76
King's (Queen's) Bench, Court of, 49, 59; prison, 132, 133, 146, 160–1
Kneebone, William, 29, 144, 145
Knill, Sir Stuart, Sheriff, 63
Knyvet, Sir Thomas, and Gunpowder Plot, 4
Konigsmark, Charles, Count, 5
Kurr, William, 85

Lamb, Anthony, 145
Lambeth, Bedlam Hospital, 18
Lambeth Palace, 134, 138
Lambeth Street Police Office (Whitechapel), 48
Lamson, Dr George, 52–3
Lane, Harriet, 86–7
Laud, William, Archbishop of Canterbury, 112, 137
Lawrence, William, 146
Le Neve, Ethel, 46, 90–1
Leaf, John, 117
Lee, John 'Babbacombe', 131
Leighton, Dr Alexander, 188
Lepidus, Jacob, 45
letter-writing, 174
Liberator Building Society, 62
Lilburne, Robert, regicide, 97
Lindsey, Joseph, 191

Littlechild, Inspector John, 43
Liverpool, Earl of, 20
Livesay, Michael, regicide, 97
Local Government Office, 43
lock-ups, 132–3
Lofty, Margaret, 106
Lollards, execution of, 115
Lollards' Prison, Lambeth Palace, 138
London Bridge, Old, cage, 133, 139; heads on gatehouse, 114
London, County of, 65
Long, PC John, 39
Longdon, John, 122
Lord Mayor of London, 49, 63, 64
Lovat, Lord, 59, 60, 110, 113
Love Lane, 16
Lowen, William, executioner, 99
Lowry, Captain James, 122
Ludgate Prison, 132, 140
Ludlow, Edmond, regicide, 97
Lumley, John, 189
Lyon, Elizabeth (Edgworth Bess), 144–5, 166
Lyttelton, Lord, 103

Macdaniel, Stephen, thief-taker, 30, 187
McDonald, William, 110
Macdonnell, George, 64
Mackay, Robert, 153
Maclane, James, highwayman, 78, 128, 162
McLean, Roderick, 21
McNaghton, Daniel, 18
Macnamara, John, 163
Maggot, Poll, 144, 145
magistrates, 24, 48; functions of, 25, 48, 67
Magistrates Courts, 48, 62, 70, 71
Malcolm, Sarah, 120–1
Malden, Daniel, 143
Man, Elizabeth, 27
Manning, Frederick and Maria, 86, 126, 130, 162
Mansfield, Earl of, Lord Chief Justice, 61
Mansion House, 64
Mapleton, Percy Lefroy, 46
Marine Police Force, 38
Markham, Mary (Moll Cut-Purse), 74
Marks, Nathan, witness, 54
Marlborough Street, Magistrates Court, 31, 71; Police Office, 25, 48
Marr, Mr., 127
marriages, clandestine, in the Fleet, 153
Marsh, Alice, 88
Marsh, Mary, 89
Marshall Hall, Sir Edward, 57, 106
Marshalsea Prison, 132, 133, 158–9
Martin, Baron, judge, 87
Martin, Henry, regicide, 97
Marvell, William, executioner, 110, 128

Price, John, hangman, 108, 128, 130
Pride, Thomas, regicide, 97
Prince, Richard, 15
Priory Church of St John of Jerusalem, 3
Prison Act (1877), 133
prisons, 132–4, 139; conditions in, 132, 133, 142–3, 147, 153, 194; convict, 195; deaths in, 184; debtor, 133–4, 135, 139–41, 147, 153–5, 158; escapes from, 143, 144–5, 161; exercise yards, 150–1, 152, 164, 169, 178; hulks, 163, 165, 191; military, 163; punishments within, 183; and reform of offenders, 132, 134, 183; regulation clothing, 181; separate and silent system, 170, 171, 174, 177, 178, *see also individual prisons*; Newgate
probation officers, 183
prostitution and prostitutes, 2, 16–17, 135
Prynne, William, 182, 186
punishments, 132, 182–3
Purefoy, William, regicide, 97
Putney Heath, 7

Quarter Sessions, 48
Queen Square Police Office, 48

rack, use of the, 183, 185
Racquets, played in the Fleet, 153
Raleigh, Sir Walter, 108, 137, 162
Ratcliff Highway, 17
Ray, Martha, 104
Raymond, Lord Chief Justice, 155
Reavil, Alice, 106
Recorder of London, 49
reformatories, 134
regicides, 97, 118
reprieves, 15, 121
Resworth, William, 189
rewards, 24–5; posters for, 44, 46
Richard II, King, 3
Richard III, King, 138
Richardson, Michael, 9
riots, 39; Battle of Cable Street (1936), 39; Gordon riots (1780), 26, 39; Hyde Park (1886), 40; Peasants' Revolt, 3, 39; Trafalgar Square (1886), 34, 40
Roberts, Mary, 110
Roberts, Richard, 146
Robertson, Lewis, 80
Robinson, PC Edward, 88
Robinson, William, 143
Roche, Philip, 122
Rochester, Robert Carr, Viscount, 101
Rocque, John, maps by, 119, 158
Roe, Owen, regicide, 97
Rogers, John, martyr, 117
'rookeries' (criminal slums), 24
Rookwood, Ambrose, Gunpowder Plot, 4
Rose, Pascha, executioner, 128

Rose, Richard, 107, 117
Ross, Donovan, 70
Routh, John, martyr, 116
Rowan, Colonel Charles, 25
Royal College of Physicians, 109
Royal College of Surgeons, 28
Royal Courts of Justice, 59, 61, 62
Royal Parks Police Force, 37
Royalist, HMS, Thames Police, 38
Rudd, Margaret Caroline, 103
Russel, Richard, 123
Russell, Lord William, 50, 116, 128
Russia, anarchist refugees from, 45
Rye House Plot (1683), 50, 116
Ryland, William Wynne, 80

Saffron Hill, rookery, 24
St Giles rookery, 24
St Martin's Round House, 133
St Marylebone watch house, 31, 133
St Paul's Churchyard, 108
St Sepulchre's Church, bells, 29, 121
Salisbury, Margaret, Countess of, 113
Salisbury, Sally, 76
Salmon, James, thief-taker, 30, 187
sanctuary, areas of, 24
Sandwich, Lord, First Lord of the Admiralty, 104
Savage, Thomas, 78, 108
Savage, Tristram, 10
Savoy Palace, 163
Say, William, regicide, 97
Sayer, John, 9
schools, adult (Wandsworth), 174
scold's bridle (brank), 184–5
Scotland Yard, 25, 32–3; New Scotland Yard, 36
Scott, Thomas, regicide, 97
Scott, William, 15
Scroggs, Lord Chief Justice, 6
Scroop, Adrian, regicide, 97
Seagoe, Mrs, *Blue Boar Tavern*, 27, 28
Searles, George, martyr, 116
Seddon, Frederick and Margaret, 57, 58
Selman, John, 74
Semple, Major James, 82
Sessions Houses, 65, *see also* Old Bailey
sewing clothing and mailbags, 194
Seymour, William, 137
Shadwell Police Office, 48
Shaw, George Bernard, 40
Sheppard, Jack, highwayman, 2, 28, 29; escapes from gaols, 144–5, 166; execution at Tyburn, 118, 120, 145
Sheppard, James, 75
Sheppard, Thomas, 144, 145
sheriffs, 24, 63, 132
ships, theft and smuggling from, 38
Shooter's Hill, 7, 123
Shrivell, Emma, 88

Sidney, Algernon, 50, 116
slums, 'rookeries', 24
Smith, Captain Alexander, on Newgate, 142
Smith, Francis, 19
Smith, George Joseph, murderer, 106
Smith, Henry, regicide, 97
Smith, John, mistaken identity, 92
Smith, John ('Half-hanged Smith'), 121
Smith, John, hanged for treason, 126
Smith, John, mutineer, 122
Smithers, Richard, 20
Smithfield, 108, 117
smuggling, 38
Soho, 16, 17
Solas, Jacob Mendez, 155
Southwark, 16, 24, 158; Horsemonger Lane Gaol, 126; Police Office, 48; prisons, 132, 158–61
Spa Fields riots (1816), 20
Spalding, Mathusalah, 125
Special Branch (Special Irish Branch), 25, 32, 35, 39, 43
special constables, 40–1
Sperlynge, William, 183
Spiggot, William, 190, 191
Spilsbury, Dr Bernard, pathologist, 90
Spink, Mary, 89
Spitalfields, 17, 22
sponging houses, 133
Spurling, Mr., Newgate turnkey, 11
Squires, Mary, 79
Stanley, Mrs., Metropolitan Women Police, 33
Stapeley, Anthony, regicide, 97
Stapleton, Walter de, 108
Statute of the Pillory (1226), 187
Stedman, Thomas, 12
Steele, John, 14
Stepney, Battle of, 45
Stepney Fields, 9
Stern, John, 5, 108
Stetham, Mrs, 28
stocks, 132, 156, 183, 184
Strafford, Earl of, 59
Strafford, Thomas Wentworth, Earl of, 112
Strange, John Shaw, Cato Street, 20, 21
Strangeways, Major George, 190–1
Stratton, Alfred and Albert, 93
Straw, Jack, 3
Stride, Elizabeth, 22
Stroud, William, 189
Stuart, Arabella, 137
suffragettes, in Holloway, 176
suicides, burial of, 82, 127
Surrey County Gaol *see* Horsemonger Lane
Surrey, Earl of, 153
Svaars, Fritz, 45
Swan, John, 77

FARRINGDON WARD
without
with it's Division *into*
PARISHES
according to a New
SURVEY.

The Arms of Richard Beckford Esq.

PART OF St ANDREWS PARISH

PART OF

Beauchamp Street

BROOK

GREVILL STREET

HATTON GARDEN

St Sepulchre's Church Yard

The Sheep Penns

Gray's Inn Lane

STREET

Furnivals Inn

ELY HOUSE

Chick Lane

Smithfield Bars

Brook House Yard

High   Holbourn

HOLBOURN

Holbourn Hill

Swan Inn

Cock Lane

LINCOLNS

Castle Yard

CHANCERY LANE

CASTLE LANE

Parish Church

St Andrew Church

Holbourn Bridge

St Sepulchre's Church

INN

Barnard's Inn

Andrew's Church Yd

FLEET

Mad House Yard

Curriers Alley

FETTER LANE

SHOE LANE

Church Yd to St Bride

MARKET

Ship Yard

The Fleet

St Dunstan

Clifford's Inn

FLEET   STREET   Fleet   Bridge LUDGATE HILL

CLEMENTS

Temple   Barr

Temple Church

St Bride

Bride well

Blackfriars

Temple

PART OF

OLD BAILEY

Dorset Street

White Friers

Exchequer Court

Cloister Court

Brick Court

Walks

The Play House

PART OF

Temple Stairs

Essex Stairs

White Friers Stairs

Dorset Stairs

Black Friers Stairs

THE   RIVER   THAMES